HIKING AND TREKKING
IN THE JAPAN ALPS
AND MOUNT FUJI

About the Authors

Tom Fay is the lead author of *Hiking and Trekking in the Japan Alps and Mount Fuji*. He is a British writer and teacher based in Osaka, and has been living in Japan for well over a decade. Growing up in the hills of North Wales, the mountains of Snowdonia were his first outdoor 'love', and he still returns there year after year. He has since hiked and climbed in many places including Scotland, Iceland, the Himalayas, China, South Korea, New Zealand and throughout every corner of Japan.

Tom writes mainly about travel and the outdoors for a variety of publications and media outlets, and is the author of a travel guidebook called *Must-See Japan*. He is a member of the Outdoor Writers and Photographers Guild.

Check out Tom's website – www.thomasfay.com – for more information.

Wes Lang has been endlessly exploring Japan's mountains since relocating to the country in 2001. In 2008 he became the first American (and one of only a handful of foreigners) to climb the *Nihon Hyakumeizan*, Japan's '100 Famous Mountains'. He has since gone on to complete the *Kansai Hyakumeizan* (100 mountains of the Kansai region) and is currently climbing the highest mountain in each of Japan's 47 prefectures.

He is the founder of 'Hiking in Japan' – https://japanhike.wordpress.com – a website providing comprehensive hiking information for the *Hyakumeizan* and beyond. His travels have taken him to the mountains of South Korea, Taiwan, New Zealand and throughout the US.

Wes lives in Osaka with his Japanese wife and young daughter.

HIKING AND TREKKING IN THE JAPAN ALPS AND MOUNT FUJI

NORTHERN, CENTRAL AND SOUTHERN ALPS

by Tom Fay and Wes Lang

JUNIPER HOUSE, MURLEY MOSS,
OXENHOLME ROAD, KENDAL, CUMBRIA LA9 7RL
www.cicerone.co.uk

© Tom Fay and Wes Lang 2019
First edition 2019
ISBN: 978 1 85284 947 4
Reprinted in 2020 (with updates)

Printed in China on responsibly sourced paper on behalf of Latitude Press Ltd
A catalogue record for this book is available from the British Library.
All photographs are by the authors unless otherwise stated.

Route mapping by Lovell Johns www.lovelljohns.com
Contains OpenStreetMap.org data © OpenStreetMap
contributors, CC-BY-SA. NASA relief data courtesy of ESRI

In memory of Michal Vojta (1986-2016),
for showing us how to dream in clouds.
'There is nothing better than waking up on top of the mountain.'

Updates to this Guide

While every effort is made by our authors to ensure the accuracy of guidebooks as they go to print, changes can occur during the lifetime of an edition. Any updates that we know of for this guide will be on the Cicerone website (www.cicerone.co.uk/947/updates), so please check before planning your trip. We also advise that you check information about such things as transport, accommodation and shops locally. Even rights of way can be altered over time.

The route maps in this guide are derived from publicly available data, databases and crowd-sourced data. As such they have not been through the detailed checking procedures that would generally be applied to a published map from an official mapping agency, although naturally we have reviewed them closely in the light of local knowledge as part of the preparation of this guide.

We are always grateful for information about any discrepancies between a guidebook and the facts on the ground, sent by email to updates@cicerone.co.uk or by post to Cicerone, Juniper House, Murley Moss, Oxenholme Road, Kendal, LA9 7RL.

Register your book: To sign up to receive free updates, special offers and GPX files where available, register your book at www.cicerone.co.uk.

Front cover: Admiring the view from the summit of Mt Tsurugi-dake in the North Alps (Trek 2, Stage 2)

CONTENTS

Mt Warusawa (Trek 11, Stage 2)

Mountain safety

Every mountain walk has its dangers, and those described in this guidebook are no exception. All who walk or climb in the mountains should recognise this and take responsibility for themselves and their companions along the way. The author and publisher have made every effort to ensure that the information contained in this guide was correct when it went to press, but, except for any liability that cannot be excluded by law, they cannot accept responsibility for any loss, injury or inconvenience sustained by any person using this book.

International distress signal *(emergency only)*
Six blasts on a whistle (and flashes with a torch after dark) spaced evenly for one minute, followed by a minute's pause. Repeat until an answer is received. The response is three signals per minute followed by a minute's pause.

Helicopter rescue
The following signals are used to communicate with a helicopter:

Help needed:
raise both arms
above head to
form a 'Y'

Help not needed:
raise one arm
above head, extend
other arm downward

Emergency telephone numbers
The standard emergency number in Japan is 110 for the police; they can then connect you to the ambulance, fire or mountain rescue services. Or dial 119 for the ambulance/fire service.

If you have trouble communicating then ring the Japan Helpline on 0570-000-911, a 24/7 emergency assistance service.

Weather reports
For up-to-date forecasts check www.jma.go.jp (Japan Meteorological Agency) or www.accuweather.com.

Symbols used on route maps

		Relief in metres	
～	route	3800–4000	
⌁	alternative route	3600–3800	
Ⓢ Ⓢ	start/alternative start point	3400–3600	
Ⓕ Ⓕ	finish/alternative finish point	3200–3400	
ⓈⒻ ⓈⒻ	start/finish & alternative point	3000–3200	
>	route direction	2800–3000	
	snowfield	2600–2800	
	woodland/marshland	2400–2600	
	urban areas	2200–2400	
▬■▬	station/railway	2000–2200	
▲	peak	1800–2000	
♠ ⚐	manned/unmanned mountain hut	1600–1800	
		1400–1600	
Å	campsite	1200–1400	
■	building	1000–1200	
)(	col or saddle	800–1000	
≍	bridge	600–800	
·	water feature	400–600	
✱	viewpoint	200–400	
🚌 Ⓟ	bus stop/parking	0–200	
·	other feature		

SCALE: 1:50,000

0 kilometres 0.5   1

0 miles   0.5

Contour lines are
drawn at 25m intervals
and highlighted at
100m intervals.

GPX files

GPX files for all routes can be downloaded for free at www.cicerone.co.uk/947/GPX.

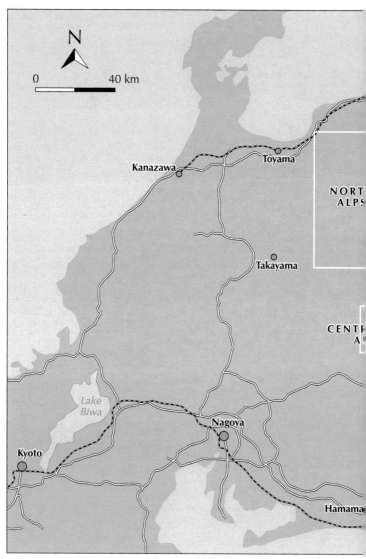

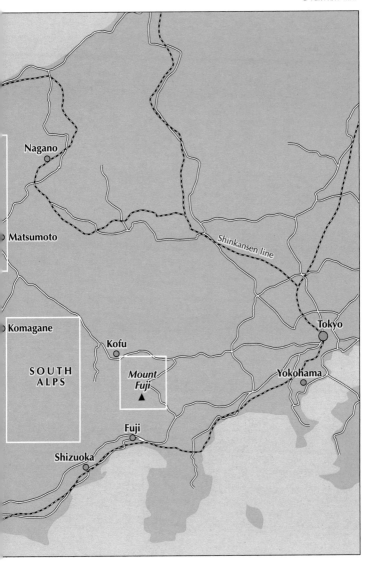

Nagano

Matsumoto

Shinkansen line

Komagane

Kofu

Tokyo

SOUTH
ALPS

*Mount
Fuji*
▲

Yokohama

Fuji

Shizuoka

Heading towards Tateyama from the Murodō bus terminal (Trek 3, Stage 1)

INTRODUCTION

Splendid views from the summit of Mt Yake-dake down towards Kamikōchi and a snow-capped Mt Hotaka (Walk 4)

Gazing south as the sky slowly fills with warm hues of orange and yellow, the distant but instantly recognisable peak of Mt Yari-ga-take pierces the crisp air like a jaunty church spire on a frosty morning. Apart from faint birdsong in the depths of the valleys and the sound of the wind as it rushes between rocks, all is silent. Down below, two sprightly 60-somethings are slowly hauling themselves up to this exposed promontory, while far away the hulking giants of the South Alps are silhouetted in the early morning sun. Beyond them, the unmistakable conical form of Fuji-san looms over all the land.

This is a sight at odds with the image of Japan as a country of cutting-edge technology, bullet trains and endless urban sprawl – yet such natural beauty is easy to find in the wild alpine high country of central Honshu. The huge mountain ranges which cut across Japan's main island from north to south are collectively referred to as the Japan Alps, and they offer a wealth of hiking and camping opportunities among some of Japan's most spectacular scenery, ranging from easy day-hikes to challenging multi-day treks. An extensive network of mountain huts service all of the trails, and with excellent bus and train links to most of the trailheads it has never been easier for visitors to explore Japan's most ruggedly beautiful regions.

The Japan Alps, or Japanese Alps (Nihon Arupusu 日本アルプス in Japanese) are a series of large mountain ranges which bisect the main island of Honshu, spanning across the centre of the country from the Sea of Japan coast in the north to the Pacific Ocean in the south. They are divided into three main ranges; the North Alps (or Kita Arupusu 北アルプス), the Central Alps (Chūō Arupusu 中央アルプス) and the South Alps (Minami Arupusu 南アルプス), all of which are home to some of the biggest mountains in the country, including 20 peaks above the 3000m mark.

Standing 50km to the east of the South Alps, imposing and alone, lies Mt Fuji or Fuji-san 富士山, the tallest mountain in Japan and a technically active stratovolcano which rises to an impressive height of 3776m. The almost perfectly symmetrical conical shape and frequently snow-capped summit has made Mt Fuji a symbol of Japan and one of the most iconic mountains in the world, and so it holds a special place in the hearts of the many Japanese and foreign visitors who come to view, photograph or climb it. The climbing season is short however, and despite its enormous popularity among people of all ages (every year up to 300,000 people attempt to reach the summit in the summer) it is not a mountain to be taken lightly. But it is an achievable goal for anyone who wishes to stand at the highest point in Japan.

This guidebook contains a variety of walks and treks in these four regions, from easy afternoon hikes to gruelling multi-day treks and climbs in high alpine terrain, so there should be something for everyone with an interest in experiencing Japan's great outdoors.

PREPARATIONS AND PRACTICALITIES

Most of the hikes in this book are intended for the summer and early autumn hiking season, although trails and some huts in the Japan Alps open from around 'golden week' in early May, through until the beginning of November. Mt Fuji's climbing season is limited to July, August and a week or two either side of this. During the summer holidays (20 July to 31 August) trails and huts are at their busiest, and public buses to trailheads usually increase in frequency, with some of the seasonal ones only operational at this time.

The Japan Alps are likely to still be very snowy earlier in the season, so if you don't have the skills and equipment for walking on snow and ice, wait until July onwards when most of the snow will have melted. June is the rainy season, but it can be a quiet and pleasant time to hike if the forecast is good, as the temperatures are a bit more comfortable than the oppressive heat and humidity of the summer. July and August are hot and sticky even in the mountains, although at heights over 2000m temperatures are cooler, and summits can be cold. Thunderstorms are common in the afternoons too. Be careful of typhoons from mid July to mid October. Late September to early November is a good time to hike, with cooler temperatures and a chance of seeing the stunning autumn colours – but check hut details carefully as many close by the end of October.

A wintery view of the Nishi-Hotaka ridgeline from Maruyama (Walk 5)

15

If you want to get away from the crowds, avoid weekends and public holidays, especially around Obon (an annual Buddhist event to commemorate ancestors) in mid August, Golden Week starting 29 April, and the cluster of holidays known as Silver Week in mid September. Transport and accommodation can be very busy throughout Japan around national holidays, including over New Year (which has been celebrated in accordance with the Western calendar since 1873) and during popular events such as cherry blossom season – known as *hanami,* when people gather outdoors to view and picnic under the cherry blossoms, usually in late March/early April.

GETTING TO JAPAN

Visas
Travellers from most Western countries will be issued a temporary visitor visa when they arrive in the country (evidence of an onward or return ticket may be required), and these are typically valid for 90 days.

By air
Narita International Airport is 1hr from Tokyo and operates daily flights from Europe, North America, Australia and many Asian countries. Some of the most popular airlines that have direct flights to and from Europe include KLM, Air France, Finnair and British Airways. Cheaper (but indirect) options include Thai Airways, Malaysia Airlines and Qatar Airways. North American routes are covered by a wide range of carriers including JAL, Continental Airlines, American Airlines, Cathay Pacific, Delta

and many others. Haneda Airport, which serves domestic routes as well as an increasing number of international carriers, is situated close to central Tokyo.

The closest international airport to the Japan Alps is Chubu Centrair International Airport in Nagoya; it serves a number of major airlines and has indirect flights from London and Manchester. Other major points of entry include Kansai International Airport near Osaka and Fukuoka Airport in northern Kyushu. Small regional airports close to the Alps include Toyama Airport and Shinshu-Matsumoto Airport.

If travelling to or from nearby Asian countries, there are a number of new 'budget' airlines that fly domestic and international routes, such as Peach, Jetstar Japan, AirAsia Japan and Vanilla Air. For airline contact details, see Appendix E.

By ferry
For those with time on their hands and a sense of adventure, it is possible to travel to Japan by ferry from China (Shanghai and Qingdao), South Korea (Busan) or Russia (seasonal services from Korsakov and from Vladivostok via Donghae in South Korea). The basic fare is often much cheaper than an air ticket. Websites such as www.aferry.co.uk and www.directferries.co.uk include most of the scheduled routes and will take reservations; and see Appendix E for further information on routes and providers.

GETTING AROUND JAPAN

Japan has some of the most reliable, clean and comfortable transport systems in the world, with even rural areas being well connected to major urban areas thanks to extensive rail and road routes. The biggest problem will often be choosing the best ways to get around! For contact details of transport providers, see Appendix E.

Rail

With arguably the world's best rail network, travelling around Japan by train is the preferred method for many visitors and locals alike. The trains are famously so efficient that on the rare occasions that they are a minute or two late it causes genuine consternation!

JR (Japan Railways) is the national rail network with six regional operators (for example JR East) which when combined cover most of the country. There are many kinds of trains, from slow and local *futsū* trains that stop at every station, to the faster *kyūkō* (ordinary express), *kaisoku* (rapid) and *tokkyū* (limited express, which is, confusingly, the fastest!) services which all have limited stops. The fastest trains of all are the famous bullet trains or *shinkansen*, which reach speeds of over 300km/h on a high-speed and supremely efficient network which now stretches right across the country. There are a few kinds of *shinkansen* services; on the Tōkaidō line between Tokyo and Kyoto, Nozomi trains are the fastest with fewest stops (making the 397km journey between the two cities in around 1hr 55min), followed by the slower Hikari and Kodama services. JR operates all bullet trains. Tourists with a 'JR Pass' have unlimited use of all JR services, including the bullet trains, while their pass remains valid (see 'Rail passes', below).

Flags blowing in the wind on Mt Fuji

The Fuji Subaru Line 5th Station is the final stop for buses to Mt Fuji's Yoshida trail (Walk 10) and is busy throughout the year

There are also a number of other train lines and operators across the country, and extensive subway systems in the big cities, and while separate tickets and passes are not typically universal, changing lines is usually straightforward. Use www.hyperdia.com to check train times and connections.

Buses

Most Japanese cities and towns, as well as more rural areas, are served by extensive bus networks, but they can sometimes be difficult for foreigners to use due to a lack of English (although this is gradually changing). In some cases there is a flat-rate fare regardless of distance travelled, while other times you have to take a ticket that shows the current zone number when boarding the bus, and you then pay the fare that matches the one for your destination,

usually displayed on an electronic sign at the front of the bus. Buses that serve popular hiking bases such as Kamikochi in the North Alps, Hirogawara in the South Alps and buses around Mt Fuji all have plenty of English signs, timetables and often even announcements and so are simple to use.

Long-distance 'highway buses', or *kōsoku basu*, can be a good way to get around the country (especially if you don't have a rail pass), as they are much cheaper than the *shinkansen* – but obviously they take much longer. Night buses are popular with hikers as they tend to arrive at the destination early in the morning, allowing for a full day of activities. Around public holidays and at weekends during the summer, long-distance buses often sell out, so try to book well in advance (reservations usually commence from one month before).

There are night buses direct to the Japan Alps from Tokyo, Kyoto and Osaka in the summer. Bus terminals tend to be located next to major train stations, and one of the best operators for non-Japanese speakers is Willer Express (www.willerexpress.com/en), which allows reservations online in English. Also on its website, foreign visitors can buy the very cheap three-, five- or seven-day 'Japan Bus Pass' for multiple long-distance day or night Willer Express buses. Many other companies also operate long-distance buses, and JR Buses (an offshoot of Japan Railways) has a nationwide network of routes, with tickets available from ticket counters at JR railway stations. As an added bonus, the JR rail pass can also be used on many JR buses.

Tourist information offices are good places to obtain bus schedules and information, and https://japanbusonline. com/en allows users to make online reservations for many bus lines and companies across Japan.

Taxis

Taxis in Japan are clean, safe and reliable, but they can be expensive. However, they can sometimes be a good way to reach awkward trailheads, especially for those travelling in a small group. The starting rate is usually around 600 yen, with a 20min journey typically costing around 4000–5000 yen. Taxis are often found outside train stations, even in rural backwaters, and while communicating with the driver can sometimes be an issue, if you have your destination written down or marked on a map then there should be no problem.

Hitchhiking

If you don't want to shell out for a taxi, then hitchhiking is widely considered to be a safe and viable option in Japan. As in any country, it is important to use common sense and to be friendly and presentable, but hitchhikers in Japan often report being recipients of generous acts of kindness. Hitchhiking (and walking) is not allowed on expressways, although service areas (with pedestrian access) are said to be good places to get a ride.

Car hire

Due to Japan's fantastic rail network, most visitors are able to easily travel all around the country using only public transport. But for those who want to really get off the beaten track and explore the remote, rural corners of Japan, then a hire car is a good option. Most of the hikes in this book are easily accessed by public transport, but there are a couple of routes where having your own wheels may be useful. Note that some roads in the Japan Alps, such as those to Murodō and Kamikōchi in the North Alps and Hirogawara in the South Alps, are prohibited for private vehicles.

You will need to obtain an international driver's licence before travelling to Japan. Two of the main car hire companies are Hertz and Toyota Rent-a-Car.

Driving is on the left in Japan, and while driving in the big cities is best avoided due to congestion, most roads are safe and the major signposts are in English. Expressways charge tolls which can be expensive if travelling long distances, and although the speed limit is 80km/h it doesn't seem to be strictly enforced, and many drive much faster.

A view of Mt Hotaka from outside Chō-ga-take Hut in the North Alps (Trek 6)

By air

It is often quicker and sometimes cheaper to travel by air in Japan. JAL and ANA are the two main domestic carriers and have regular flights between Tokyo and major hubs such as Osaka, Sapporo, Sendai, Fukuoka and Naha, as well as flights to more regional airports. In recent years the number of low-cost carriers has increased, with the likes of Peach, Skymark and Jetstar Japan all offering relatively cheap flights across the country. The small airport at Matsumoto has seasonal flights to and from Sapporo, Osaka Itami and Fukuoka, while Toyama Airport can be reached from Tokyo Haneda, Sapporo and a handful of destinations in Korea and China.

By ferry

Japan is a country made up of islands, and there is a huge amount of ferry services between them. Although not applicable to any of the hikes in this book, if you plan to travel around Japan during your stay, then a ride on a ferry is a relaxing and unique way to get around. JR operates a handful of ferries (most notably between Hiroshima and Miyajima) for which the JR rail pass is valid. Ask locally for details.

RAIL PASSES

To make best use of the extensive rail network, a variety of rail passes are available for visitors to Japan, and purchasing one can certainly save you money, depending on your itinerary.

JR rail pass

JR is the national rail network which includes the *shinkansen* and covers the entire country. This rail pass is available to anyone visiting Japan on a tourist visa. Japanese nationals living abroad may also be eligible. See www.japanrailpass. net/en for detailed information.

There are two types of JR pass on offer: ordinary or green (the latter allowing use of the premium green cars on long-distance trains, which along with the slightly extra room can often have free seats available during busy periods), and these are available for durations of 7 days, 14 days or 21 days, costing from 29,000 yen to 80,000 yen. Prices for children are roughly half those for adults.

The JR pass is valid for travel on all JR trains (as well as JR buses and ferries). It is valid for *shinkansen* trains but not the faster Nozomi or Mizuho services.

Until recently, a JR pass had to be bought prior to arrival in Japan, but on a trial basis until the end of March 2019 (and possibly beyond that in the future) it is possible to obtain one at the ticket counter in most major stations, although it costs a little more. However, it's still cheaper and easier to buy one beforehand; purchase an 'exchange order' from a designated sales office or agent in your country before travelling to Japan (search the internet for reputable agents or check www.japanrailpass. net/en – select 'JAPAN RAIL PASS: From purchase to travel' – for lists of sellers). You should turn in your exchange order along with your passport at the Japan Rail Pass exchange office at any major JR station (including Narita Airport, Tokyo, Shinjuku, Shibuya, Kansai Airport,

Osaka and Kyoto stations). You will then be presented with your JR pass and are free to use it from that point on for its full duration. Be aware that your exchange pass must be turned in for a JR pass within three months of the date of purchase, so don't buy one too far ahead of your trip's starting date.

To use your JR pass, don't enter the automatic ticket gates at stations, but simply show your pass at a staff-attended gate. You can also go to the reservation office (*midori-no-madoguchi*) to reserve seats ahead of time.

If you plan on travelling around the country during your trip then the JR pass is a good investment. When you consider that the average price of a one-way *shinkansen* ticket between Tokyo and Kyoto is around 13,000 yen, then a single trip to Kyoto and back costs almost the same as a seven-day JR pass, which also saves the hassle of buying tickets.

Regional passes

There are a wide variety of other rail passes available which cover certain cities or areas, allow travel on railways or subway lines not covered by the JR pass, or include entry or discounts to some attractions. JR East (www.jreast.co.jp/e) and JR West (www.westjr.co.jp/global) have a number of region-specific passes which may suit your needs if you're mostly staying in one area or have a few days before/after your main JR pass has activated/expired.

There are also a bewildering number of city-specific passes, but they can be a little pricey; it is difficult to know what exactly is covered and they are probably not worthwhile unless you're using the trains almost all day.

For the Japan Alps region, the 'Alpine-Takayama-Matsumoto Area Tourist Pass' is an interesting option, as it provides foreign visitors with five consecutive days' unlimited use of JR trains between Nagoya and Toyama and Nagoya and Shinano-Omachi, along with transportation along the popular Tateyama Kurobe Alpine Route (a sightseeing route using trains, buses and ropeways which cuts through the North Alps). The ticket costs around 17,500 yen. There is also a three-day 'Mt Fuji Area Pass', allowing unlimited use of JR trains; see http://touristpass.jp/en for details of both. Another option, the 'Fuji Hakone Pass', can be used for travelling from Tokyo and includes use of non-JR lines and buses along with discounts at many attractions in the Mt Fuji and Hakone areas. Check www.odakyu.jp/english (select 'Discount Passes') for full details.

Prepaid IC cards

Prepaid IC cards are contactless smart-cards which make getting around quick and easy. IC cards don't give you any discounts, but they are convenient as you can ride almost any train or bus (JR, subways, other train lines) in the city without buying a ticket, and they can even be used to pay for items in many shops.

IC cards can be purchased at ticket machines or ticket counters for a refundable deposit of 500 yen, plus an initial amount to be charged onto the card. You can then top up the cards at machines as and when you need to. To use them, just touch the card onto or hold above the reader as you pass through an automatic ticket gate; your current balance will flash up on the small screen too.

Different cities and regions have separate IC cards, but in 2013 Japan's most popular cards were made compatible, so you can now use just one card wherever you go in the country. Cards include Suica (JR East in Tokyo and Tohoku), Pasmo (Tokyo's other operators), Icoca (JR in western Japan) and Toica (JR in Nagoya and Shizuoka).

ACCOMMODATION

Accommodation options are plentiful in the big cities, but rooms can often sell out, especially around public holidays and special events such as cherry blossom season, so always try to book well in advance.

The big international hotel reservation websites such as www.booking.com and www.expedia.com have a wealth of accommodation options from hostels to hotels, but there also some Japan-specific websites such as www.japanican.com and www.jalan.net/en, both of which have some *ryokan* and *minshuku* listings (see below). Two websites that specialise in *ryokan* information and bookings are www.ryokan.or.jp/english and www.japaneseguesthouses.com.

Hotels

Hotel prices vary greatly, with basic 'budget' hotel rooms starting from around 3000 yen a night, to luxury first-class hotels costing around 15,000 yen and upwards. Cheap business hotels can frequently be found close to train stations and so are useful for travellers, although rooms can sometimes smell a bit of old cigarette smoke, so try asking

Narada – a hot spring village near Hirogawara in the South Alps (Trek 9)

for a *kinen* room (non-smoking) when booking.

Capsule hotels are mostly found in big cities and they are a uniquely Japanese experience and good for those on a budget. Rooms are small body-length pods with just enough room to sleep and sit up in, and they come with a TV, wireless internet and a curtain for a door. Some have separate male and female areas. Luggage is stored in lockers and there are communal bathrooms and shower facilities.

Love hotels are used by couples for a bit of 'private time', and can often be identified by their garish, Disneyland-like façades and themed rooms. They are designed with privacy in mind and charge hourly 'rest' rates along with overnight options. They sometimes pop up on hotel listings websites, and are acceptable places to stay, but children are prohibited.

Hostels

Hostels and backpackers' guesthouses are another cheap option and can be found all over Japan. With a bed typically costing around 3000 yen per night, they tend to be very popular with young Japanese students. Dormitory-style rooms with bunk beds are the norm, although some places offer private lodgings, and there is often a curfew of around 11pm. Toilets and bathrooms are usually shared, and towels are not always provided (but can be rented for a small fee). A full list of official youth hostels can be found at www.jyh.or.jp/e.

Renting apartments

In recent years Airbnb (www.airbnb. com) has taken off in Japan (although new restrictive laws mean that it is less widespread than in many other countries) and visitors rarely run into problems. Many houses and apartments are available to rent for one night or longer, mostly in inner-city locations but with an increasing number in more rural areas too. They are good for budget travellers; the property's owners can often impart useful local information and there is often free wi-fi available.

Ryokan

Ryokan (旅館) are traditional Japanese inns usually found in rural hot spring areas, and they offer the quintessential Japanese experience, with a focus on service and polite hospitality. Rooms are traditionally furnished with tatami floors and futons to sleep on and guests can enjoy fine seasonal and locally sourced *kaiseki ryori* (multi-course haute cuisine) typically served in the room, and make use of the hot spring baths. *Ryokan* come in many varieties, from small relatively affordable family-run establishments, to eye-wateringly expensive and luxurious retreats. While they are hardly a budget option with prices starting at around 10,000 yen per person, a stay in one is a memorable experience and can seem like absolute heaven after a few days spent roughing it in the mountains.

Minshuku and pensions

Minshuku (民宿) are family operated, bed-and-breakfast style establishments, frequently found in hot spring resorts, ski areas, seaside villages and mountain hamlets. In many ways they are like slightly downscale *ryokan*, with tatami-floored rooms, futons and sometimes shared bathroom and dining rooms, and there is usually a hot spring bathhouse adjacent or very nearby. Prices range from around 3000 to 10,000 yen per person, often with the option of dinner and breakfast.

MOUNTAIN HUTS AND CAMPING

Japan has a large and well-maintained network of mountain huts (*yamagoya* 山小屋), particularly throughout the Japan Alps and all the way up Mt Fuji. These can vary from basic emergency shelters to fully staffed huts that charge for meals and accommodation. Huts are generally open from May to late October (check Appendix C and the route descriptions for details). Prices tend to vary, but expect to pay in the region of 6000 to 10,000 yen per person per night, including two meals (dinner and breakfast). It is possible to pay for accommodation only (*sudomari* 素泊まり in Japanese), which brings the price down to around 4000 to 7000 yen.

Warm futons and small pillows are provided, with hikers usually crammed together in dorm-style tatami rooms, although a few of the bigger huts do have small, private rooms. If possible it's best to call ahead to make a reservation, but huts will always make space and never turn people away, so booking is not necessary (with one or two exceptions, such as Kitazawa-tōge in the South Alps and Kisodono sansō in the Central Alps; booking is also highly advisable on Mt Fuji during peak season). Latecomers tend to get the worst sleeping spots though, so get there early if possible. Mountain huts can be difficult places to get a good night's sleep, with noisy snorers, people shuffling around at night, and many hikers getting up as early as 3am to catch the sunrise, so take earplugs if you're a light sleeper.

Sleeping quarters in a mountain hut

When entering a hut, go to the desk or counter (taking off your boots if necessary) and you will be required to fill out a form with your name, contact address and hike plan, and then you pay upfront (cash only).

Mountain huts tend to operate on fairly rigid schedules, with dinner served from 5pm (you may miss out if you arrive after 6pm), lights out at 8 or 9pm and breakfast from around 4.30am! If you take your own food you can stay in bed longer and leave at a more leisurely hour, and there is usually a space for doing your own cooking. For wet gear, there is often a heated drying room (called *kansō shitsu* 乾燥室) where you can hang your wet items.

Most huts have plenty of snacks, noodles and drinks (including beer) for sale, but expect to pay higher 'mountain

prices' as everything has to be flown in by helicopter. Some huts have free water (usually collected rainwater) while others charge a couple of hundred yen per litre. Hut staff are knowledgeable and are worth consulting about trail conditions and weather forecasts, with the younger ones in particular often speaking a smattering of English.

There are a number of unmanned emergency huts (*hinan-goya* 避難小屋) on a few routes in the Japan Alps. They are free to stay in (some have a donation box) but rarely have any amenities at all, so you must take all your own sleeping gear and food.

Providing you have all the equipment, camping at (or in the region of) a mountain hut is a cheap option, with prices around 500 to 1000 yen per person per night. Just say *tento* テント (tent) or *kyampu* キャンプ (camp) at the hut's reception, pay your fee and choose your spot. Campers can use the hut facilities (including drinking water and toilets) too. Campsites are sometimes situated a fair distance away from mountain huts, and come in all shapes and sizes; some are grassy and spacious, others small, rocky and very exposed – both to the weather and in terms of steep drops. Some of the campgrounds in the North Alps in particular are perilously exposed on narrow windy ridges, so make sure you have a decent three-season tent with plenty of guy lines. Free-standing tents can be very useful for setting up on hard, stony ground.

Note that wild camping is prohibited in national parks and protected areas (which includes most of the Japan Alps), with camping only allowed at the designated campsites. There are often campsites close to trailheads, and in many parts of Japan (even in towns and cities) 'stealth camping' – setting up late, leaving early – is generally not frowned upon in local parks, on beaches and at other quiet spots.

Dinner time in the South Alps

FOOD AND DRINK

One of the great joys of visiting Japan is sampling the many kinds of unique foods and dishes on offer, with most regions very proud of their local and seasonal specialities.

Izakaya 居酒屋 are almost like Japanese pubs, serving a number of dishes and lots of alcohol: they range from small and smoky hole-in-the-wall places to refined establishments. *Shokudō* 食堂 and *shokujitokoro* 食事処 are all-round restaurants with varied menus and represent good value.

Some of the most well-known staples of Japanese cuisine include fresh sushi (寿司) and sashimi (刺身), while noodle dishes such as ramen (ラーメン) and udon (うどん) come in many variants, are a cheap meal and restaurants can be found almost everywhere. Other popular dishes include:

- *kushikatsu* (串かつ): deep-fried bite-size pieces of meat, seafood or vegetables on skewers
- *yakitori* (焼き鳥): grilled chicken on skewers cooked over a charcoal fire and seasoned in a sweet and thick soy sauce called *tare* (たれ) or salt (塩)
- *yakiniku* (焼肉): meaning 'grilled meat', customers cook various cuts of meat over a grill at the table,

often with helpings of fluffy white rice and a sauce for dipping

- *shabu shabu* (しゃぶしゃぶ): a hot-pot-style dish where thin slices of beef and pork along with vegetables are swirled around in boiling water and then eaten after dipping in a *ponzu* (citrus-based) or sesame sauce
- *sukiyaki* (すき焼き): similar to *shabu shabu* except the ingredients are simmered in boiling water with soy sauce, sugar and *mirin* (sweet rice wine) and are then dipped into a bowl of beaten raw eggs before eating.

Teppanyaki is a general style of Japanese cuisine based on food that is cooked on an iron griddle. The high-end version typically includes *wa-gyu* (premium-quality beef such as Kobe beef, known for its marbling and exquisite taste), seafood and seasonal vegetables all cooked by a chef in front of the customer. These are multi-course menus and usually command a high price (anything from about 5000 to 25,000 yen). The lower-end version of *teppanyaki* features cheaper and more regional dishes such as *okonomiyaki* (お好み焼き), which is a kind of pancake stuffed with cabbage and meat or seafood, famous in Osaka and Hiroshima, and a fried noodle dish called *yakisoba* (焼きそば).

In the Takayama region of the Japan Alps you can find local specialities which include Hida beef (another highly prized variety of marbled meat), *goheimochi* (pounded rice or 'mochi' grilled on a skewer and glazed with sesame sauce) and many varieties of sake, while Matsumoto is famous for raw horse meat sashimi known as *basashi* (馬刺し), buckwheat noodles called *soba* (そば) and *Shinsu miso* (味噌), a paste made from fermented soybeans. For more adventurous eaters, some traditional rural mountain foods include *inago* (いなご) which are grasshoppers boiled in soy sauce and sugar, and *hachinoko* (蜂の子) is bee or wasp larvae often served in a sweet marinade; neither are as bad as they sound!

The Mt Fuji region has a few local delicacies to lookout for including chewy Yoshida udon noodles, often served with cabbage and cooked horse meat. Houtou Fudou is a speciality chain found only in the Fuji Five Lakes area, which serves thick white noodles in big iron pots. The local Koshu (甲州) grape is used to make a dry white wine which goes well with Japanese food.

Mountain huts have a decent selection of food and drinks available, the most typical meals being curry rice (カレーライス), ramen or oden (おでん), which is a one-pot dish consisting of boiled eggs, vegetables and processed fishcakes in a light broth. Beer, tea, water and soft drinks are usually sold, but expect to pay more than at lower elevations. It's always best to stock up at supermarkets or convenience stores before leaving town (or to take some of your favourites from home), as most rural areas and trailheads have few shops.

Vegetarian and vegan hikers can find meat-free options in most major metropolitan areas, but you should consider taking your own food when heading into the mountains. Meals at mountain huts usually consist of at least one meat or fish product, and most soup broths are made from either a fish or meat base.

HOT SPRINGS

As a seismically active country, geothermal hot springs, or *onsen* 温泉 can be found all over Japan, and taking a soak in their mineral-enriched waters is not just a relaxing pastime but something approaching a national obsession and a key component of Japanese culture. Hot springs come in many varieties, from indoors to outdoors, basic to lavish, and the word *onsen* can refer to a single bathhouse or an entire resort town. The thermally heated water is pumped up from the ground and is believed to have healing qualities, and hot springs differ by their mineral content, temperature (although they're all usually red hot!) and even water colour. In the past, many hot springs were mixed gender, but these days the sexes are far more likely to be segregated, and as everyone is naked it is a great social leveller.

Free footbath (ashiyu) at Hakuba-Yari Onsen (Trek 1, Stage 2)

There is a certain *onsen* etiquette which it is important to follow: take off all of your clothes in the changing area and put them in a basket along with your towel (note that at mixed *onsen* women tend to wear a swimming costume or cover up with a towel; in gender-segregated hot springs wearing anything at all is almost unheard of for both males and females). Before entering the bath, wash your body using the showers or washbowls and be careful to rinse off all the soap and shampoo. You can then enter the bath and soak for as long as you like. You can take a small towel into the bath and bathing area to protect your modesty, or do as the locals do and dip it in the water, rinse it out and then put it on your head (this is thought to help stop you passing out from the heat).

One point to note is that many bathhouses won't admit entry to people with tattoos due to their long-rooted association with the *yakuza* (organised crime syndicates), although the situation is slowly changing. Look out for signs that make this explicitly clear, or if in doubt, ask at the counter. Some *onsen* are fine with tattoos, others may ask you to cover them up (with plasters/band-aids) but some will refuse entry full stop.

Many Japanese hikers will aim to visit a hot spring at the end of a long day in the hills, with the *onsen* often being as important as the hike itself, and certainly the rejuvenating effects of a long soak on weary limbs can't be underestimated. Luckily there are many hot springs in the mountains, often connected to *ryokan* (traditional Japanese inns) and they are frequently found near trailheads, with a number of mountain huts even having their own indoor, or occasionally out-door bath. There are even natural hot springs on lonely trails deep in the wil-derness, so it's always worth checking the maps for the hot spring symbol (♨). The Japan Alps are blessed with many bathhouses and famous *onsen* resorts, while areas around Mt Fuji such as Lake Kawaguchi-ko and Hakone have been attracting people for centuries due to their natural beauty and abundant hot springs. So forget your inhibitions and experience a uniquely Japanese activ-ity that is entwined with the country's mountain culture.

MONEY

Japan is thought of as an expensive country, and while this can often be true, it is possible to travel on a 'budget' with just a little planning. When hik-ing, the biggest expenses will usually be transport and accommodation, but a rail pass can save a lot of money (see 'Rail passes', above) and camping is much cheaper than staying in mountain huts. Affordable hotels and hostels are to be found in most urban areas, and eating out can actually be cheaper than in many other developed countries, espe-cially for noodle or rice-based dishes. Also remember there is no culture of tip-ping in Japan.

The Japanese currency is known as 'yen' (円), and notes come in denomi-nations of 1000, 2000 (very rare), 5000 and 10,000. Coins are 500, 100, 50, 10 and 1. (Bear in mind that a stock of 100-yen coins may be useful for entry to the toilets in some of the mountain huts.)

The rate does vary, so always check before converting (see www.xe.com for

the latest rates). Currency exchange can be expensive in Japan, so it is often best to change some money into yen before your arrival.

In 2019 the exchange rates are approximately:
£1 = 140 yen
€1 = 120 yen
$1 = 110 yen

The best option, however, is to have a credit or debit card from your own country which doesn't charge for cash withdrawals at foreign ATMs. Japanese banks don't usually accept foreign cards, but Mastercard and Visa cards can be used to withdraw cash from ATMs at post offices, 7-Eleven stores and some banks, such as Citibank. Most machines have an English-language option. Post offices and 7-Elevens can be found in almost every town and decent-sized village, so get cash before setting out on your hike. Be aware that not all ATMs function 24/7, and some may limit the amount you can withdraw at any one time.

Japan is still very much a cash-based society, and it is always a good idea, if not essential to have some on you. Japan is very safe, so you don't need to worry about carrying large amounts of cash around, but always use com-mon sense. Coins are useful for buses, snacks and drinks. Many places don't accept cards, including some hotels and restaurants, and this is even more likely to be the case in the countryside. Credit cards are not accepted at mountain huts, so always take enough cash to cover the entire hiking trip. For those hiking in the popular Hotaka area of the North Alps, note that Kamikōchi has no ATMs or convenience stores.

Creeping pine grows in vast swathes on many mountain tops in the Japan Alps (Trek 8, Stage 2)

COMMUNICATIONS

Japan is a technologically advanced country, and in the big cities internet and mobile phone coverage is good, with many cafés, shops, tourist information offices and even some train stations offering free wi-fi. In the countryside it can be another story entirely, with far patchier mobile coverage, and in the mountains there is often no coverage at all.

Pre-paid SIM cards are useful if you want to use your smartphone when travelling around Japan. Your phone must be unlocked and you can then purchase a 'visitor SIM card' at the airport or at any big electronics store (such as Yodobashi Camera, Softmap). There are a number of service providers to choose from, and prices vary wildly depending on coverage, duration and data usage. A popular SIM card is PAYG SIM by b-mobile,

which has good coverage across Japan and provides 3MB of data for seven days' use.

Pocket wi-fi devices are a simpler option, as there is no need to mess around with SIM cards, they work with locked phones and wi-fi can be used with multiple phones, tablets etc. It does mean carrying and charging another device, but they are cheap to rent and very reliable, even in the mountains. They can be ordered online before your trip, to be ready for pickup at the airport or hotel, and they come with a pre-paid envelope, so returning them couldn't be easier. Prices vary but typically start from around 4000 yen for a week's rental. Two of the most popular providers are Japan Wireless (www.japan-wireless.com) and GAC (www.globaladvancedcomm.com/pocketwifi.html).

LANGUAGE

Japanese is the national language of Japan (although the Japan archipelago is also home to a handful of minority languages including the Ryūkyūan languages spoken in southern-lying Okinawa and the Amami islands). The standard form of Japanese is called *hyōjungo*, which originates from the upper-class areas of Tokyo and is now the form taught in schools, used in all official communications and mass media and is understood by everyone. Many distinct dialects (*~ben* in Japanese) exist however, the most well-known being *Kansai-ben*, which is the regional dialect of Osaka and Kyoto. Dialects from more peripheral regions may be unintelligible to people from other ends of the country, with big differences in tone, accent and sometimes vocabulary.

Japanese has a famously complex writing system which uses three different elements. By far the most difficult to learn is *kanji* (漢字), a script with Chinese origins that has thousands of logographic characters, each one of which can have multiple pronunciations depending on context – meaning even Japanese people can often struggle to read or remember them. *Hiragana* (ひらがな) is a phonetic syllabary (symbols representing syllables) with only 46 basic characters: it is usually attached to the end of *kanji* to form grammatical conjugations, or is sometimes used for words with no (or obsolete) *kanji* readings. *Katakana* (カタカナ) is similar to *hiragana* except it is used to write foreign loan words (e.g. ビール/*biiru*/beer) and non-Japanese names and can be used to provide emphasis.

If you are keen to study a little Japanese before your trip, then both *hiragana* and *katakana* can be memorised fairly quickly, and they are very useful for reading things like station names on signs or items on restaurant menus.

With a complex grammar that is very different to English, multiple levels of polite and humble speech and the convoluted writing system, Japanese can seem intimidating to non-speakers. However, most Japanese people will be very pleased and impressed if a foreigner manages to fumble through even a single word of Japanese, so just give it a go! A glossary of useful vocabulary and phrases along with notes on pronunciation can be found in Appendix D.

Despite the fact that English is a core subject in schools and Western influences are to be found everywhere, many Japanese people do not speak or understand English well. Always speak slowly and clearly when trying to communicate, and write things down if necessary, as many Japanese people find it easier to read English as opposed to speaking or listening. The honorific suffix '~san' is often added to the end of people's first names or surnames when speaking or referring to them, and it is also an alternative reading of the *kanji* character for 'mountain' (山), eg. Fuji-san (富士山).

Note that some of the websites provided in this guide are in Japanese. In such cases there may be an English-language option clearly visible at the top of the page. Where this option is not available it is worth using an automatic translation tool such as Google Translate; this should at least enable you to obtain the required information.

The final climb towards the summit of Mt Yake-dake (Walk 4)

TOURIST INFORMATION OFFICES

Most towns and cities usually have at least one tourist information office; they tend to be located either inside or very close to train stations, and are always worth checking out. They are called *kankō-annai-jyo* (観光案内所) in Japanese and can be identified by the large question mark sign at the entrance. They often have free English-language maps of the area, and while the staff are not always fluent English speakers, they tend to be very helpful and can offer advice on local hotels, restaurants, hot springs, events and attractions, as well as things like bus routes, times and schedules. However, due to the recent boom in overseas visitors, offices in sightseeing hotspots can be very crowded and understaffed.

WHAT TO TAKE

The Japanese summer is hot and humid down near sea-level, but alpine peaks can be cold both during the day and at night, and this is especially true towards the beginning or end of the main hiking season, so you need to wear layers and pack for all weathers. It may be shorts and t-shirt weather at the trailhead, but at elevations over 2000m a fleece, light down jacket and/or windbreaker are often needed, while gloves and a hat are good for staying warm. The sun can be very strong, so always have sunglasses and sunscreen (convenience stores usually sell UV lotion in small, easy-to-carry bottles). While sunny days are fairly frequent, mountain areas are subject to localised weather fronts meaning there is always a chance of rain, so it is essential to pack a waterproof jacket and pants. Take a small towel for wiping sweat away, drying camping gear and using at an *onsen*.

Comfortable hiking boots or sturdy trail-running shoes are a must; ideally they should be 'broken in' well before a big trip to avoid developing painful blisters on the trail. For multi-day hikes it is a pleasant luxury to have a pair of light shoes, crocs or sandals for use around the hut or camp. Gaiters may be useful on muddy or stony trails, and a couple of pairs of thick hiking socks are mandatory. Early in the season (late May through June) there may be still be substantial snow patches at higher elevations, so a pair of simple crampons or snow spikes could prove useful.

Trekking poles are very popular in Japan, and they can help with balance and reducing wear-and-tear on the knees. (Rubber caps should be attached to the tips to prevent damage to the trails.) A decent sized rucksack (15L to 35L) should suffice for day-hikes, while a bag of 35L to 70L is better for multi-day treks, although if you plan to stay in mountain huts then a smaller pack will do. A small first-aid kit should always be carried, and it's best to take medications from home (although be careful as there are some common cough and cold medications which are illegal to take into Japan, so do check beforehand).

In addition, inside your rucksack you should carry a headtorch (even in the summer it gets dark early in Japan), spare batteries, clean clothes (in a waterproof stuffsack), a map, water, snacks and a compass. Many Japanese hikers carry a bear bell attached to their rucksack, and while the constant jingling sound can be annoying at first, you soon get used to it. Your chances of running into a bear are slim however, so whistle or sing to make your presence known on quiet stretches of the trail.

If you are staying only in mountain huts, then you won't need a sleeping bag because futons are provided, although if you're a light sleeper then earplugs are a must to block out the noise of snoring hikers!

If you are camping then you'll need to take a good, lightweight three-season tent – the smaller the better as some campgrounds can be narrow and cramped, and as the ground is often hard and rocky, a freestanding design can make life easier. You'll also need a sleeping bag, sleeping mat and cooking equipment (although if camping near huts you can usually buy some hot food and snacks from there). It is prohibited to take gas canisters on airplanes, but Japanese outdoor shops stock a variety of cooking stove fuels from the likes of Primus and Coleman.

In the big cities there are numerous outdoor shops (pronounced *outodoā shoppu*) such as ICI Sports (now known as Mt Ishii Sports, Mt 石井スポーツ) and Kojitsu Sanso (好日山荘). They have a wide range of hiking goods and stock most of the famous Western brands as well as Japanese makes, but the prices are often expensive. Sizes tend to be on the small side too, especially for hiking boots. It is possible to rent clothing, boots and equipment after arriving in Japan at some hiking stores and from www.yamarent.com (English-language option); they have a shop in Shinjuku, and also at Kawaguchiko and Mt Fuji's Subaru Line 5th Station during the summer season.

Yakushi-tōge campground (Trek 3, Stage 3)

For hiking food, outdoor stores sell an increasing variety of lightweight freeze-dried foods, but it is cheaper to visit a supermarket before setting off and stock up on things like pasta, instant noodles, chocolate, dried fruits etc. Almost all huts and campgrounds have drinking water available, while most people happily drink water from designated springs and streams without treating it, so water purification tools are probably unnecessary.

LUGGAGE FORWARDING

If you are hiking in the mountains then it can be good to travel lightly by having your luggage forwarded to your next hotel or destination. Japan has many companies that offer a simple and efficient service called *takkyubin*,

collecting and delivering to addresses all over the country. You can send luggage from your hotel, or even to and from convenience stores and airports, and prices range from around 1000 to 5000 yen per item, depending on size. Deliveries can usually be made by the next day, or for a specified time and date within seven days of pickup, and hotel staff are usually happy to help with the logistics.

In the Japan Alps it is possible to get your luggage sent to and from hotels in Kamikōchi (for staying guests), and the Tateyama Kurobe Alpine Route has its own forwarding service (see www.alpen-route.com/en).

Two of the most popular luggage forwarding services are Yamato www.kuronekoyamato.co.jp/en and Sagawa www.sagawa-exp.co.jp/english.

MAPS AND GPS

For almost all of the walks in this book, the Yama-to-kōgen series (山と高原地図) produced by Shobunsha are the most comprehensive, high-quality and popular hiking maps, covering all of the major mountains in great detail. Unfortunately they contain very little English, but the trails (with walking times), huts, campgrounds and water sources are clearly marked, and when used in conjunction with the maps in this book, they should be relatively straightforward to use. Most of the maps are at a scale of 1:50,000 and are reasonably priced. They are updated every year, with new maps occasionally added to the line-up, so be aware that the map numbers quoted here (correct as of 2018) may change in future years. The maps are difficult to come by outside of Japan (although

it may be possible to order online from www.amazon.co.jp) but are easily available after arrival in most hiking stores and from most major book shops – the biggest and best-known being Junkudo and Kinokuniya, both of which have many branches in the big cities.

Maps in the series numbered 34 to 43 cover the Japan Alps in their entirety; see the information at the beginning of each chapter for details of which map(s) to use. Mt Fuji is covered by map 32. The outdoor book and magazine specialist Yamakei (ヤマケイ登山地図) also produces a small range of good-quality maps at 1:25,000 for areas of the Japan Alps, and although less common, they may be found in some Japanese book stores and hiking shops, and online.

Those who like to use a GPS device while hiking don't have a great deal

Metal climbing aids in the Central Alps

of options when it comes to English-language maps for Japan. Probably the best one available for Garmin devices is the Japan Map V2 from UUD (www.uud.info). It is not especially cheap to download but it covers the entire country and has most of the main hiking trails and peaks marked in English. There are also a few free open-source maps of varying quality available for Garmin and other devices if you search online.

WAYMARKING

Paths and trails, even rugged and remote ones, are usually fairly well-maintained and clearly marked and most trails, junctions and landmarks are signed, but often not in English. Exceptions to this are around popular mountain hubs (Murōdo, Kamikōchi), Mt Fuji and much of the South Alps where many signs are bilingual.

Hikers should pay close attention to markings on rocks; arrows are self-explanatory, 'O' means good, 'X' means don't proceed. Small bits of colour-ful tape attached to trees and branches are used to mark the paths, and most Japanese hikers very rarely leave the marked trails intentionally; often due to the nature of the terrain and the thick vegetation it is almost impossible to do so anyway.

THE TYPICAL HIKING DAY

Some of the walks and individual stages of treks in this book are long mountain days where it is important to start early. Many Japanese hikers also set off early with an aim to finish walking by mid afternoon so as to avoid the clouds

and storms that can often roll in later in the day. As the sun sets relatively early at these latitudes (around 7.30pm), it makes sense to make the most of the daylight hours by setting off as early as possible in the morning. So an early 'alpine' start involves waking up at (or even before) sunrise at around 4.30am, and being on the trail by around 5am or certainly no later than 6am. Mountain huts usually serve breakfast around 5am, so you will often have no choice but to conform if staying in a hut!

In the summer months, trains, buses and ropeways tend to start running quite early, so check the timetables beforehand and aim to ride the earliest one available if you have a long day planned. Otherwise camp or stay in accommodation close to the trailhead to ensure an early start. The route information boxes in this guide give an indication of accommodation options at or near the trailhead (and at points along the route).

MOUNTAIN ETIQUETTE

Japanese society has many deeply rooted social expectations and behaviours, often most clearly witnessed by visitors in cultural practices such as *omotenashi*, the rather vague term that describes the selfless humility, hospitality and respect shown to a customer or guest. In all levels of society, etiquette depends on someone's age or status in relation to others: even in the mountains these social behaviours can be seen, particularly among groups of Japanese hikers who often have a leader and a singular group mentality. However, generally speaking, out in the wilds the normal

Tozan-post *for registering hike details*

rules and expectations of everyday life are slightly less rigid, and foreigners are rarely expected to conform to or even be aware of such social nuances.

Although many Japanese people are rather reserved and shy in everyday life, while out hiking it is almost customary to greet other hikers with a friendly *konnichi-wa* (hello), or *ohayo-gozaimasu* (good morning) between the hours of 1am and 7am.

There are a few rules and practices that everyone should try to follow when hiking in Japan. Firstly, at the start of many hikes you will often find a post box-like 'mountain climbers register' or *tozan post* (登山ポスト), where hikers can write down their name, dates and hiking plan, and while this may not be checked regularly it gives the authorities something to go on if a person goes missing. In addition, some forms of hiking insurance may require you to fill out your hiking plan for the insurance to remain valid.

On narrow sections of trails and when using chains and ladders it is good practice to give way to those descending, and some popular mountains (notably Mt Fuji and Yari-ga-take) have separate, clearly marked paths for ascent and descent which should always be used.

If you use trekking poles, remember to attach rubber caps to the tips to prevent damage to the trails, and all rubbish should be packed out and disposed of after the hike. Fires are strictly prohibited in the Japan Alps and indeed in most outdoor areas, and wild camping is only allowed at designated sites.

On mountain summits there is usually a sign or post indicating the peak's name and height and these obviously make for great photo opportunities, so on popular peaks always try to move away from these points to allow others a good shot.

Toilets in the mountains are maintained by the authorities, and most require a donation of 100 yen to be popped in the honesty box. Inside mountain huts, if there is a raised floor and shelves or room for boots nearby then you must take off your shoes before entering, and use the slippers if any are provided.

HEALTH AND SAFETY

Hiking in Japan is generally a safe activity but as with anywhere it pays to plan properly and prepare for any eventuality. When walking and trekking in mountain areas it is important to have clothing to protect you in cold and wet weather, always be aware of your current position, and only choose routes that suit your abilities and the conditions. Leave plenty of time to complete the day's hike – it can start getting dark by around 7.30pm, even in the height of summer, and in the summer months afternoon electrical storms are fairly common in the mountains so it is probably good practice to have most of the hike finished by mid afternoon, if not earlier. Always carry a headtorch and spare batteries.

Heatstroke and sunburn are a real risk on blazing sunny days, particularly in the thinner air at higher altitudes, so drink plenty of fluids and pack sunscreen and a hat.

Although well marked, many Japanese trails are rocky, rough and steep, knotted with tree roots or pass through thick vegetation, and there is always a risk of slipping or twisting an ankle. Loose and crumbling rocks are common, especially after heavy rainfall.

Altitude sickness is rarely a severe problem in Japan, but its effects can be felt from about 2500m upwards, which includes many of the big peaks in the Japan Alps and certainly near the top of Mt Fuji at 3776m. Symptoms include headaches, nausea, dizziness, tiredness and shortness of breath and the only cure is to descend to a lower altitude as soon as possible. To avoid altitude problems it is recommended to ascend slowly, stay hydrated and keep an eye on party members for any possible symptoms.

Japan has almost no serious infectious diseases to worry about (such as malaria or rabies), but there may be a very small risk of contracting Japanese encephalitis – a serious but very rare viral brain infection spread by mosquitos. It is predominantly found in rural regions in the west of the country. There is no cure available, but Japanese people are vaccinated against it in childhood; travellers and hikers shouldn't require a vaccine unless planning to spend a lot of time (at least a month) in rural farming areas.

Volcanoes, earthquakes and typhoons
There are a number of risks and dangers specific to Japan which you may not have faced back home. Situated on the Pacific Ring of Fire, Japan is one of the most geologically active places on Earth. In reality the danger posed by volcanoes is very low; a more likely potential risk is that of inhaling poisonous gases, particularly on some of the routes in the more volcanically active North Alps. Always pay attention to signs and warnings and never enter restricted areas, especially around craters and fumaroles (openings in the ground on or near a volcano through which gases emerge).

Another result of the movement of tectonic plates are the thousands of earthquakes Japan experiences every year. Most of them are too small to notice without sensitive recording equipment, but occasionally they can shake with a violent ferocity, setting off tsunamis and causing widespread damage and destruction. If you are indoors when an earthquake strikes, take cover under a doorway, table or next to a supporting pillar and watch out for falling debris if you're out on the street. In the mountains earthquakes can cause avalanches, rockfall and landslides, fell trees and damage bridges and trails. It is best to avoid hiking in areas recently hit by an earthquake as trails may be closed or altered and there is a high chance of aftershocks, which can sometimes be as severe as the main event.

Every year from around late June to October approximately 15 to 20 typhoons swing north from the tropics, causing damage and disruption particularly in Okinawa, Kyushu, Shikoku and the Pacific side of western and central Honshu. Landslides and flooding are commonplace, while the heavy rains and strong winds cause travel havoc which usually lasts for a couple of days. Hikers should avoid setting out and be prepared to change plans if a typhoon is forecast, as paths and roads may be washed away and rivers can turn into dangerous overflowing torrents. Conversely, the days immediately after a typhoon blows over often feature a period of fine and settled weather, but always do some research online or call mountain huts to check the current trail conditions. (See Appendix C for mountain hut contact details.)

It is always good practice to check online for the latest weather updates and for warnings on volcanic and earthquake activity before setting off on a hike. The Japan Meteorological Agency has some useful information in English on their website at www.jma.go.jp/jma/indexe.html, while www.mountain-forecast.com has weather forecasts for many Japanese peaks.

Wildlife

There is little dangerous wildlife in Japan, although Asiatic black bears are occasionally spotted in remote areas, including the Japan Alps. They can be aggressive and strong and on extremely rare occasions have been known to

Japanese macaques are frequently seen on the trails around Kamikōchi (Trek 5, Stage 1)

attack and kill people. Mothers can be fiercely protective of their cubs, particularly if startled, so the best way to avoid coming across a bear while hiking is by making noise such as talking or clapping, or do as many Japanese hikers do and wear a bear bell. If you happen to encounter a bear the advice is to back away slowly and quietly without making eye contact. Don't run or climb a tree (bears are faster and better climbers than humans).

Large troops of Japanese macaques are a common sight in the wooded lower elevations of the Japan Alps: while they don't pose any danger, you should avoid eye contact, getting too close or feeding them. Monkeys have been known to steal items from tent vestibules (particularly things in plastic bags) at campsites in the valleys, so store everything securely at night.

Venomous snakes such as the *mamushi* マムシ / 蝮 (Japanese pit viper) are found on forested hillsides, often close to water sources where they feed on frogs. This small greyish-brown snake is shy and will only bite if stepped on, so always be alert when walking. Deaths are not unheard of but a good antivenin is available in hospitals.

The *suzumebachi* (スズメバチ) or Japanese giant hornet is a subspecies of the world's largest hornet, and adults often grow to about 2 inches in length. They are very aggressive and have painful stings, which can occasionally cause death even for people who are not allergic. They mostly live in forests and mountain areas, so if you see one, remain still and don't provoke it, and stay away from their nests. They are also said to be attracted to black clothing.

Ticks and leeches can be found in low-lying undergrowth, so wear thick socks and cover up exposed skin. Mosquitoes and other biting insects are mostly just an annoyance, so take insect repellent during the height of summer.

EMERGENCIES

In the case of an emergency, the number for the ambulance and fire services is 119, and for the police it's 110. The operator should understand very simple English, but in case of difficulties call the Japan Helpline on 0570 000 911; it provides emergency assistance and advice in English 24 hours a day, seven days a week.

If you or someone in your party has an accident on the trail then try to get to the nearest mountain hut, as the staff will be able to call for further help. Other hikers may also be able to call the emergency services, but many mountain areas have limited mobile reception. Ensure you convey the most vital information including where the accident happened and the person's condition. If you need to signal for help then the international distress signal is six blasts per minute on a whistle, or six torch flashes after dark, followed by a one-minute pause, and then repeat. The reply is three blasts or flashes followed by a minute's silence.

The local police generally handle mountain rescues; they have specially trained mountain rescue units and rescue helicopter services. Some callouts are totally free, while there are horror stories of hikers having to pay millions of yen to cover the costs of rescue, so always make sure you are covered. Most people's travel insurance doesn't include cover for things like helicopter rescue, so specific hiking insurance is recommended. Worldwide coverage is available and can be bought in advance from specialist providers such as the British Mountaineering Council (www.thebmc.co.uk). At Kamikōchi it is possible to buy insurance (hoken 保険) from a machine at the bus terminal for a reasonable daily rate (500 yen). For long-term residents or those planning on spending a lot of time in the mountains there are a number of comprehensive options including JRO (www.sangakujro.com) and Mont Bell (www.montbell.jp) (Japanese-language websites). Some insurance policies require hikers to fill out their hiking intentions at a *tozan post* (mountain climbers' register) at the trailhead for the coverage to remain valid, so always check the small print.

USING THIS GUIDE

The aim of this book is to show the reader some of the best and most scenic hikes in central Japan's most spectacular mountain regions. Easy options include short hikes on popular and well-defined mountain paths, while some of the more challenging treks can involve multiple long days at altitude with steep ascents and descents, sustained scrambling and walking on rocky and exposed ridges. Some of these also involve the occasional use of fixed chains and ladders, and there are some traverses over snow and ice. Unlike treks in many other parts of the world where trails tend to be steady and take 'the path of least resistance', treks in the Japan Alps often follow rugged, steep trails which rise and fall over multiple peaks, so good levels of fitness and stamina may well be required. Read the descriptions carefully in advance of

Looking back down towards Murodō from the lower slopes of Mt Jōdo-san (Trek 3, Stage 1)

your outing and choose the best hike for your experience and ability.

The Japan Alps are presented in three main areas, arranged geographically from north to south. The Mt Fuji area is included after the South Alps section.

Each route description is preceded by a range of information to help you choose a suitable walk or trek. Bus access is noted and accommodation/facilities are described in brief, while information on distances, ascents, descents and the nature of the terrain should allow you to make informed choices. Times quoted are approximations only, and do not allow for breaks or photo stops.

Route maps are provided at a scale of 1:50,000. In the route descriptions, places or features that are also shown on the route map are shown in **bold** to aid navigation.

Some things may change over time; paths may be re-routed, signs and landmarks may disappear and huts, buses and facilities can go out of service. So always try to check online for the latest information before setting out, or search Facebook groups to ask about the latest trail conditions and for useful advice from likeminded and knowledgeable individuals. See also this guide's updates page on the Cicerone website (www.cicerone.co.uk/947/updates).

Grades

The following grades have been used in this guidebook:

Grade 1: Relatively short and/or easy, steady or small amount of ascent/descent on well-defined paths and mostly easy terrain.

Grade 2: Medium length, moderate amount of ascent/descent, possible short scrambling/ladder sections and areas of difficult terrain.

Grade 3: Long and/or strenuous, large amount of ascent/descent, long sections of exposed and/or challenging terrain.

A plus sign indicates that a route is at the upper end of that particular grade.

Scrambling and exposure

The grade system above is primarily based on how strenuous the route is, taking into account distance, ascent and terrain. Some routes have also been assigned an additional rating, which reflects the amount of scrambling and exposure involved. Those with a fear of heights or lacking experience on steep terrain and rock should avoid routes with a high scambling and exposure rating.

*   Short or easy scrambling/ladder/fixed chain sections.
**   Relatively steep and exposed terrain, fairly lengthy scrambles/ladders/chains.
*** Very steep/vertical scrambles and climbs, sustained and challenging, lots of exposure.

GPX tracks

GPX tracks for the routes in this guidebook are available to download free at www.cicerone.co.uk/947/GPX. A GPS device is an excellent aid to navigation, but you should also carry a map and compass and know how to use them.

ALL ABOUT THE JAPAN ALPS AND MT FUJI

Located to the east of China and the Korean Peninsular, Japan forms a chain of over 6000 islands which jut up from the depths of the Pacific Ocean. The archipelago covers almost 380,000km² (a bit larger than Germany) and stretches almost 20 degrees of latitude, from the sub-arctic northern frontier with Russia to the balmy sub-tropical climes of Okinawa and the Southwest Islands. The four biggest islands are Honshu, Hokkaido, Kyushu and Shikoku and they make up about 97% of Japan's land area, with the main island of Honshu being roughly the same size as Great Britain. Although Japan is home to some of the world's most populous and densely packed cities, over 70% of the land is rural and mountainous. Sandwiched between the sprawling cities of Tokyo in the east and Kyoto/Osaka in the west is Honshu's central region, known as Chūbu, and this is where the great mountain ranges of the Japan Alps and Mt Fuji are situated.

Due to its geography and the length of the archipelago, Japan has a wide range of climates and environments, and much of Honshu lies within the northern temperate zone, with four distinct seasons and a rainy season lasting from June until mid July. The rainy season always varies in intensity and duration, but expect frequent rainy days with some occasional heavy downpours and a chance of flooding.

Above a sea of clouds on Tateyama (Walk 2)

43

Mt Fuji's highest point, Mt Ken-ga-mine

Even mainland Honshu has a complex climate; along the south-facing Pacific side summers are hot and humid, with typhoons regularly battering the coast from late July to October, while winters are generally cool and dry. The northern side of Honshu is hit with Siberian weather systems which pick up moisture over the Sea of Japan, resulting in long, freezing-cold winters with huge dumps of snow, including some of the deepest recorded snowfalls in the world. Tall mountains such as those in the Japan Alps are covered in snow for half of the year, so the main hiking season is relatively short, starting in mid May and finishing in November. Mt Fuji's hiking season is even shorter, with hikers only officially permitted in July, August and the beginning of September.

GEOLOGY AND LANDSCAPE

The islands of Japan formed as a result of oceanic and plate movements over hundreds of millions of years in this highly active region of the Pacific Ring of Fire. Japan was originally connected to the eastern coast of the Eurasian continent, but the subduction of the Philippine Sea Plate and the Pacific Plate pulled Japan eastwards, separating it from the mainland and forming the Sea of Japan about 15 million years ago. Just off the eastern coast of Japan are some of the deepest sea trenches in the world, formed by the tectonic plates moving under one another, and so making Japan one of the most seismically and volcanically active regions on Earth. With over 100 currently active volcanoes (accounting for 10% of all active volcanoes in the world), the Japanese landscape is always in a state of change.

Thanks to their location at the meeting point of multiple fault lines, the Japanese islands have a very complex geological makeup, with igneous and metamorphic rocks attributable to volcanism and substantial sedimentary deposits as a result of plate tectonics. For many years there was some debate about whether Japan's mountains had been influenced by glacial action; it is now generally agreed that a number of cirques and valleys were carved out by the action of ancient glaciers, of which some small remnants still just about remain in the high and shaded hollows of the alpine regions.

The three main mountain ranges of the Japan Alps comprise some of the most rugged landscapes in the country, bisecting the central part of Honshu from coast to coast, north to south. They roughly follow the Itoigawa-Shizuoka Tectonic Line which separates Japan into east and west, and has helped to form these huge mountain chains which are home to 20 peaks over 3000m in height. The North Alps are predominantly volcanic in origin, as evidenced towards the northern end of the range by the boiling water and sulphur deposits at Jigokudani (hell valley) near Murodō, while the caldera at Mt Tateyama is the largest non-active crater in Japan. Further south, Mt Yake near Kamikōchi regularly bellows steam and poisonous gases, and two great volcanoes – Mt Norikura and Mt Ontake – lie at the far southern end of the range; they are colossal island peaks, independent and imposing. The bulky and remote South Alps in contrast have no volcanoes, instead being formed at the bottom of the ocean and pushed skywards by tectonic activity (and they are still rising at a rate of about 5mm per year). These granite giants, layered with limestone, chert and other sedimentary rocks and minerals are home to a variety of environments favourable to rare alpine flowers, giving the South Alps a notable abundance of unique plant life.

Mt Fuji lies on the Pacific coastal plains about 100km southwest of Tokyo, and is an active stratovolcano (a volcano built up of alternate layers of lava and ash), although it is currently considered as having a low risk of eruption. Its almost symmetrical volcanic cone is mostly formed of basalt, and it is the 35th most prominent mountain in the world, owing to its height (3776m) and isolation from other peaks. It first formed following eruptions hundreds of thousands of years ago, and has been through multiple phases of volcanic activity since, with the most recent eruption taking place in December 1707. This formed a new crater and a small secondary peak called Mt Hōei halfway down its southeastern flank.

PLANTS AND WILDLIFE

Japan has a wide variety of climates and environments, making for a huge diversity of animal and plant life. Central Honshu is mostly in the East Asian warm-temperate zone, with the high mountains of the Japan Alps being home to species typical of the alpine and semi-alpine zone.

Trees and flowers
Up to 70% of Japan is forested, but little of the natural virgin forest now remains.

Alpine flowers bloom in the summer

After the Second World War the government initiated a widespread reforestation policy which involved planting vast swathes of uniform, red-barked cedar trees (*Cryptomeria japonica*, otherwise known as *sugi* スギ/杉) to be used in construction, most notably for building traditional Japanese houses. Cedar is bad for those with allergies and bad for the environment, as the monoculture forests drain hillsides of water, loosening the topsoil and increasing the risk of landslides, and even as demand for cedar has waned, the cedar plantations have remained.

In spite of the cedar problem however, there is a great variety of tree and plant life in Japan, especially in remote areas such as the Japan Alps. Evergreens, including many different kinds of fir (*momi* モミ/樅) and pine tree (*matsu* マツ/松) grow at various elevations, and cypress (*hinoki* ヒノキ/檜/桧) is a fragrant tree with beautiful red-coloured bark, often used to make traditional-style baths. On wooded mountainsides there are deciduous trees including birch (*kaba* カバ/樺), beech (*buna* ブナ/撫) and oak (*kashiwa* カシワ/柏), while Japanese maples (*momiji* モミジ/椛) blaze with colour in the autumn, and cherry (*sakura* サクラ/桜) and plum (*ume* ウメ/梅) trees delight with their pink and white blossom in the spring. Mountain trails often weave through thick swathes of bamboo grass (*sasa* ササ/笹), while higher up around the alpine zone Japanese fir (*momi* モミ/樅) can endure the harsh winters and low-lying creeping pine, also known as Siberian dwarf pine (*haimatsu* ハイマツ/這松), can grow in abundance even on exposed peaks and ridges.

Japan has a rich and bewildering array of wildflowers, with the alpine regions home to some unique and rare varieties. Large yellow daylilies with trumpet-like flowers bloom on sunny slopes in early summer, and other kinds of mountain lilies include a striking black variety known in Japanese as *kuroyuri* クロユリ/黒百合. Thickets of fringed galax are fairly common, while alpine woodlands are home to a frilly pink Shortia called 'Nippon-bell', along with the white, stem-like snakeberry (*Maianthemum dilatatum*) and white and yellow fairy bells, which are pretty woodland flowers found throughout Asia. Anemones, saxifrage and dazzling blue gentians add a dash of colour to grassy steppes, and at higher elevations stony, wet slopes are laced with white and yellow Aleutian avens, while *nadeshiko* ナデシコ/撫子 is a sweetly scented pink flower associated with feminine beauty. Entire meadows of alpine flowers and mountain herbs can be found blooming in the Japan Alps during high summer, with cheery yellow cinquefoils brightening up many mountain summits. Familiar plants often spotted alongside mountain trails include buttercups, pink geraniums and wild raspberries and bilberries. On wooded lower slopes and valley floors a myriad of ferns, mosses and fungi favour the cool, damp conditions near streams and springs.

Birds and animals

Japan is a haven for birds with over 600 species recorded, many of which are migratory species stopping over en route between Siberia and Southeast Asia or beyond. The unofficial symbol of the Japan Alps is the ptarmigan or *raichō* 雷鳥 (meaning 'thunder bird'), a charming member of the grouse family which changes from a speckled brown colour

The rock ptarmigan, or raichō, is frequently spotted in the Japan Alps

in the summer to all white in the winter. It can often be seen scurrying about on barren slopes at high elevations, and is surprisingly approachable. In alpine forests look out for the green woodpecker, the Japanese robin, brown- and grey-coloured accentors and the spotted nutcracker, a medium-size brown bird common throughout Europe and Asia which mostly feeds on pine seeds.

Of the native animals, bears are the largest carnivores, and two species reside in Japan. The large and sometimes aggressive brown bear (*higuma*) is only found in Hokkaido, whereas the smaller and mostly crepuscular (active at dawn and dusk) Asiatic black bear (*tsukinow-aguma*, or often simply referred to as *kuma*), is found in the mountains of Honshu, Shikoku and Kyushu. Adults grow to around 1.5m in height and can weigh up to 200kg, and they exist on a diet of berries, roots, acorns and insects. Whilst common in the Japan Alps, encounters with hikers are quite rare, but you will still see written warnings (クマ or 熊 on signs) and many walkers carry bear bells to avoid startling them.

The Japanese serow (*kamoshika* カモシカ) is an unusual kind of goat-antelope most frequently found in dense woodland around the semi-alpine zone, where it feeds on leaves, shoots and acorns. It has good hearing and eyesight, so often steers clear of hikers. Large groups of Japanese macaque (*saru* サル/猿), a medium-size grey-brown monkey, can be observed in the forests of mainland Japan, foraging, grooming or even enjoying a hot spring bath. In the Japan Alps, macaques are frequently encountered around Kamikōchi. Wild boar (*inoshishi* イノシシ) are nocturnal

and can be found in forests all over Japan, apart from in Hokkaido. They grow to about 1.2m in length and are a pest to farmers as they are omnivorous, eating everything from berries, bark, roots and shoots to earthworms and crops. Other mammals sometimes seen in the mountains include the red fox, stoats, sika deer and the Japanese pine marten.

Reptiles and amphibians are well represented in Japan and in the summer months they can be found at lower elevations in the alpine regions. Snakes are frequently spotted near riverbeds and rarely pose any threat to humans, although the small and reclusive Japanese pit viper (*mamushi* マムシ/蝮) has powerful venom and likes to sit camouflaged on forested hillsides. Frogs and salamanders are common in damp and shaded areas, while the Japanese giant salamander (*ōsanshōuo* オオサンショウウオ) is a subspecies of the largest amphibian in the world, and spends the day hiding away in clear, fast-flowing mountain streams: it can live for 80 years and grows up to an impressive 1.5m in length.

HISTORY OF HIKING IN JAPAN

Since ancient times the mountains of Japan were traditionally seen as dangerous and mysterious places, and no place for ordinary folk to venture. Farmers would sometimes make forays into the mountains to forage for mountain vegetables and shrubs (*sansai*), and hunters would be familiar with the terrain but rarely scaled the largest peaks, while hermits and mystics would occasionally disappear into the mountains to commune with the gods. For much of recorded history, it was mostly for religious and spiritual reasons that people climbed mountains.

Shintō (meaning 'way of the gods') is an indigenous religion connected to nature. Its practices were first recorded around the eighth century, but it existed in a less distinguished form at least two centuries earlier. Gods (*kami*) were believed to be manifested throughout nature and could be found in rocks, trees, rivers, animals and even people. So the mountains were considered a sacred refuge of the gods, and a place where they could descend to earth, with shrines built to honour them on mountain tops and at other sacred spots.

Buddhism, on the other hand, was introduced to Japan from Korea in the sixth century, and over the years a unique Japanese form of the religion developed, with many of its facets combining harmoniously and even complimenting the native Shintō beliefs. As Buddhism gradually gained recognition, temples were built, often close to existing shrines.

During the Heian period (794–1185) Shintō beliefs and the Buddhist pursuit of enlightenment came together to form a unique branch of mountain asceticism called Shugendō. Other religious sects also developed pilgrimage routes, often over remote, arduous terrain to temples at the tops of mountains. In time, *yado* or pilgrims' inns popped up on some of the more popular routes to provide relief for weary travellers.

By the Edo period (1600–1867) outdoor recreation was becoming more popular among Japanese people, partly

Entrance to Oyama's summit shrine (Walk 2)

inspired by the writings of famous wanderers such as the haiku poet Matsuo Bashō (1644–1694). Sightseeing trips to the mountains became fashionable: visiting quaint countryside shrines, relaxing at mountain hot springs or viewing cherry blossom (*hanami*), fireflies (*hotaru*) and autumn leaves (*kōyō*) all became popular seasonal activities, and remain so to this day.

It is believed that by the start of the Meiji period (1868–1912) most of Japan's big peaks had been climbed by an assortment of surveyors, hunters and ascetics, but hiking and climbing mountains purely for the sake of it was still uncommon. It wasn't until 1888 that an Englishman called Walter Weston first began travelling and climbing in Japan's most rugged mountain areas, with his writings opening up the region to the West, and introducing the Japanese to hiking as a form of recreation. He was an influential figure and helped to establish the Japanese Alpine Club in 1905. At Kamikōchi in the North Alps, Weston is honoured with a bronze plaque and a festival in his name.

Around this time, new magazines and books began to extol the Japanese landscape and nature, fostering an ever-increasing interest in the outdoors. The Second World War brought recreational activities to a halt, but soon afterwards the Japanese government began promoting outdoor activities as healthy and educational, and with the advent of the automobile, camping trips became an affordable and popular pastime.

In 1964 a celebrated author and mountaineer called Fukada Kyūya released a book titled *Nihon-Hyakumeizan* 日本百名山 ('100 Famous Mountains of Japan'). It wasn't supposed to be a definitive list, but merely the mountains which he considered interesting due to their stature, history or character. The list caught the imagination however, and climbing them became the goal of many hikers. During the 1980s and 1990s there was a real outdoor boom as people became eager to get back to nature, and hiking has been popular ever since. The noughties saw a '*yama*-girl' (mountain girl) boom, as young women in their 20s donned the latest mountain fashions and took to the trails. University hiking clubs are a common sight in the Alps, but most of the hikers you meet will be retirees from Japan's aging population, many of whom show remarkable energy and stamina!

THE NORTH (KITA) ALPS –
北アルプス

The ridge connecting Mt Yakushi-dake's two main summits (Trek 3, Stage 2)

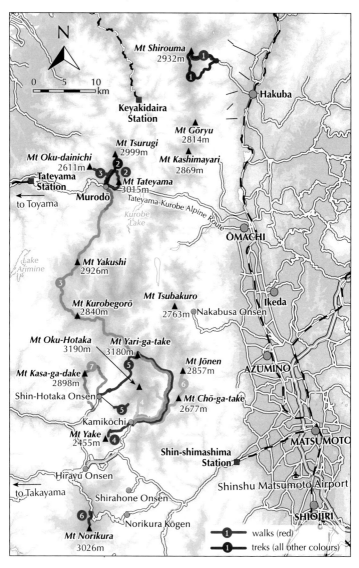

THE NORTH (KITA) ALPS – 北アルプス

The rugged and magnificent North Alps (Kita Arupusu in Japanese) run from the border between Toyama and Niigata prefectures on the weather-beaten Sea of Japan coast, stretching southwards into Gifu and Nagano for nearly 100km in a roughly Y-shaped formation of huge rocky ridges and windswept summits. Also known as the Hida Mountains, the Kita Alps lie entirely within the limits of the Chūbu Sangaku National Park and cover over 1740 square kilometres, with many of the peaks reaching around 3000m in height. The mountains create a barrier separating the historical and rural provinces of Hida-Takayama in the west and Shinshū in the east, with the remote Kurobe river valley and its enormous lake and dam nestling near the centre of the range.

Due to their size and location, the North Alps are buffeted by harsh Siberian weather fronts in the winter, resulting in some of the deepest snowfalls in the world. Originally formed by volcanic activity and still smouldering in places, these mountains are home to much of Japan's most spectacular alpine scenery, with year-round snowfields, deep valleys and remote gorges, tall and craggy peaks and some exhilarating hiking trails. Easy access and numerous transport options mean that the North Alps are popular with serious outdoor enthusiasts and day-trippers alike, with a vast range of walks and multi-day treks to suit all abilities, especially from the main mountain hubs of Murodō in the north and Kamikōchi at the southern end of the range.

OVERVIEW	
Location:	Chūbu region of central Honshu, encompassing parts of Toyama, Nagano and Gifu prefectures, and the western corner of Niigata Prefecture.
Information:	www.japan-alps.com/en
	For **bases**, **access** and **maps**, see Hakuba, Tateyama, Hotaka and Norikura chapters.

HAKUBA AREA – 白馬エリア

Mt Shakushi-dake and Mt Yari-ga-dake, two of Mt Shirouma's three peaks (Trek 1, Stage 2)

Rising up from the Sea of Japan, the northeastern spur of the North Alps is home to a large and spectacular range of mountains, buffeted by harsh winter weather fronts, and where snow remains throughout the year in deep snow valleys. Situated north of Matsumoto in a once remote area, Hakuba is a small village at the foot of Mt Shirouma (the mountain having the same *kanji* characters as the village, but pronounced differently; one of the idiosyncrasies of the Japanese language) which rose to prominence during the 1998 Winter Olympics. Thanks to the deep and high-quality powder snow that blankets the region, Hakuba is one of Japan's premier ski resorts, attracting people from all over the world during the winter season. In the summer time the area is somewhat quieter, and giant alpine mountains such as Mt Shirouma (2932m), Mt Goryū (2814m) and Mt Kashimayari (2889m) provide plenty of great hiking, with a long and exciting traverse of the entire ridge (all the way from the Kurobe Dam to the Sea of Japan) a possibility. The old town of Ōmachi lies at the southern end of the range, and is the starting point or terminus of the Tateyama-Kurobe Alpine Route (www.alpen-route.com/en) – a popular tourist trail that cuts across the Alps via a series of tunnels, cable cars, ropeways, buses and trains.

Hakuba village 白馬村 is the main base in the region, with regular trains taking about 1hr 30min from Matsumoto (change at Shinano-Ōmachi) on the JR Oito Line. (There are direct trains from Tokyo and Nagoya to Matsumoto, and express buses from Tokyo, Kyoto and Osaka.) There are also express buses from Nagano, and highway and night buses from Tokyo and Kyoto/Osaka. The village has an alpine feel and is packed with skiers in the winter, but is more relaxed during the summer, with plenty of places to stay and a number of relaxing hot springs to revive weary limbs. It is possible to rent crampons during the summer season from Kita

Alps sōgō-annaijyo 北アルプス総合案内所, the tourist information centre just outside Hakuba Station (open 5am to 7.30pm in summer). The cost is 1000 yen, with 300 yen cashback upon return.

Ōmachi大町 is a traditional town at the foot of the Alps, well known for its hot springs and *ryokan* (traditional inn) accommodation. The main train station is called Shinano-Ōmachi and it is almost halfway along the JR Oito Line between Matsumoto and Hakuba.

Both Walk 1 and Trek 1 are covered at 1:50,000 by the Yama-to-Kōgen (No. 35) Shirouma-dake 白馬岳 sheet.

Alpine flower meadows above the Daisekkei (the great snow valley) (Walk 1)

WALK 1
Mt Shirouma-dake 白馬岳

Start/finish	Sarukura 猿倉
Alternative start/finish	Upper ropeway station, Tsugaike Nature Park 栂池自然園
Distance	14km (8½ miles) or 18km (11 miles) via Hakuba Ōike
Total ascent/descent	1700m (5580ft) or 1080m (3550ft) via Hakuba Ōike
Grade	2
Time	9hr 30min (return) or 12hr (return) via Hakuba Ōike
Terrain	Gravel track and rocky path up the valley, followed by a long, relatively steep climb on snow/ice (simple crampons recommended). Rough rocky trails near Shirouma's summit.
Access	Buses from JR Hakuba Station to Sarukura daily from early July until end of August, otherwise only on weekends and holidays from Golden Week (late April) until mid October; journey time 30min, first bus from 5.55am. See www.alpico.co.jp/access/hakuba/sarukura (Japanese) for bus schedule. Taxis take 25min from Hakuba to Sarukura. Parking spaces at Sarukura trailhead. For Tsugaike, see below.
Accommodation	Huts and camping near the trailhead and below Mt Shirouma's summit
Facilities	Water, food and toilets at huts. Restaurant at Hakuba-sansō hut. Medical clinics at summit huts during height of summer.
When to go	Early July to early October are the best times to climb; lots of snow before this

Mt Shirouma-dake (2932m) is the northernmost and highest peak in the Hakuba region, and is well known for its year-round snowfields and beautiful alpine scenery. The name means 'white horse mountain', possibly due to the shape of the long lingering snow patches on its upper slopes. The mountain is frequently enveloped in clouds, and tends to take the brunt of the weather fronts that come rolling in from Siberia and pick up moisture as they cross the Sea of Japan. This results in huge dumps of snow in the winter, although most of the main trails are clear by early July. The most popular approach is from the east via the Daisekkei ('the great snow valley'), a long glacial valley where snow remains throughout the year. The huts near the summit are some of the largest in Japan, with capacity for over 1000 hikers, but despite the mountain's popularity (particularly in August) the setting still feels grand and remote.

The Daisekkei is a relatively easy climb, although simple four-point crampons are highly recommended to avoid slipping (they can be bought for a very reasonable price from Hakuba-jiri-goya hut). Landslides and crevasses can occur along the Daisekkei, but officials regularly check and mark the best course up the snow valley, so stick to the main route for safety. Beware of rockfall from the steep valley sides (the snowfield is littered with rocks and boulders) and be alert at all times.

With good fitness and an early start it is easily possible to do the Daisekkei route as a day-hike, but many people like to split it over two days to enjoy the wonderful scenery at a more leisurely pace.

The trail starts to the left of the **Sarukurasō** hut 猿倉荘 and leads into the forest. Gently climb over rocky and sometimes muddy ground to meet a gravel track in about 5min. Turn left and follow the track as it winds up the valley along a slight incline, using wooden boards to ford a stream that falls into the river far below and to the right. ▶

There are good views of Mt Shirouma and a huge concrete dam on the other side of the valley.

Sarukurasō hut at the Mt Shirouma trailhead

57

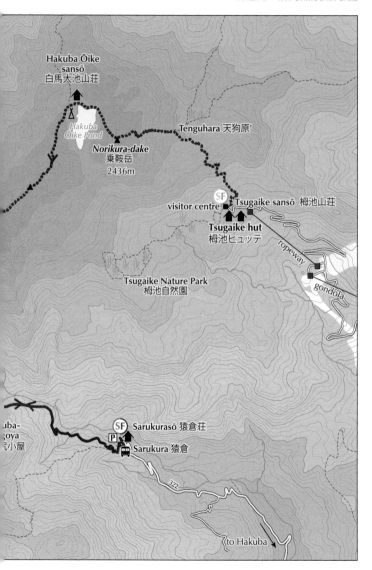

Hakuba Ōike
sansō
白馬大池山荘

Hakuba
Ōike Pond

Tenguhara 天狗原

Norikura-dake
乗鞍岳
2436m

SF

visitor centre

Tsugaike sansō 栂池山荘

Tsugaike hut
栂池ヒュッテ

ropeway

gondola

Tsugaike Nature Park
栂池自然園

uba-
goya
小屋

SF Sarukurasō 猿倉荘

P

Sarukura 猿倉

322

to Hakuba

59

*The path leading to
Hakuba-jiri-goya (hut)*

Cross another small stream and continue along the gravel track to its end. After climbing wooden steps that cut through thick undergrowth you'll soon arrive at a plank bridge to cross a small gushing stream. Follow more wooden steps and then a stony path, and cross another narrow stream. Continue up stony steps to arrive at a clearing in front of the two huts of **Hakuba-jiri-goya** 白馬尻小屋. Maps indicate 1hr to get here, but it can be done much quicker if you're fit.

The lower hut is where the reception and shop is; the other one is only for staying guests. The clearing serves as the camping spot and has great views of the rocky riverbed leading up the valley. ◄

*The hut also sells
simple crampons if
you need them.*

Ascend the stone steps next to the signboards and to the right of the huts. (The signs have lots of information in Japanese about the snow conditions further up the valley.) Cross a small stream and climb wooden steps, then follow the stony path up through the undergrowth to emerge at the foot of the famous **Daisekkei** 大雪渓, or 'great snow valley'.

Depending on the time of year and how much snow remains, you can either follow the path directly onto the snow or ascend the rocky trail up the left side of the valley

for a short while. Cracks and crevasses can cause alterations to the snow route many times during the season, but
the well-trodden and clearly marked path is usually obvious
and generally sticks close to the left side of the valley. Rocks
of all sizes litter the snowfield, so pay attention to your surroundings in case of rockfall. From the hut it can take around
2hr of steady climbing to reach the top end of the snowfield.

TRAVERSING THE DAISEKKEI

Most people wear crampons for this part of the route, as the surface can be more
like ice than snow after repeated melting and freezing. It is also deceptively steep
in places (often only noticed when looking back down the valley), and is very
occasionally closed off if the snow conditions are considered too dangerous or if
the risk of rockfall is high.

Leave the snow on the right side of the snowfield and
follow a stony and steep path up the valley side. Yellow paint
marks show the way across loose scree and between large
boulders, and to the left torrents of water disappear into dark

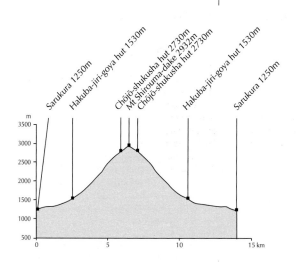

61

Approaching the top of the Daisekkei

The crumbling stony turrets of Mt Shakushi-dake 杓子岳 loom above to the left.

snow tunnels at the crevassed top end of the snowfield. Hop over rocks and carefully traverse narrow wooden planks to cross a cascading river which can flow heavily depending on conditions. On the other side, follow a stony path which twists and turns up the now much greener hillside, and enjoy the spectacular views back down the valley. ◄

Climbing steadily, pass a huge brown-coloured boulder lodged halfway up a rocky gully where rotting snow clings to the steep walls, before drifting left and scrambling over rocks and past lush patches of yellow mountain violets. Clamber across an area of rocky streams to reach flatter ground and then follow the path through head-high foliage to reach a tiny emergency hut nestled below a big rock.

The path is less steep now and follows a rocky course uphill through glorious meadows of long grass and colourful alpine flowers. After passing a large sign with lots of Japanese writing below a rocky outcrop, climb over boulders and sturdy wooden stairs and follow the rocky path all the way up to the **Hakuba-chōjō-shukusha** hut 白馬頂上宿舎, which can be reached about 1hr 30min–2hr after leaving the snowfield.

There is a rocky campground directly behind the hut. Ascend the stony path to the right which leads to the even bigger **Hakuba sansō** hut 白馬山荘 in about 15min.

Hakuba sansō hut is one of the largest in the Alps and it sits high on the grassy and windswept slopes below Shirouma's summit. From the top of the steps, the building directly ahead is the main reception, the building to the right is called 'Skyplaza Hakuba' スカイプラザ白馬 and serves as a shop and restaurant, and the impressive long building to the left has sleeping space for hundreds of hikers.

To continue, head uphill on the stony path behind the buildings to reach the summit of **Mt Shirouma-dake** 白馬岳 (2932m) in 10min. ▸ The panoramic views from the summit are outstanding on sunny days. To return to the **Sarukurasō** hut 猿倉荘, descend the mountain by the same route in about 3½–4hr.

About halfway along the path just off to the right is a relief of Teiitsu Matsuzawa, a local man who founded the first mountain hut here in 1906.

Alternative approach via Hakuba Ōike ('big pond') 白馬大池

This is a scenic and popular, but longer approach to Mt Shirouma, avoiding the climb up the Daisekkei snow-field. Starting from the ropeway station at 1850m, the trail crosses wetlands and high alpine meadows before arriving at Hakuba Ōike, a large picturesque pond in a wonderful mountainous setting, then continues along the ridge to the summit. This 9km (5½ miles) route is a bit too long to do as a there-and-back day-hike as it takes roughly 7hr one way with 1080m (3550ft) of ascent, so it's best to stay at a hut overnight or camp. It is also easy to combine with the previous Daisekkei route for an enjoyable two-day hike starting and ending at Hakuba Station with no backtracking.

Tsugaike Kōgen can be reached by bus from JR Hakuba Station in 25min; see www.alpico.co.jp/access/hakuba/tsugaike (Japanese) for the bus timetable. From Tsugaike Kōgen the Tsugaike Panorama Way (栂池パノラマウエイ) whisks hikers up the mountain via a combination of gondola and ropeway in 40min. See www.tsugaike.gr.jp/english for details. Parking is also available at Tsugaike Kōgen.

Exit the upper ropeway station and follow the paved road towards **Tsugaike Nature Park** 栂池自然園. There are pleasant marshland nature trails leading west, but take the path immediately next to the visitor centre marked by a brown sign 登山道入口. Enter woodland and climb steadily, over rocks in places, passing birch trees and then going up a series of zigzags. After reaching a flat marshland area called **Tenguhara** 天狗原 (about 1hr), follow the trail across wooden boardwalks and through low forest. Ignore the junction leading north for Kazafuki Ōike 風吹大池 and begin climbing the rocky trail towards and over a snowfield that often lingers well into August to reach the top of **Mt Hakuba Norikura-dake** 白馬乗鞍岳 (2436m), marked by a summit post and large stone cairn.

The rocky path descends very gradually to the north shore of **Hakuba Ōike** (meaning 'Hakuba big pond', although it could easily be called a lake), which is famed for its beautiful reflections. Follow the path as it skirts the water's edge around to **Hakuba Ōike sansō** 白馬大池山荘, a cosy hut on the pond's northwest side and about 3hr from the trailhead. (Its campground is in a nice spot down by the pond, where purple primulas and yellow and white Aleutian avens bloom close by.)

The summit of Mt Shirouma

From the hut, ascend the path up the ridge, keeping an eye open for rock ptarmigan (*raichō* in Japanese), often spotted among the creeping pine on these slopes. Follow the ridgeline which is dotted with flowers and offers fine views of the Daisekkei snow valley far below, and reach the stony summit of **Mt Korenge-san** 小蓮華山 (2766m) in around 2hr.

Continue west for 30min along a trail with great views of the nearby peaks, and then ignore the trail coming in from the right. Follow the bare rocky ridge south, staying away from the cliffs that drop away to the east, to arrive at the summit of **Mt Shirouma-dake** 白馬岳 (2932m) in 1hr. A descent via the same route takes about 5hr, and the ropeway usually operates until just after 4pm (varies by season, check the schedule beforehand).

Mt Shirouma's unmistakable summit plinth

TREK 1
Mt Shirouma-dake and Hakuba-Yari Onsen
白馬岳~白馬鑓温泉

Start/finish	Sarukura 猿倉
Distance	20.5km (12½ miles)
Total ascent/descent	2100m (6890ft)
Grade	2+ *
Time	2 or 3 days
Terrain	Well-marked paths on rocky ground, sometimes steep and undulating. A long walk up a snow valley and lingering snow patches likely in other places (simple crampons recommended). Includes a section of short scrambles on exposed rocks secured by fixed chains.
Access	See Walk 1
Accommodation	Huts and camping along the way
Facilities	Huts sell food, drinks and some mountain goods. Crampons available at Hakuba-jiri hut. Hot spring at Hakuba-Yari Onsen.
When to go	Apart from the Daisekkei snow valley, most of the trails will be clear of snow by mid July. The hut at Hakuba-Yari Onsen closes (and is completely dismantled for the winter) in mid to late September, although it is still possible to camp there (and use the hot spring!) after this.

This trek climbs to the summit of Mt Shirouma (2932m) and then continues south along the ridge before looping back to Sarukura via an open-air hot spring. Taking in all three of Shirouma's major peaks, it is one of the most satisfying and varied two- or three-day treks in the entire Japan Alps, with magnificent ever-changing scenery throughout the route.

Having summited Mt Shirouma there is the option of climbing over or skirting past the second peak of Shakushi-dake 杓子岳 (2812m). This is followed by a short ascent of Yari-ga-take 鑓ヶ岳 (2903m – not to be confused with the more famous Mt Yari-ga-take of the Hotaka region – see Treks 5 and 6) before heading back down to Sarukura via Hakuba-Yari Onsen 白馬鑓温泉, where the soothing waters offer very welcome respite for weary limbs.

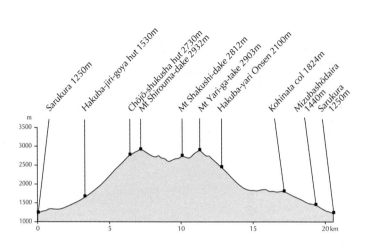

STAGE 1
Sarukura to Hakuba sansō 猿倉~白馬山荘

Start	Sarukura 猿倉
Finish	Hakuba sansō hut 白馬山荘
Distance	7.5km (4½ miles)
Total ascent	1700m (5580ft)
Total descent	Negligible
Time	6hr
Terrain	Gravel track and rocky path up the valley, followed by a long, relatively steep climb on snow/ice (simple crampons recommended). Rough rocky trails near the summit.
Accommodation	Huts and camping near the trailhead and below the summit

A hike up a spectacular snow valley, and then along fairly steep and rocky paths passing through meadows rich with alpine flowers. The day's objective is the summit of Mt Shirouma, and accommodation can be found at one of the enormous huts there.

This stage follows the same course to the summit of Mt Shirouma as Walk 1. With a very early start (and if staying at one of the huts near the trailhead the night before), it is possible to do Stage 1 and Stage 2 of this trek in one day, although it would make for a long one.

TRAVERSING THE DAISEKKEI

Most people wear crampons for this part of the route, as the surface can be more like ice than snow after repeated melting and freezing. It is also deceptively steep in places, and is very occasionally closed off if the snow conditions are considered too dangerous or if the risk of rockfall is high.

The trail starts to the left of the **Sarukurasō** hut 猿倉荘 and leads into the forest. Gently climb over rocky and sometimes muddy ground to meet a gravel track in about 5min. Turn left and follow the track as it winds up the valley along a slight incline, using wooden boards to ford a stream that falls into the river far below and to the right.

Cross another small stream and continue along the gravel track to its end. After climbing the wooden steps that cut through thick undergrowth you'll soon arrive at a plank bridge to cross a small gushing stream. Follow more wooden steps and then a stony path, and cross another narrow stream. Continue up stony steps to arrive at a clearing in front of the two huts of **Hakuba-jiri-goya** 白馬尻小屋 (about 1hr).

Ascend the stone steps next to the signboards and to the right of the huts. (The signs have information in Japanese about the snow conditions further up the valley.) Cross a small stream and climb wooden steps, then follow the stony path up through the undergrowth to emerge at the foot of the famous **Daisekkei** 大雪渓, or 'great snow valley'.

Depending on the time of year and how much snow remains, you can either follow the path directly onto the snow or ascend the rocky trail up the left side of the valley for a short while. The well-trodden and clearly marked path is usually obvious and generally sticks close to the left side

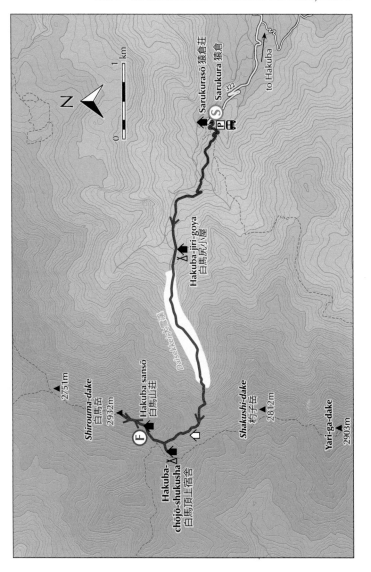

Walking up the Daisekkei 'great snow valley'

There are usually a number of crevasses at both the top and bottom ends of the Daisekkei, but the path is routed to avoid them.

of the valley. Rocks of all sizes litter the snowfield, so pay attention to everything around in case of rockfall. From the hut it can take around 2hr of steady climbing to reach the top end of the snowfield.

Leave the snow on the right side of the snowfield and follow a stony and steep path up the valley side. Yellow paint marks show the way across loose scree and between large boulders. ◄ Hop over rocks and carefully traverse narrow wooden planks to cross a cascading river which can flow heavily depending on conditions. On the other side, follow a stony path which twists and turns up the green hillside.

Climbing steadily, pass a huge brown-coloured boulder lodged halfway up a rocky gully where rotting snow clings to the steep walls, before drifting left and scrambling over rocks and past lush patches of yellow mountain violets. Clamber across an area of rocky streams to reach flatter ground and then follow the path through head-high foliage to reach a tiny emergency hut nestled below a big rock. The path becomes less steep and follows a rocky course uphill through glorious meadows of long grass and colourful alpine flowers.

After passing a large sign with lots of Japanese writing below a rocky outcrop, climb over boulders and sturdy wooden stairs and follow the rocky path all the way up to **Hakuba-chōjō-shukusha** hut 白馬頂上宿舎 (1hr 30min–2hr from the snowfield). ▶

There is a rocky campground directly behind the hut.

Ascend the stony path to the right which leads to the huge **Hakuba sansō** hut 白馬山荘 in about 15min.

Hakuba sansō is one of the largest huts in the Alps and it sits high on the grassy and windswept slopes below Shirouma's summit. From the top of the steps, the building directly ahead is the main reception, the building to the right is called 'Skyplaza Hakuba' スカイプラザ白馬 and serves as a shop and restaurant, and the impressive long building to the left has sleeping space for hundreds of hikers.

Head uphill on the stony path behind the buildings to reach the summit of **Mt Shirouma-dake** 白馬岳 in 10min. Enjoy the panoramic views, which are outstanding on sunny days, and then return to the huts or campsite.

Hakuba-chōjō-shukusha hut and the ridgeline to Hakuba-Yari

STAGE 2
Hakuba sansō to Hakuba-Yari Onsen
白馬山荘~白馬鑓温泉

Start	Hakuba sansō hut 白馬山荘
Finish	Hakuba-Yari Onsen-goya hut 白馬鑓温泉小屋
Distance	6.5km (4 miles)
Total ascent	310m (1010ft)
Total descent	750m (2460ft)
Time	5hr
Terrain	An undulating ridge walk along stony paths. Rough and rocky descent to Hakuba-Yari Onsen, including short scrambles on exposed rocks secured by fixed chains.
Accommodation	Hut and camping at Hakuba-Yari Onsen

This stretch follows the ridge along a stony path, with several short ascents and descents of Mt Shirouma's satellite peaks. The trail then heads down into a remote valley below towering rocky crags, where alpine flowers provide a dash of colour. The climb down to Hakuba-Yari Onsen is a little precipitous in places, with fixed chains adding security on slippery, exposed rocks. But the wonderfully secluded surroundings and revitalising outdoor hot spring bath at Hakuba-Yari Onsen hut make for a great end to the day.

From **Hakuba sansō hut** 白馬山荘, follow the path back down to **Hakuba-chōjō-shukusha hut** 白馬頂上宿舎, but instead of turning left for the hut simply follow the path straight on along the ridge. If you stayed at **Hakuba-chōjō-shukusha hut** then follow the path up behind the back of the hut, passing the campsite to gain the ridge.

Follow the stony path up a small grassy knoll, looking back for great sweeping views of Mt Shirouma's shapely summit. Walk south along the relatively flat but twisting path, with views of Shirouma's other two peaks looming straight ahead. To the southwest, the unmistakable pointy peak of Mt Tsurugi and the vast snow patches on Mt Tateyama will be visible in the distance if the weather is fine.

Drop between jumbles of rocks and gently descend the grassy slope on a stony path. The trail briefly flattens and then

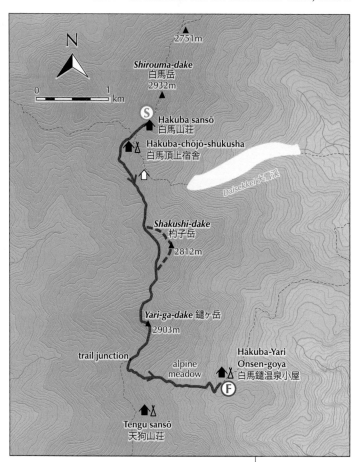

descends into a saddle via a stony zigzagging path, and the Daisekkei snow valley can be seen far below to the left.

Climb out of the saddle up another bendy and stony path, and sweep left around a rocky corner to see the jagged cliffs and grey scree slopes of Mt Shakushi-dake straight ahead. Drop down into another shallow saddle and walk across a flattish area through low-lying creeping pine, and

The saddle before Mt Yari-ga-dake

If the weather is good, the angular landscape of colourful and snow-dabbled mountains both near and far is splendid.

then onto a slope of rust- and grey-coloured scree. The path splits 1hr from the hut, so either follow the left trail for a short stony ascent to the top of **Mt Shakushi-dake** 杓子岳 (2812m), followed by a brief walk along the ridge; or take the right-hand branch for a less tiring traverse along the side of the mountain. Both paths meet back up shortly afterwards so take your pick. Once the trails meet again, descend slightly to a small and narrow col where there are good views east towards Hakuba.

The path up Mt Yari-ga-dake climbs quite steeply from here, with many twists and turns and the splintered cliffs of Yari's east face always to the left. After a brief respite at a stony flat shoulder where a wooden pole juts out of a stone cairn, climb a short rough path through creeping pine to the top of a small rocky arête. From here drop down to a small grassy saddle, and then begin a zigzagging climb on a stony path. Continue upwards along pale scree, ignoring any trails leading off to the right, to arrive at the summit of **Mt Yari-ga-dake** 鑓ヶ岳 (2903m) about 2hr after leaving the hut. ◄

Walk beyond the small summit post to find a faint path that zigzags down the steep white scree slopes, and then onto a flatter rocky path. You will arrive at a sign and **trail junction** after about 20min.

> The path ahead leads uphill and across to **Tengu sansō** 天狗山荘, a hut and campground 20min away, and a good option if it is getting late in the day. From Tengu sansō a path continues south to Mt Karamatsu-dake 唐松岳 and then further down the ridge for a long, arduous multi-day trek over two giant peaks, Mt Goryū 五竜岳 and Mt Kashimayari-ga-take 鹿島槍ヶ岳.

Turn left at the junction and meander down the rocky slope on a well-marked stony path to reach a level section of tussocky grass and large boulders. Continue down the valley, and follow the rough path through green bushy vegetation and thickets of trees. About 1hr 30min from the junction you'll arrive at a small open glade with rocks to sit on among rich **alpine meadows** of buttercups, lilies and lilac geraniums.

Carry on downhill along a narrow stony path which cuts through low trees, ferns and thick undergrowth. After

Snow valley leading to Hakuba-Yari Onsen hut

descending steps and skirting over a stream, grab onto chains to traverse and descend a series of rock sections, including a precarious spot above a waterfall (can be very slippery when wet).

Continue over rough ground, down wooden stepladders and chunky wooden stairs, and pass the foot of the waterfall. The stony path swings left just before a steep snow gully. Cross a stream and follow the narrow trail to wind along a steep slope above the gully, soon reaching the hut and campsite at **Hakuba-Yari Onsen-goya** 白馬鑓温泉小屋.

The outdoor **hot spring** at Hakuba-Yari Onsen hut is a great place to soothe aches and pains while enjoying the sunset or sunrise. It is a mixed-gender *onsen*, so swimwear is permitted but not compulsory. Pay the small bathing fee at the hut beforehand. There is also a small indoor bath for women only, and a free-to-use *ashiyu* (footbath).

STAGE 3
Hakuba-Yari Onsen to Sarukura 白馬鑓温泉~猿倉

Start	Hakuba-Yari Onsen-goya hut 白馬鑓温泉小屋
Finish	Sarukura 猿倉
Distance	6.5km (4 miles)
Total ascent	90m (300ft)
Total descent	1350m (4430ft)
Time	3hr 30min
Terrain	An up-and-down descent on rugged, narrow paths, crossing occasional gullies, streams and possible snow patches. Ends with a steady and long descent on a rough forest path.
Accommodation	Hut at Sarukura trailhead

The return to Sarukura is fairly straightforward, following a winding trail down and then across a remote high valley, with a fair bit of up and down. There are snow and scree gullies to cross, and great views of the rugged east face of Mt Shirouma's extensive ridgeline which looms high above.

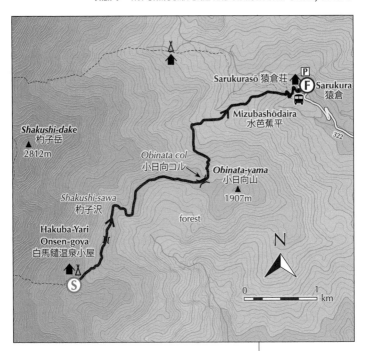

The trail down the valley starts from the campsite just in front of **Hakuba-Yari Onsen-goya hut**. Cross the small bridge over the steaming stream (this is run-off from the hot spring) and follow a narrow path steeply downhill to reach the side of the impressive gully which holds snow until late in the season. Drift left at a post with a yellow sign, descend briefly to a rocky river gully, and cross the water on a narrow wooden (and sometimes slippery) bridge with no handholds.

On the other side, climb the stony path up and over a small brow to reach another rocky river gully, where deep snow often lingers and the river carves impressive snow tunnels. Reach the bridge and cross it, then traverse across the snow carefully, being sure not to stray from the markers (there is a risk of avalanche here, particularly early in the season). The route continues along a relatively flat and stony path, which twists and turns along the hillside, before

Take care on the bridge over the stream

crossing a small steep stony gully on a narrow and eroded path at a place marked as 崩沢 (Kuzuresawa) on a yellow sign.

Follow the path around a corner and then cross a much bigger rock gully called Ochiishi-sawa 落石沢 roughly 1hr from the start. You will arrive on a brow overlooking the rocky ravine of **Shakushi-sawa** 杓子沢 where waterfalls tumble down from the left and snow lingers above and below. Early in the season a path across the snow offers the most direct route across, but if it is roped off walk down to the left and use a narrow wooden bridge to cross the river. Swing right and climb a stony path up the other side of the ravine, affording great views of the peaks and ravines back towards the hut.

Follow the path up the thickly vegetated hillside to arrive on the rim of a green and forested bowl-shaped valley. The rough, winding and gently undulating stony path crosses numerous tiny streams (which serve as good water sources) and leads to a sign 三白沢 marking the valley's name, Sanjiro-zawa.

Continue along the mostly flat trail of gravel and rocks, which sometimes also serves as the course for a shallow stream. After passing through an area of bushy undergrowth and small trees you will reach a stony clearing next to a shallow pond less than 2hr after leaving the hut.

Follow the stony path as it gradually climbs before crossing a grassy, boggy spot using wooden logs. At **Obinata col** a sign reads 小日向コル and this place marks roughly the halfway point of the route. Pass a small pond and go through a lightly wooded area of bamboo grass to reach an open hillside of gravel paths and wetland grasses. ▶ The long descent to the bottom of the valley starts from here.

The path winds its way downhill. Descend steep zigzags and clamber over rocks on an obvious but narrow and rough trail, and then follow the gently undulating and stony path through forest and brush to reach a flat shaded glade marked as 水芭蕉平 (**Mizubashōdaira**). ▶

Continue steadily down a stony path through pleasant woodland with ferns and *sasa* grass, and eventually emerge back at the gravel track close to the trailhead. Turn right and walk down the track for a few minutes, then take a right onto the path leading into the forest to soon reach the hut and bus stop at **Sarukura** 猿倉.

There are clear views of Mt Shirouma's jagged east face across the valley to the left.

The name Mizubashōdaira alludes to the Asian skunk cabbage which grows here, a white flowering plant found in wet areas.

TATEYAMA AREA – 立山エリア

Paved paths between Murodō and Raichōdaira (Trek 2, Stage 1)

The northwestern end of the North Alps is a land of verdant alpine uplands and distinctive rocky peaks, where snow falls deep in the winter and remains in shaded gullies and depressions throughout the summer. As evidenced by the calderas and lava-formed plateaus, the mountains here were created by volcanic forces long ago, and there are still places today where steam and poisonous gases bellow from deep underground.

Tateyama is a revered mountain which dominates the skyline above one such plateau at Murodō, a spot now home to a huge hotel complex and bus terminal. This rather ugly building serves the thousands of sightseers making their

way along the Tateyama-Kurobe Alpine Route which cuts across this part of the Alps. The road opens in late April and has to be dug out from underneath the snow, creating a winding corridor with snow walls up to 20m high – a tourist attraction in its own right. The majority of day-trippers, however, don't make it much further than Mikuri-ga-ike Pond just beyond the hotel, and on the myriad mountain trails leading away from Murodō in all directions you may only have yourself for company.

Despite its rocky profile, Tateyama is a popular peak with hikers of all ages and abilities during the summer months, with a straightforward scramble leading up to a Shinto shrine perched on one of its prominent summits. Nearby Mt Tsurugi-dake is an altogether different beast, its serrated ridges and sword-shaped crown demanding respect from even seasoned mountaineers, and it is widely regarded as the most challenging of Japan's '100 Famous Mountains' to climb. In 2012 it was announced that a perennial snow patch on Tateyama and a couple more on Mt Tsurugi are actually tiny remnant glaciers, the southernmost in East Asia.

Just a short walk from Murodō there are plentiful huts, hot springs and a large campsite at Raichōsawa, making the area a good base for exploring the surrounding mountains. It is also the starting point for a number of day-hikes and longer treks, including the classic multi-day alpine traverse of the North Alps from Tateyama to Kamikōchi (Trek 3).

BASES

Murodō 室堂 is located on an ancient lava plateau which is green in the summer and buried in deep snow during the long winter months. At 2400m it is the highest point on the Tateyama-Kurobe Alpine Route, and one of the most popular stops along the way, with a large hotel and many facilities including restaurants, shops and coin lockers as well as the busy bus terminal. Be aware that there is no ATM here (or anywhere along the Alpine Route).

Mikuri-ga-ike is a large pond 10 minutes' walk from the hotel, and is famous for beautiful reflections of the nearby mountains. Just a bit further north is Jigoku-dani (Hell Valley), a sulphur-stained crater site which continually spurts out steam and poisonous gases. The four huts in this area make the most of the geothermal activity, using the naturally heated water in their hot spring

The main route up to Oyama, one of Tateyama's three peaks (Walk 2)

SHORT WALKS FROM MURODŌ

- **Mikuri-ga-ike:** 40min. Gentle loop around pond on cobbled paths.

- **Mt Jōdo-san:** 2–3hr. Small peak with exceptional views. Loop back via Ichinokoshi hut; see first part of Trek 3, Stage 1.

- **Mt Oyama (Tateyama):** 3–4hr. Popular route up to the southernmost summit of Tateyama and back down the same way; see first part of Walk 2 description.

baths (making them the highest *onsen* in Japan), with the well-known Mikuri-ga-ike Onsen open to non-staying guests. Raichōsawa campground 雷鳥沢キャンプ場 is a popular spot for campers, located in a picturesque dell at the foot of Tateyama, and is a 40min walk north of the bus terminal.

Murodō is easily reached from the west on the Alpine Route by taking a train on the Toyama Chihō Railway from Dentetsu Toyama Station to Tateyama Station (1hr), then a cable car up to Bijodaira (8min) for a bus to Murodō (1hr). If approaching from the east there are buses from Shinano-Omachi to Ōgisawa (45min), followed by a trolley-bus (20min), a walk across Kurobe Dam (10min), a cable car (5min), ropeway (7min) and finally another trolleybus (10min) passing under Tateyama itself to arrive at Murodō. The whole Alpine Route takes about 6–7hr to complete, or longer during busy periods. There are English pamphlets and timetables at train and bus stations along the route, or check www.alpen-route.com/en for more information. For drivers there are parking spaces near Tateyama Station and at Ōgisawa, as private vehicles are not permitted on the roads to Murodō.

Toyama 富山 lies on the Sea of Japan coast and is the main city of Toyama Prefecture. Although about 55km from Murodō, it is located at the start of the Alpine Route and has far more facilities and accommodation options than anywhere else, making it a good place to start or end a hiking trip. It is even possible to do either Walks 2 or 3 as day-trips from Toyama if you catch one of the earliest trains. The city has good rail links to Kanazawa and Kyoto/Osaka in the west, and Tokyo, Nagano, Niigata heading east.

There are also a few places to stay around **Tateyama Station** at the terminus of the Toyama Chihō Railway.

MAPS

The walks and treks in this chapter are largely covered at 1:50,000 by the Yama-to-Kōgen (No. 37) Tsurugi/Tateyama 剱・立山 sheet, and at 1:25,000 by the Yamakei – Tsurugi/Tateyama renpō 剱・立山連峰 map. Stages 4 and 5 of Trek 3 are covered by Yama-to-Kōgen (No. 38) Yari-ga-take and Hotaka-dake 槍ヶ岳・穂高岳, and Yamakei – Yari-ga-take and Hotaka-dake 槍・穂高連峰.

WALK 2
Mt Tateyama 立山

Start/finish	Murodō 室堂
Distance	9.5km (6 miles)
Total ascent/descent	900m (2950ft)
Grade	1+ *
Time	6hr 30min
Terrain	A flat, easy start on a paved path, climbing gently before a steep and rocky scramble. Then a rough and rocky ridge path on sometimes steep and loose ground, followed by stony undulating paths and a rugged descent.
Access	See Tateyama chapter introduction
Accommodation	Huts en route and around Murodō; camping at Raichōsawa
Facilities	Shops, restaurants, coin lockers and toilets at Murodō. Baths at huts near Mikuri Pond and Raichōsawa. Huts sell snacks and refreshments.
When to go	Although there are buses along the Alpine Route from mid April, the mountains remain covered in deep snow until mid June at the earliest. The best time for hiking is from July until the end of October.

Tateyama is the name of the sacred mountain looming high above Murodō, and with a highpoint of 3015m it is one of the tallest mountains in the Hida Range. A jagged and rocky massif formed of granite and gneiss, Tateyama is one of Japan's 'Three Holy Mountains' (along with Haku-san and Mt Fuji), with a small Shinto shrine perched on top of Oyama, one of the three main peaks. From Murodō it is only a 2hr hike up to the summit shrine, making Tateyama a very popular day-trip.

The route described here is a longer loop hike, leaving the majority of the crowds behind at the shrine for a traverse along the rocky ridgeline to the mountain's true highpoint. There are then a few easy scrambles, glimpses of spectacular snow gullies and distant peaks, finishing with a classic view of Mt Tsurugi before returning to Murodō. This full loop is doable as a day-trip from Toyama (or with a stopover if travelling all the way along the Alpine Route), and there is a possible shortcut after summiting Tateyama for those short on time. The walk can also be combined with an ascent of Mt Tsurugi (Trek 2) for an enjoyable and thrilling two- or three-day adventure.

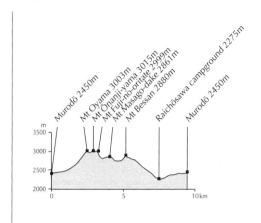

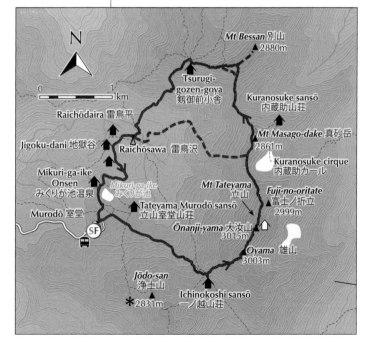

Leave the hotel and bus terminal complex at **Murodō** 室堂 and walk over to the prominent rock feature gushing with water. ▶ Climb the steps to the right of the water source and follow the paved walkway across grassy flatlands, soon turning right at a junction. Keep walking straight and follow the signs for 一ノ越・立山 (Ichinokoshi and Tateyama).

This is a good place to fill up your bottles.

Shortly after passing a turnoff to the left for Tateyama Murodō sansō hut 立山室堂山荘, ignore a path to the right which leads up to the small peak of Jōdo-san 浄土山. Continue straight along the sturdy stone path and start climbing to reach a shallow gully where there is often a small snowfield to be crossed. The path swings left and rises steadily up some zigzags. Pass a small shrine encased in rocks and a patch of marshy ground to the right, then head up another short series of zigzags to arrive at **Ichinokoshi sansō** hut 一ノ越山荘, about 1hr from the bus terminal.

Another path leads southwest in the opposite direction up to Jōdo-san 浄土山 in 40min; useful if carrying on to Goshiki-ga-hara on the long North Alps traverse (see Trek 3).

The path to the summit is to the left of the toilet block across from the hut and begins climbing immediately. ▶ Scramble up loose stones, staying close to the crest of the broad ridge. Despite the route's popularity it's a steep climb over surprisingly rough ground, but in less

Looking back to the summit shrine at the start of the Tateyama ridge traverse

than 1hr you will arrive at **Oyama** 雄山 (3003m), one of Tateyama's three main peaks.

There are toilets next to the hut, and refreshments are available. Just beyond is a *torii* gate (traditional and sacred shrine entrance) leading to the small summit shrine (small entrance fee charged) on the pointy peak. Most walkers turn around and head back to Murodō here, but the path along the ridge continues down to the left just in front of the *torii* gate, marked by a wooden sign for 大汝峰 (Ōnanji-mine) in 20min.

From this point the walk becomes a bit more exciting. Follow the narrow trail down over awkward rocks, and go along just below the crest of the ridge, taking care not to slip down the steep scree slope that falls away to the left. There is a bit of up and down and some light scrambling, then a steady ascent to reach Tateyama's highest peak, **Ōnanji-yama** 大汝山 (3015m). Scramble up to the summit post hidden among a jumble of boulders and admire the jagged ridgeline leading back towards the shrine. ◄

The mountain falls away precipitously on its eastern side, and below it is a snowy cirque called Gozenzawa 御前 沢 where Tateyama's small glacier lies.

Just below the north of the summit is a flat shoulder with a small weathered building called Ōnanji-kyūkei-sho 大汝休 憩所. This hut (open from early July to late September) sells tasty hot meals and refreshments and even has a full English menu, but it is not possible to stay here.

To continue, follow the yellow paint marks to navigate the boulder field beyond the hut and climb a rocky path hugging the left side of the ridge to reach a small flat stony spot below Tateyama's third peak, **Fuji-no-oritate** 富士ノ折 立 (2999m). It is a 5min scramble up to the summit, from where there are magnificent views across to Mt Tsurugi-dake. Return to the small clearing, then follow the path heading left down the west side of the mountain and descend steeply for 20min across stones and scree, taking care not to slip.

It is estimated that some of the ice in this cirque is around 1500 years old.

The path leads to a saddle and narrow ridge with a long scree slope falling away left, and the impressive snow-filled **Kuranosuke cirque** 内蔵助カール on the right. ◄ Continue climbing gently along the top of the ridge, ignoring a very faint path that heads left down the scree slope partway along – this leads to nowhere.

Just before the short ascent to Masago-dake, the path splits near a wooden post and weather-beaten map. The left branch traverses the scree along the side of the mountain before turning left for a 1hr 30min descent to Raichōsawa

campground. This is a steep but quicker way to return to Murodō if time is running short, involving a steep zigzagging descent on loose stones, then a rough path down past a snow-filled ravine, before a nice walk through a flat alpine meadow to the campground, where the main route description can be picked up.

For the main route, however, head straight for a gentle 10min climb to the top of **Mt Masago-dake** 真砂岳 (2861m). Continue beyond the summit – passing a trail on the right leading to a hut, Kuranosuke sansō 内蔵助山荘, in 5min – and follow the stony ridge as it drops gently and then climbs to the south summit of Mt Bessan 別山 (2874m) 1hr from Masago-dake. The views across to the serrated turrets of Mt Tsurugi are outstanding.

An optional path to the right goes past a small pond and reaches Bessan's north and main summit, Kita-mine 北峰 (2880m), in 10min. Otherwise head left along the ridge and meet a path coming up from the valley on the right. ▶ Continue along the ridge for a further 15min and then drop down to **Tsurugi-gozen-goya** 劒御前小舍, a hut

Views of Masago-dake, Mt Bessan and Mt Tsurugi-dake in the distance

If continuing on towards Mt Tsurugi, take this path for a steep descent to Tsurugi-sawa campsite in 40min (see Trek 2).

Panoramic autumn view of Raichōsawa campground

that sits in a high saddle on the main route from Murodō to Mt Tsurugi and is a popular resting spot.

Walk between the hut and the toilet block and go down the stone steps to begin the 1hr descent to **Raichōdaira** 雷鳥平. The path zigzags down almost immediately, the ground steep and loose underfoot. There is some respite at a small stony shoulder among creeping pine. Continue downhill on a rocky but well-defined path, brushing past small trees and bushes towards the bottom end of the valley, to emerge near a river. Turn left and head to the bridge leading to **Raichōsawa campground** 雷鳥沢キャンプ場.

Trails through the desolate landscape of Jigoku-dani are usually off-limits due to the poisonous fumes.

Walk through the campsite and turn right at its centre on the cobbled stone path, then follow the path left up the hill, passing two huts on the right. At the top of the hill pass the large Raichōsō 雷鳥荘 hut sitting just above the steaming pits of **Jigoku-dani** 地獄谷 (Hell Valley). ◄

There is a bit of up and down before arriving at **Mikuri-ga-ike Onsen** みくりが池温泉, a popular hut with a nice indoor hot spring bath. Carry on past the famous **Mikuri-ga-ike Pond** to soon reach the bus terminal at **Murodō**, a 50min walk from Raichōsawa.

WALK 3
Mt Oku-dainichi-dake 奥大日岳

Start/finish	Murodō 室堂
Distance	10km (6¼ miles)
Total ascent/descent	580m (1900ft)
Grade	1
Time	6hr
Terrain	An undulating stone track, then a narrow and rough path with a steady climb to the summit
Access	See Tateyama chapter introduction
Accommodation	Huts at Murodō and Raichōsawa; camping at Raichōsawa
Facilities	Shops, food and baths at huts around Murodō and Raichōsawa. Medical centre at campground from mid July to end of August.
When to go	Trails mostly clear of snow from mid July until mid November

Clearly visible to bus passengers on the long and winding road up to Murodō, an impressive ridge of mountains runs just north of the Midagahara and Murodō plateaus. This is not a chaotic, rocky ridgeline like many others in the area; the slopes look green and inviting, with softer lines and friendlier undulations. The tallest peak of Mt Oku-dainichi-dake 奥大日岳 attains only a modest height of 2611m, making it less imposing than some other nearby mountains. But the views from this ridgeline are wide and interesting, allowing you to really see and understand the geography of the area. The route from Murodō is pleasant and fairly gentle, a steady climb with no nasty scrambles, and so this is a good alpine walk for those with little experience.

Leave the hotel and bus terminal at **Murodō** 室堂 and enter a rock garden with lots of people milling about. Take the cobbled stone path heading left of the water source and turn left again to reach **Mikuri-ga-ike Pond** みぐりが池 in a few minutes. Descend into a small dip and walk past the pond viewing point, then climb the steps to **Mikuri-ga-ike Onsen** hut みくりが池温泉.

Follow the path left past the hut for views of the grey and barren **Jigoku-dani** (Hell Valley), a scorched area of active vents and steaming fumaroles. Bear right and descend a knobbly shoulder, passing a small marsh and the reddish-brown Chi-no-ike pools on the right, and then descend stone steps to reach a saddle where there is a windsock and a warning system for the poisonous gases that occasionally blow over. ◄

The pond down to the left is called Rindō-ike.

From the saddle, climb the stone steps and walk past Raichōsō hut 雷鳥荘, then descend stone stairs, passing two more big huts just off to the left. The valley you are now walking in is called **Raichōdaira** 雷鳥平. Turn right to reach **Raichōsawa** campground 雷鳥沢キャンプ場 around 45min after leaving the bus terminal.

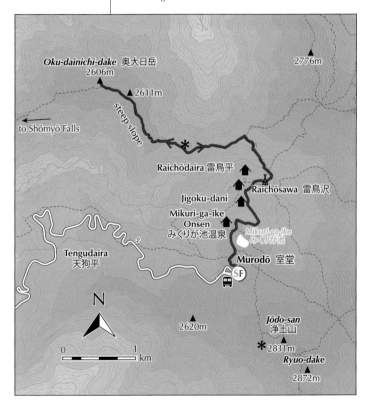

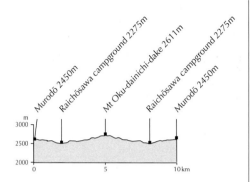

Walk through the campsite and head left. Go down log steps and cross the river via a wooden plank bridge, then turn left and follow the path downstream. A rocky trail leads up to the right, but carry on straight. Continue along a rough path covered with large stones, drifting right up a creek thick

The bridge over the river at Raichōdaira

with knotweed. On reaching a fairly flat grassy meadow mottled with wildflowers, walk over narrow wooden boards.

The route rises gently and then more steeply up a stony path for 15min to reach the brow of a hill. A path heading right leads up towards Mt Bessan and Mt Tsurugi, so turn left and follow the relatively flat dirt path that skirts along the rolling grassy slopes with wonderful views of Tateyama and across to the steaming pits of Jigoku-dani.

Continue on the path as it bends right and meanders gently up through swathes of low-lying *sasa* grass. You will arrive at a stony clearing **viewpoint** with a good glimpse of Mt Tsurugi's jagged profile. From here, follow the stony path up and around the next hill, passing through thick grass and alpine brush.

There are excellent views across to the expansive Tengudaira plateau; see if you can spot the hotels along the snaking Alpine Route road.

A short, easy scramble is required at a patch of whitish-coloured rocks, after which the narrow path continues (can be muddy in places). Rise gently through low creeping pine and meander up a grassy hill, where the path becomes more stony. ◀

At the top of the hill, follow the fairly flat path along the other side of the grassy ridge. Mt Tsurugi looms majestically

Splendid views of Tengudaira and the Alpine Route road

to the east and narrow snow-filled ravines are visible across the valley. Cross a small saddle and carry on steadily upwards, brushing through thick grass and pine. You will need to negotiate a few spots of loose scree and rocks; be careful (especially if there is remaining snow) as the slopes fall away steeply down into the river valley far below.

At the top of the ridge a path to the right is closed off – this leads to the true highpoint in a couple of minutes, but the path beyond there has eroded away so is now a dead-end. Instead head left and follow the gently undulating trail along a nice ridge of low grass with a real alpine feel. Skirt past a minor pond to arrive at the small summit of **Mt Oku-dainichi-dake** 奥大日岳 (2606m – not the official true high point), about 2hr 30min from Raichōsawa campsite. After enjoying the views, simply retrace your steps back to the bus terminal at **Murodō**.

Optional extension to Shōmyō Falls (6hr)

A path continues west down the ridge from the summit of Oku-dainichi-dake to Dainichi-goya 大日小屋 in about 2hr. This hut sits in a saddle just below the summit of another mountain in the range, Mt Dainichi-dake 大日岳 (2498m). The trail then descends for a further 4hr or so all the way down to Shōmyō Falls 称名滝, a four-stage 350m waterfall, the tallest in Japan. There is a bus from there to Tateyama Station.

TREK 2
Mt Tsurugi-dake 剱岳

Start/finish	Murodō 室堂
Alternative start/finish	Bambajima-sō 馬場島荘 (see Stage 2)
Distance	14km (8¾ miles) or 16.5km (10 miles) from Bambajima
Total ascent/descent	1590m (5220ft) or 2250m (7410ft) from Bambajima
Grade	3+ *** or 2+ ** for Bambajima route
Time	2 or 3 days
Terrain	An easy start on a solid stone path, followed by a steep ascent and short descent on a rough and stony trail. Then prolonged and exposed scrambling on very steep, rocky and potentially dangerous terrain, with a number of vertical climbs and descents using fixed chains and bolts. The Bambajima route is a steady climb through forest and up a rugged ridge, with some scrambling and fixed chains near the summit (less intense than the standard route).
Access	See Tateyama chapter introduction. For Bambajima, see Stage 2.
Accommodation	Huts at Murodō and near Mt Tsurugi; camping at Raichōsawa and Tsurugi-sawa. Huts and camping at start and midpoint of Bambajima route.
Facilities	Shops, restaurants and baths at Murodō. Huts around Mt Tsurugi have showers for guests and sell food and refreshments. Medical centres at both campgrounds from mid July to end of August. Standard hut facilities on Bambajima route.
When to go	There are buses along the Alpine Route from mid April but lots of snow remains until mid summer. The trail to Mt Tsurugi is mostly clear of snow from mid July until the end of October.

While Tateyama may have long been revered in the past by priests and ascetics for religious reasons, Mt Tsurugi-dake (2999m) is a peak that now elicits similar levels of reverence among modern-day climbers and mountaineers. A pyramidal spear of rock, with brutally serrated ridges emanating from the sword-shaped summit (*Tsurugi* alludes to 'sword' in Japanese), the mountain resisted all earlier attempts to

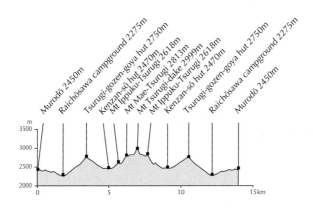

Murodō 2450m
Raichōsawa campground 2275m
Tsurugi-gozen-goya hut 2750m
Kenzan-sō hut 2470m
Mt Ippuku-Tsurugi 2618m
Mt Mae-Tsurugi 2813m
Mt Tsurugi-dake 2999m
Mt Ippuku-Tsurugi 2618m
Kenzan-sō hut 2470m
Tsurugi-gozen-goya hut 2750m
Raichōsawa campground 2275m
Murodō 2450m

climb it until a team of surveyors finally reached the summit in 1907, making it the last mountain in the Japan Alps to be officially climbed. The surveyors were greatly surprised,

Sweeping views of Tateyama and beyond from Mt Tsurugi-dake's summit (Stage 2)

View of Mt Tsurugi-dake from Tsurugi-sawa campsite

however, to find the tip of an ancient priest's staff and an old rusty spearhead nestling among the summit rocks, so seemingly they weren't the first to conquer this challenging peak.

These days there are a number of routes to the summit, but even the easiest of these involves scaling chains and ladders on exposed and near-vertical sections of rock, and Tsurugi-dake is widely regarded as the most 'dangerous' mountain climbable in Japan. There is a mountain rescue base close to the foot of the mountain to deal with the large number of accidents and incidents that occur every climbing season, but despite its somewhat fearsome reputation, Mt Tsurugi is a fantastically thrilling climb for anyone with scrambling experience and a taste for adventure. The alternative Bambajima route is long and involves a huge elevation gain, but the scrambling is much easier and not nearly as intense as the main route.

STAGE 1
Murodō to Kenzan-sō 室堂~剣山荘

Start	Murodō 室堂
Finish	Kenzan-sō hut 剣山荘
Distance	5km (3 miles)
Total ascent	490m (1610ft)
Total descent	425m (1400ft)
Time	4–5hr
Terrain	A solid stone path, then a long and steep ascent followed by a shorter descent on a rough and stony trail
Accommodation	Huts around Murodō and near Mt Tsurugi; camping at Raichōsawa and Tsurugi-sawa

A relatively easy start, although the climb to Tsurugi-gozen-goya is long and tiring, especially if you are carrying a heavy backpack. There are plenty of interesting sights along the way and a variety of birdlife can be spotted among the creeping pine. The views of Mt Tsurugi as it draws nearer are awe-inspiring and intimidating in equal measure.

Exit the hotel and bus terminal at **Murodō** 室堂 and emerge in front of a prominent water feature and water source. Take the cobbled stone path heading left and soon turn left again to reach **Mikuri-ga-ike Pond** みくりが池 in a few minutes, continuing past benches at a viewing spot in a small dip before climbing up past Mikuri-ga-ike Onsen hut みくりが池温泉 on your left.

Turn left to follow the path beyond the hut, with views down into the charred grey and steamy moonscape of **Jigoku-dani** – an active crater. Then swing right and descend a bushy shoulder, passing a marshland and the reddish-brown Chi-no-ike pools on the right. After descending stone steps to reach the bottom of a saddle, pass a windsock and warning system for poisonous gases which sometimes blow over from the crater area.

The route now climbs to reach Raichōsō hut 雷鳥荘; walk past the hut and descend stone stairs, passing two more

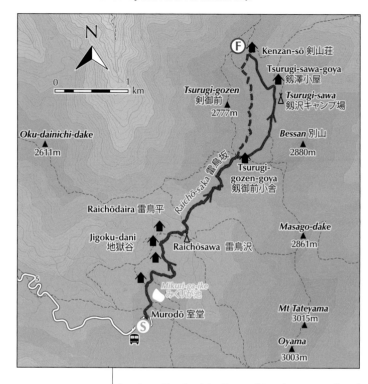

huts just off to the right. Descend into the scenic valley of
Raichōdaira 雷鳥平 and turn right at the bottom to reach the
Raichōsawa campground 雷鳥沢キャンプ場, about 45min
from the bus terminal.

> The **campsite** is in a great spot at the foot of
> Tateyama, with plenty of space for tents. A small hut
> at the west side of the campsite has toilets, water
> and also serves as the reception, although there is
> no shop.

Take the path east out of the campsite, then walk down
steps to a river and cross the bridge. Turn left and follow the
path downstream, and soon turn right at a small wooden

sign to begin climbing a rough and rocky path known as the Raichō-saka 雷鳥坂.

The route continues through head-high creeping pine and across a meadow of knotweed on a stony path; veer right to climb loose rocks, crossing a bushy rib and cutting through more pine and brush to emerge on the other side. Follow the long stony path uphill, climbing a few small switchbacks and grassy slopes, home to delicate yellow and white anemones.

The path broadens and the gradient softens briefly at a rocky shoulder, then climbs abruptly again on loose rocks. Ascend steep zigzags and rough stone steps, taking care not to slip on loose scree. Continue upwards and out of the creeping pine, up a few more stony zigzags, and climb sturdy stone steps to arrive at **Tsurugi-gozen-goya** 劔御前小舎 (1–2hr from the campsite).

The hut is a popular rest spot, with many paths converging and splendid views east and west. Past the toilet block a trail to the left (not part of this trek) climbs along the crest of the ridge to the minor summit of Mt Tsurugi-gozen 劔御前 (2777m) just to the north. ▶

For the campground and the best views of Mt Tsurugi, turn right just beyond Tsurugi-gozen-goya. A path climbs right and leads up to Mt Bessan 別山 and onwards to Tateyama 立山; do not follow this. Instead follow the stony path downwards, skirting above a big permanent patch of snow in the hollow down to the left.

Scramble easily over rocks and pass a big rock with a metal relief attached to it, then follow the stony path and wind gently down to a flat and grassy boulder-strewn plateau with spectacular views of Mt Tsurugi towering up ahead. After about 20min you will arrive at a stony clearing with a wooden signpost and a path coming in from Mt Bessan up to the right. The campground and huts should be visible further down the valley, so follow the stony path downhill, cutting through a thicket of creeping pine and then descending to reach the **Tsurugi-sawa** campground 劔沢キャンプ場 in a further 15min.

The **campsite** is spacious and rocky, has a water source and offers great views across to the towering and imposing Mt Tsurugi-dake. A small hut with a red cross painted on it serves as the reception, summer medical centre and mountain rescue base, but

A narrow alternative trail to Kenzan-sō descends the side of this ridge, skirting across scree and winding down to the hut in 1hr. It is the quickest direct route.

Great views on the approach to Mt Tsurugi

there is no shop. There are toilets in the stone building across to the right.

The route continues on a narrow stony path that leads down from the small hut to **Tsurugi-sawa-goya** 劔澤小屋 in 10min. This nice, friendly hut is the place to buy supplies if you are camping and is a good place to stay in itself.

To continue towards Kenzan-sō, take the path left of Tsurugi-sawa-goya and cross a small rocky gully. Traverse a field of boulders and rocks, carefully following paint marks and trail markers, before regaining the path and following it through low-lying creeping pine and patches of wildflowers. Pass a small pond and arrive at **Kenzan-sō** 劍山荘 in 30min. This hut is a convenient starting base for climbing Mt Tsurugi.

STAGE 2
Kenzan-sō to Murodō via Mt Tsurugi-dake summit
剣山荘~剱岳~室堂

Start	Kenzan-sō hut 剣山荘
Finish	Murodō 室堂
Distance	9km (5¾ miles)
Total ascent	1100m (3610ft)
Total descent	1165m (3820ft)
Time	7–8hr
Terrain	Steep, rugged paths and lots of up-and-down between summits. Plenty of scrambling on very exposed, rocky and potentially dangerous terrain, with a number of vertical climbs and descents using fixed chains, bolts and ladders.
Accommodation	Kenzan-sō hut is passed again on the return to Murodō
Warning	There are some long sections on almost vertical rock, with metal chains and bolts fixed in place to aid along the most difficult parts. Many Japanese people opt to wear a helmet. Competent scramblers and those with a head for heights should be fine, but less experienced hikers should stay away. The route should not be attempted in bad weather, as the polished rock becomes lethal when wet.

This is the most popular route on the mountain, following the Bessan Ridge 別山尾根 (Bessan-one) virtually all the way from the hut to the summit. Two minor summits are traversed along the way, and the going gets tough almost from the off, with steep terrain and plenty of scrambling up and down rocky crags, some parts more akin to rock climbing. Lots of incredibly exposed sections and big drops make this one of the most thrilling and challenging 'standard routes' on any mountain in Japan.

Follow the gravel path down the side of **Kenzan-sō hut** 剣山荘 and climb steps next to a stone wall. Turn right at the signpost for 剱岳方面 (Tsurugi-dake-hōmen); the stony path immediately starts climbing the grassy hillside, and there are good views east towards the distant pointy summit of Mt Kashimayari-ga-take 鹿島槍ケ岳.

There are 13 sets of chains along this route, and they are all marked with metal plaques indicating their number.

Continue to a stretch of angular rocks laced with chains – an easy first scramble. ◄ Follow paint marks and clamber over brown-hued rocks to almost gain the top of the ridge, then skirt across loose scree to another chain section traversing narrow rock platforms. From here scramble easily up rocks to the bouldery summit of **Ippuku-Tsurugi** 一服剱 (2618m), 30min from the hut.

The next summit (Mae-Tsurugi 前剱) now looms into full view, looking almost impossibly high and steep. Drop down rocks and descend a steep and rough path through a thicket of creeping pine to reach a stony saddle, and then ascend sloping grey scree, bearing right about halfway up. Follow the stony path, scrambling upwards over rocks and paying attention to paint marks – the correct route winds left and right and is easy to lose. Be alert also to tumbling rocks if people are above.

At a steep and narrow rocky gully with a huge boulder wedged partway up, climb with the aid of a long chain to emerge at the top on a narrow ridge. Now bear right, traverse the easy fourth section of chains and follow the narrow rocky path, soon ascending a short but vague route up to the crest of the ridge (be careful not to miss this; there is a faint red 'x' painted on a rock to warn against going too far). ◄ The path

From the exposed and windy crest the views back towards Tateyama are wonderful.

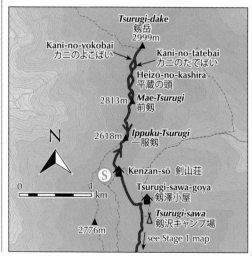

splits, so head right along the 'up' route to scramble along the spine of the ridge to the summit of **Mae-Tsurugi** 前劍 (2813m) around 40min from Ippuku-Tsurugi.

Walk along the ridge and scramble down to a rocky saddle with a narrow metal bridge hanging over a gully. Cross the bridge and head right for a very exposed traverse of the cliff face using a 20m-long fixed chain. Scramble down steep rocks with more chains to reach another small rocky saddle, then ascend loose scree and clamber over rocks, and follow the rough path up the side of the ridge. ▶ Scramble up and along the ridge crest, and bear left at a metal sign indicating a dead-end ahead.

Follow the rough path along the other side of the ridge to a rugged, rocky place where chains dangle down and the trail splits. Head right for the 'up' route, and climb using the chain and metal bolts screwed into the rock face. Once up, use chains to descend steeply 20m down the other side of the outcrop on slippery polished rock, shuffling carefully left and then down to a stony col. This steep and bare fin of rock is known as **Heizō-no-kashira** 平蔵の頭.

Traversing an exposed section with the help of fixed chains

Early in the season snow can remain along here and is prone to avalanche.

Climbers at the top of the infamous Kani-no-tatebai

There is a variation route up this valley, but it is strictly for experts only.

Follow the pale scuff marks across steep rocks and clamber up the eighth set of chains. At the top of these, walk along a flat rock ledge and admire views of tumbling scree slopes leading down to a secluded snow valley. ◄

Cross the scree slope to reach one of Mt Tsurugi's most notorious points, the **Kani-no-tatebai** カニのたてばい, which loosely translates as 'place to scuttle up like a crab', roughly 40min from Mae-Tsurugi. This is a 50m climb up an almost vertical rock face, protected only by metal handholds and chains. It is straightforward but requires confidence and sure-footedness. At the top of the climb, edge right and scramble up a steep and narrow chimney, then scramble up and around to gain the ridge.

Follow paint and scuff marks up over jumbles of rocks just below the crest of the ridge, then clamber upwards and hop over larger rocks to reach the small shrine housing a metal sword at the summit of **Mt Tsurugi-dake** 剱岳 (2999m), from where there are far-reaching views in every direction. Over on the far western side of the summit ridge a signpost marks the way for the trail up the Hayatsuki ridge 早月尾根 (see alternative approach from Bambajima).

For the return, head back along the ridge and down the same boulder-strewn slope. Where the ridge narrows, instead of turning left where you came up, descend chains straight down to an exposed cliff-edge. This awkward spot is called **Kani-no-yokobai** カニのよこばい, or 'place to scuttle sideways like a crab'. Grab the chains and carefully lower yourself over the cliff-edge, shimmying left to safety. Use a sturdy metal ladder to descend 15m down a sheer rock face, and then use chains to climb another 15m down a very steep rocky notch. Pass a small wooden shack that serves as a toilet and then scramble down left to rejoin the 'up' path.

Back at the fin-shaped **Heizō-no-kashira** the 'up' and 'down' paths split again, so ascend the chains heading straight up and over the fin of rock, loop around the back of the outcrop and then descend a steep 10m chain to rejoin the main trail.

Continue back along the way you came, but where the path splits for the final time take the right-hand branch up some steep rocks and the 13th set of chains. This is followed by another down-climb, then follow the rough path as it skirts across the steep slope below the summit of **Mae-Tsurugi**. Both trails converge again, so follow the path back down to **Kenzan-sō** hut, from where you can retrace your steps to the bus terminal at **Murodō** (allow at least 3hr 30min from Kenzan-sō).

Alternative approach from Bambajima (8–9hr) 馬場島

Those with an aversion to heights and crowds may want to consider climbing via Hayatsuki-one 早月尾根, a strenuous but less terrifying route that follows a northwestern spur ridge from Bambajima at 750m all the way to the summit over a distance of 8.2km. Most people break up the hike by staying at Hayatsuki-goya hut before carrying on to the summit the following morning. Access is by car (parking available) or taxi (40min from Kamiichi Station on the Toyama Chihō Railway, return booking recommended, tel 0120-490-151) and despite the remoteness, the route is marked with metal signposts every 200m of vertical elevation gain, providing an easy way to measure your progress.

Start by walking up the paved forest road away from **Bambajima-sō** hut and campground to reach an etched granite signpost marked 剱岳. Enter the forest and zigzag for 3hr up through large cedar trees and over protruding tree roots to

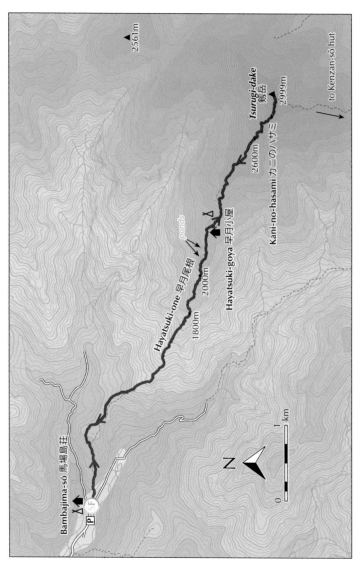

reach a **1800m** signpost. From here it is a short 30min climb to an unmarked summit at the top of the ridge with views towards Mt Tsurugi-dake. The rout now flattens and skirts past two **ponds** and then a short ascent leads to **Hayatsuki-goya**早月小屋, a hut with camping spots 4–5hr from the trailhead.

Climb the steep spur to the left of the hut for 90min along a ridge of stunted hardwood trees and winter-hardened dwarf pine. At a **2600m** signpost, skirt by the edge of a snow-field and climb fixed ropes to boulder fields at the base of the summit wall. A 2800m signpost marks the final 1hr push and the beginning of the **Kani-no-hasami** カニのハサミ, or 'crab claw traverse'. Head left for the first set of horizontal chains, and then go right and up the next set to reach a junction with the main trail coming in from Kenzan-sō. Turn left for the short climb to the summit of **Mt Tsurugi-dake** 剱岳 (2999m). From here, retrace your steps to return to **Bambajima** or follow the description in Stage 2 for the route to Kenzan-sō.

The small summit shrine at the top of Mt Tsurugi-dake

TREK 3
North Alps traverse 北アルプス縦走

Start	Murodō 室堂
Finish	Kamikōchi 上高地
Distance	63km (39 miles)
Total ascent	4365m (14,320ft)
Total descent	5295m (17,370ft)
Grade	3 **
Time	5–7 days
Terrain	Rugged but well-marked paths with lots of ups and downs, including a few straightforward but long climbs. Mostly simple walking, staying above 2000m all the way until the final day. Occasional short passages of easy scrambling and fixed chains, but overall few overly technical or challenging sections. Note, however, that snow can lie late in the year in places.
Access	See Tateyama chapter introduction. For Kamikōchi, see Hotaka introduction.
Accommodation	Hotels, huts and camping at start and finish, huts and camping at regular intervals along the route.
Facilities	Shops, restaurants and hot spring baths at Tateyama and Kamikōchi. Drinks, snacks and meals available at huts.
When to go	Mid July to the beginning of October is the best time to hike. Most of the huts are open by mid July, but there can still be substantial patches of snow covering the path, especially at the Tateyama end, so a pair of light crampons may be useful. Huts close early to mid October, some even earlier, and winter conditions can be expected by the end of the month.

One of Japan's classic multi-day treks, this week-long, high-altitude route traverses the undulating western spine of the North Alps, connecting two of the Alps' main mountain hubs: Murodō in the north, and Kamikōchi in the south. A network of mountain huts and campgrounds, located at regular intervals along the entire route, mean it is possible to enjoy wonderfully secluded alpine scenery without any logistical problems. Murodō and Kamikōchi are always

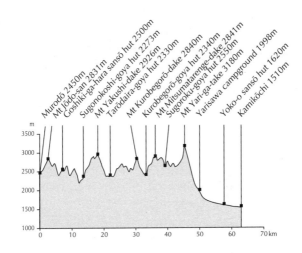

Murodō 2450m
Mt Jōdo-san 2831m
Goshiki-ga-hara sansō hut 2500m
Sugonokoshi-goya hut 2273m
Mt Yakushi-dake 2926m
Tarodaira-goya hut 2330m
Mt Kurobegorō-dake 2840m
Kurobegorō-goya hut 2340m
Mt Mitsumatarenge-dake 2841m
Sugoroku-goya hut 2550m
Mt Yari-ga-take 3180m
Yarisawa campground 1998m
Yoko-o sansō hut 1620m
Kamikōchi 1510m

Walking towards the high plateau of Goshiki-ga-hara (Stage 1)

swarming with people, but once those two touristy areas are left behind the trails soon become much emptier, with the long section between Goshiki-ga-hara and Kurobegorō-goya particularly quiet and remote. There are good transport links at either end of the trek, so getting to and from the mountains is easy, and there are a few detours and escape routes along the way if you want to change plans.

The trek starts at Murodō and gradually winds southwards, up and down many minor peaks, climbing the two bulky and remote giants of Mt Yakushi-dake and Mt Kurobegorō-dake, and meandering through the scenic heart of the North Alps and up to the summit of the region's most iconic peak, Mt Yari-ga-take. It is also just as viable to start the trek from Kamikōchi and do the route in reverse (south to north), although as Kamikōchi (1505m) has a lower starting altitude than Murodō (2420m) there is a bit more 'up', with the total overall ascent being somewhat higher than for the route described here. Adventurous types can also combine the North Alps Traverse with the challenging and committing scrambles between Yari-ga-take and Oku-Hotaka (see Trek 5, Stage 2), or the ascents of Tateyama (Walk 2) and Tsurugi-dake (Trek 2) for longer and even more exciting expeditions.

Mt Yari-ga-take looms ahead along the Nishikama ridge (Stage 4)

STAGE 1
Murodō to Goshiki-ga-hara 室堂~五色ヶ原

Start	Murodō 室堂
Finish	Goshiki-ga-hara sansō hut 五色ヶ原山荘
Distance	7km (4¼ miles)
Total ascent	700m (2290ft)
Total descent	680m (2230ft)
Time	5–6hr
Terrain	Flat paved stone path, becoming more rugged and undulating. Some gradual climbs and steep descents, and a few short fixed chains and ladders. Snow can remain in some spots until early autumn.
Accommodation	Huts and camping at start and end of stage

Once the crowds around the busy hotel complex at Murodō have been left behind, the trail soon becomes much quieter and more remote, traversing a few minor peaks to reach Goshiki-ga-hara, a beautiful highland plateau covered in wildflowers and formed by lava flows from the nearby Tateyama caldera. Snow often lies late in these parts, particularly between Mt Jōdo-san and Zara-tōge, and although crampons are not usually required, a light pair of four- or six-pointers may prove useful.

Aim to arrive at Murodō by mid morning at the latest to allow ample time to reach the end of the stage before dark, perhaps even spending a day or two beforehand exploring the peaks and hot springs around Tateyama.

Leave the large hotel and bus terminal complex at **Murodō** 室堂 and walk over to the rock feature gushing with water. ▶ Climb the steps to the right of the water source and follow the paved walkway across grassy flatlands, soon turning right at a junction. Keep walking straight and follow the signs for 一ノ越・立山 (Ichinokoshi and Tateyama).

Just after a turnoff to the left for Tateyama Murodō sansō hut 立山室堂山荘, take the path going right signposted 室堂山・浄土山 for a short climb up Mt Jōdo-san, a rugged little peak with fantastic views. (Alternatively you can carry on straight along the main path for 1hr to Ichinokoshi sansō hut 一ノ越山荘 and then turn right for a 40min climb to rejoin the route on the far side of Jōdo-san.) ▶

This is a good place to fill up your bottles.

If you opt for the Ichinokoshi route you can also make a quick detour climb up to Oyama 雄山 (3003m), one of the main summits of Tateyama (see Walk 2).

111

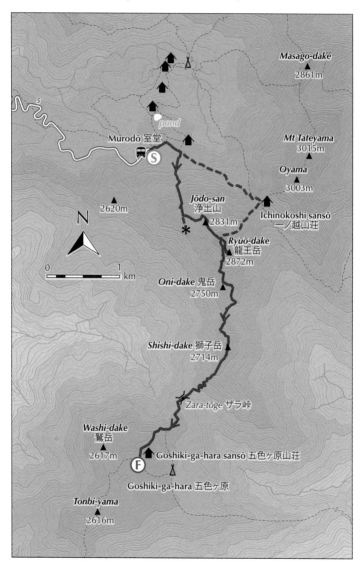

The path up Jōdo-san starts relatively flat and cobbled, but soon starts to climb steadily and becomes more rugged. In around 40min the trail branches left but you can leave your rucksack here and carry on straight for a 5min stroll to Murodōyama-tenbōdai 室堂山展望台, a dead-end **viewpoint** with superb panoramic views of the Tateyama caldera, Goshiki-ga-hara and the distant bulk of Mt Yakushi-dake.

Back at the trail branch, head left to start scrambling easily over rocks up the mountainside, steep in places. Follow the paint marks and after 30min arrive at the north summit (北峰) of **Mt Jōdo-san** 浄土山 (2831m), a peak with great views of the nearby Tateyama massif. ▶ From here veer right across the undulating summit area to the open and expansive south summit (南峰), and turn right after passing a walled-off Toyama University snow research facility building.

Stroll down to a saddle below the small, jaunty summit of **Mt Ryūō-dake** 龍王岳 (2872m). A narrow path leads to the top if you fancy a quick detour climb; otherwise follow the path right (left takes you to Tateyama, or back to Murodō via Ichinokoshi if you are just doing the short Jōdo-san loop – see Tateyama Area introduction) and ease downhill on a rocky, rugged path to a pleasant saddle.

The trail briefly climbs and then drops around the east side of another minor peak called **Mt Oni-dake** 鬼岳 (2750m). Snow can linger on the traverse down its steep slopes until September, but a clear path and steps have usually been cut out (although light crampons may be useful).

Carry on south for a steady climb to the summit of **Mt Shishi-dake** 獅子岳 (2714m), crossing wooden boards through patches of buttercups and mountain lilies before a rugged climb. After dropping from the summit the path briefly flattens, with views east down to the large Lake Kurobe. Descend a few short fixed chains and ladders. The path then zigzags steeply down to reach **Zara-tōge** ザラ峠, a saddle near the edge of the Tateyama caldera and the lowest point of the stage at 2348m, 2–3hr from Jōdo-san.

The last part of the stage is a steady 40min climb on a stony path up the grassy green slopes to the plateau, passing safely to the left of the impressive crumbling red cliffs which you may have spotted earlier in the day. Wooden boardwalks signal your arrival at Goshiki-ga-hara 五色ヶ原 – an expansive ancient lava plateau and a wonderful habitat for many

A stone memorial near the summit of Jōdo-san was built to commemorate the 2595 men of Toyama who died in the Russo-Japanese War (1904–1905).

Approaching Goshiki-ga-hara sansō hut

The bath is filled with water from melted snow, so in years of lower snowfall the bath may be out of use by the end of August.

alpine flowers such as Aleutian avens, black lilies and pink geraniums.

A path leading left goes directly to the camping ground (which has toilets and a water source, pay fee at hut), but carry on for 10min along wooden boardwalks to arrive at **Goshiki-ga-hara sansō** 五色ケ原山荘, a white-walled, red-roofed hut at 2500m, with the chance of a hot bath for staying guests. ◄

STAGE 2
Goshiki-ga-hara to Yakushi-dake 五色ケ原~薬師岳

Start	Goshiki-ga-hara sansō hut 五色ケ原山荘
Finish	Yakushi-dake sansō hut 薬師岳山荘
Distance	12km (7½ miles)
Total ascent	1335m (4390ft)
Total descent	1085m (3560ft)
Time	10–11hr
Terrain	Rugged mountain path with many ups and downs, briefly dipping below the tree line. The second part is a long climb up and across the rocky and undulating summit ridge of Yakushi-dake, followed by a short stony descent.
Accommodation	Huts and camping at beginning, middle and end of stage

A long stage with lots of ups and downs, ending with a big climb up and over Mt Yakushi-dake (2926m). As such, it requires an early start and a decent level of fitness, although many people split the stage in two by staying at Sugo-no-koshi-goya スゴ乗越小屋, a hut and campground conveniently located halfway along the route (closes mid to late September).

This is a wonderfully remote area, with large humpbacked mountains that are more reminiscent of the South Alps than the craggy peaks that the North Alps are famous for, and you may not bump into many other people on the trail for most of the day.

Leave **Goshiki-ga-hara sansō hut** 五色ケ原山荘 and rejoin the wooden boardwalks of the main trail heading south. Rise gently through alpine meadows and climb past possible late-lying snow patches on the sloping flanks of **Mt Tonbi-yama** 鳶山 (2616m), whose grassy summit is reached in around 40min. From here it is possible to trace the route for the next couple of days along the mountains if the weather is clear to the south. ▶

Continue along the narrow stony path, following the steep ridge down to a **col** at 2356m, then go over boardwalks into low forest. You will emerge onto a wide slope of creeping pine; steadily climb the stony trail for 1hr to the top of

There are views of the huge lake formed by the Kurobe Dam way down in the valley to the east.

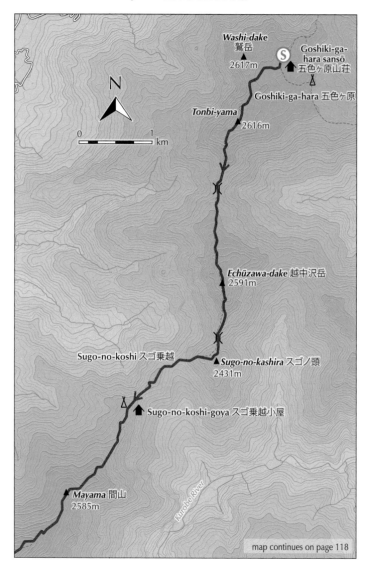

map continues on page 118

Mt Echūzawa-dake 越中沢岳 (2591m), marked by a wooden summit post.

After admiring the views, follow the ridge along the path which is rough and quite steep in places, sometimes scrambling over rocks. Beyond another remote **col** you will regain about 100m of altitude as you ascend the rugged stony path to reach a wooden post close to the summit of the small, lonely peak of **Sugo-no-kashira** スゴノ頭 (2431m).

Follow the path as it drops right through the creeping pine, descending the lightly wooded slopes for 30min to a flat, bouldery pass and good rest spot called **Sugo-no-koshi** スゴ乗越 – the lowest point of the trek so far (2130m). There is one more steady but undulating climb through the trees and alpine brush for 1km before reaching **Sugo-no-koshi-goya** スゴ乗越小屋 (2273m).

This is a small, quirky **hut** decorated with Himalayan prayer flags. There are plenty of spaces for tents nearby. It is a good place to break up the stage, but be aware that it closes around mid to late September, earlier than most other huts. Many

Don't forget to turn around and admire the views behind

hikers finish the day here, and as this is roughly the halfway point of the stage in both distance and time, you should decide whether to continue or not. The second half of the stage has far fewer exhausting up-and-downs, but it is a long, steady climb up and over the bare rocky bulk of Mt Yakushi-dake.

From the hut, the onward path climbs the patchily wooded ridge, soon passing above the tree line and becoming stonier, climbing along a broad, open shoulder with extensive views. After about 1hr you'll reach a tiny pond with a dead-end path leading just a few metres right to the summit marker of **Mt Mayama** 間山 (2585m).

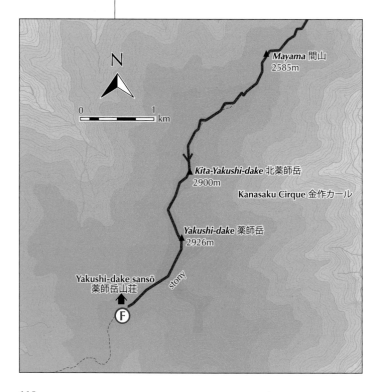

Getting close to the true summit of Mt Yakushi-dake

Continue past the pond for a steady but enjoyable climb up the wide stony ridge for about 1hr 30min, scrambling over rocks and boulders before reaching Yakushi's northern summit, Mt **Kita-Yakushi-dake** 北薬師岳 (2900m). There are wonderful sweeping views of the large scree-filled Kanasaku cirque 金作カール below, where patches of snow last almost throughout the year.

Continue along the rocky, undulating ridgeline, which is narrow and a little exposed in places, to arrive at the true summit of **Mt Yakushi-dake** 薬師岳 (2926m) in about another 1hr. This is one of Japan's '100 Famous Mountains' and is capped with a small Shintō shrine and a wooden summit post. ▶

The final part of the stage is a 40min descent on a stony zigzagging path, passing the remains of an old stone emergency shelter on the way, to arrive at **Yakushi-dake sansō** 薬師岳山荘 – a nice modern hut with beautiful sunset views on a saddle below the summit. If you are camping then the campsite is another 1hr or so down the trail.

Expect to see more people from this point onwards, as many hikers climb Mt Yakushi as a one- or two-day hike from Oritate.

STAGE 3
Yakushi-dake to Kurobegorō-dake 薬師岳~黒部五郎岳

Start	Yakushi-dake sansō hut 薬師岳山荘
Finish	Kurobegorō-goya hut 黒部五郎小舎
Distance	14km (8¾ miles)
Total ascent	865m (2840ft)
Total descent	1230m (4040ft)
Time	7hr
Terrain	Wooden boardwalks at the start, stony mountain paths later. Undulating route through hilly grasslands, with one big climb up Kurobegorō. Steep and rugged descent into the cirque.
Access	If you take the early escape route from near Tarōdaira-goya down to Oritate, there are a few buses to Toyama (or Arimineguchi Station) every day between mid July and the end of August, and then only at weekends until early October. Ask at Tarōdaira-goya hut for the bus schedule, or check www.chitetsu.co.jp (Japanese link – click on バス then in sidebar 夏山バスのご案内 and 富山-有峰線 for timetable).
Accommodation	Huts and camping at beginning and end of stage

Another remote section of the trek with some more ups and downs along the way, but thankfully these are far less demanding than those of the previous stage. The trail follows a pleasant broad ridge through stunning alpine grasslands as it curves around to the east for a steady climb to the summit of Mt Kurobegorō-dake, another big mountain with a spectacular cirque on its northern side. Most people drop down into the cirque but you can also scramble along the ridgeline to reach Kurobegorō-goya, an attractive and comfortable hut in a secluded alpine setting.

From **Yakushi-dake sansō hut** 薬師岳山荘 head southwest down the stony trail, descending the hillside to reach a broad flat plateau with alpine flowers. Proceed along boardwalks to enter the top of a mostly dry rocky river gully and follow the markings downstream into forest, hopping over rocks and crossing the stream in places.

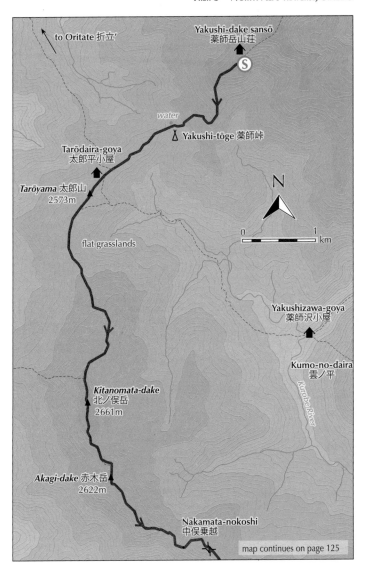

to Oritate 折立

Yakushi-dake sansō
薬師岳山荘
S

water

Yakushi-tōge 薬師峠

Tarōdaira-goya
太郎平小屋

Tarōyama 太郎山
2573m

flat grasslands

Yakushizawa-goya
薬師沢小屋

Kumo-no-daira
雲ノ平

Kurobe River

Kitanomata-dake
北ノ俣岳
2661m

Akagi-dake 赤木岳
2622m

Nakamata-nokoshi
中俣乗越

N

0   1 km

map continues on page 125

You will eventually emerge out of the trees at a low 2294m saddle called **Yakushi-tōge** 薬師峠 where there is a large stony campsite with water, toilets and a small reception where you can pay the camping fee and buy drinks (open until late afternoon; otherwise pay fee at Tarōdaira-goya). From here it is a 20min stroll uphill on wooden boardwalks to **Tarōdaira-goya** (sometimes called Tarōbei-goya) 太郎平小屋, a hut at 2330m on a broad grassy shoulder and the meeting point for a few trails.

To leave the trail
In front of the hut a trail to the right leads west down to Oritate 折立 in around 3hr. This is a relatively popular path for hikers climbing Mt Yakushi as a one- or two-day trip, but Oritate is a fairly remote trailhead where you can find a basic shelter, campground, water and parking. From mid July to late August a few buses a day leave for Toyama 富山 or Arimineguchi Station 有峰口 (on the Toyama Chihō Railway Line running between Tateyama and Toyama), and then only on weekends until early October. Use this trail if you need to escape the mountains early or to turn this into a shorter trek, but ask at Tarōdaira-goya for the bus schedule before setting off.

Just past Tarōdaira-goya the boardwalk trail splits.

Optional variant to explore Kumo-no-daira
The branch leading left goes to Yakushizawa 薬師沢 down in the valley. Beyond there you can carry on east for a few hours to one of the most remote areas of the North Alps: **Kumo-no-daira** 雲ノ平. Sometimes referred to as 'Japan's last unexplored region', it is a beautiful and isolated highland plateau surrounded by hidden valleys and the source of the Kurobe-gawa river. Pristine alpine gardens, secret outdoor hot springs and many interesting trails lie waiting to be discovered, and there are some nice huts along the way. A trip through Kumo-no-daira from Tarōdaira-goya all the way to Mitsumata sansō (see Stage 4) by the most direct route takes 9–10hr, but would be best split over a couple of days to enjoy the remote setting.

Follow the main trail to the right for Kurobegorō-dake 黒部五郎岳, climbing gently and skirting past the small peak of

Mt Tarōyama 太郎山 (2373m) before continuing on for 1hr or so to gradually ascend the broad ridge. This is a beautiful and remote area of undulating small peaks, patches of creeping pine, and flat grasslands home to many kinds of wildflowers. Ignore a trail turning right and soon arrive at the stony bald summit of **Mt Kitanomata-dake** 北ノ俣岳 (2661m).

From here there is a bit of up and down, but very gentle compared to the previous day. Descend very gradually and walk along a winding path for 30min, hopping over large rocks to skirt around the minor peak of **Mt Akagi-dake** 赤木岳 (2622m). It is another 30min down to a broad flat saddle covered in grass and creeping pine (**Nakamata-no-koshi** 中俣乗越, 2450m), followed by a short climb on a stony path to a small unnamed **peak** (2578m).

Drop gently to another broad saddle before passing a rocky outcrop and starting the main ascent of the day, to the top of **Mt Kurobegorō-dake** 黒部五郎岳 (2840m). The steep, stony climb should take around 40min. At a rocky shoulder just below the summit the path splits; if you intend to take the main cirque route to Kurobegorō-goya hut you can leave

Looking back up towards the bowl-like cirque walls of Mt Kurobegorō

The huge cracked rock in Kurobegorō Cirque

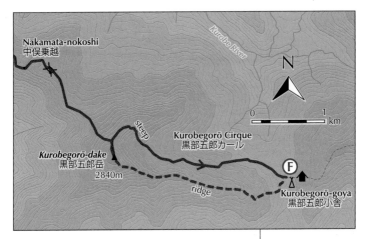

your rucksack here and head right for the easy 10min clamber up to the summit. ▶

Note that from the summit a rough path continues east along the ridge and leads to Kurobegorō-goya in 2hr 30min, but this is not the route most people take (although it is sometimes recommended if the cirque is cloaked in mist). Instead return to the junction and walk northeast along the ridge, soon turning right to descend steeply into the cirque.

The **Kurobegorō Cirque** 黒部五郎カール route takes about 1hr 30min and is a splendid walk through glorious surroundings passing snow patches, gurgling rivers, alpine flower meadows and the steep-sided cliffs of the cirque wall. ▶

Follow the rugged path along the floor of the cirque, crossing streams and hopping over rocks, then cut through a forest of birch and brush before emerging into an open meadow for a short walk to **Kurobegorō-goya** 黒部五郎小舎, a distinctive and attractive red hut with good food and a friendly atmosphere. There is a campground nearby. If you still have time and energy then it is feasible to carry on to Sugoroku-goya 双六小屋 (3–4hr) or detour to Mitsumata sansō 三俣山荘 (2hr 30min).

Mt Kurobegorō is another of the 100 Famous Mountains, and from the summit the unmistakably pointy Mt Yari is visible to the east.

Look out for a rock the size of a house which has a massive crack down the middle, said to be caused by a lightning strike!

STAGE 4
Kurobegorō-dake to Yari-ga-take 黒部五郎岳~槍ヶ岳

Start	Kurobegorō-goya hut 黒部五郎小舎
Finish	Yari-ga-take sansō hut 槍ヶ岳山荘
Distance	12km (7½ miles)
Total ascent	1365m (4470ft)
Total descent	625m (2040ft)
Time	9hr
Terrain	A steady climb to the top of the ridgeline, dropping down to a saddle by way of either an undulating ridgeline or a lower-level meadow walk. A long traverse along a narrow ridge, exposed in places with occasional fixed chains, followed by a long, steep stony ascent.
Access	You can cut the trek short by leaving the trail at Sugoroku campsite and walking to Shin-Hotaka Onsen; there are hourly buses to and from Takayama (1hr 30min) and Hirayu Onsen (30min, for bus connections to Matsumoto and Shinjuku) leaving from Shin-Hotaka Ropeway. See www.nouhibus.co.jp/english (select 'Route Bus') for schedules.
Accommodation	Huts and camping at Sugoroku-goya, Mitsumata sansō (off route) and at end of stage

Leaving the relative solitude of the trek's middle section behind, the route winds over towards Mt Yari via minor peaks and high alpine meadows, passing the hut and major trail junction at Sugoroku, where more traffic is usually encountered. This is still deep in the heart of the North Alps though, with nothing but endless mountain views in every direction, and the stage ends just below the spire-like summit of one of the most iconic and instantly recognisable peaks in the whole of Japan: Mt Yari-ga-take (3180m).

It is possible to split this stage in two by staying at Sugoroku-goya, making more time for a short detour to Mt Washiba-dake 鷲羽岳 (2924m), a handsome mountain with a small crater lake and another one of Japan's 100 Famous Mountains. You could also opt to stay at Mitsumata sansō hut (or campground) close to the foot of Washiba-dake.

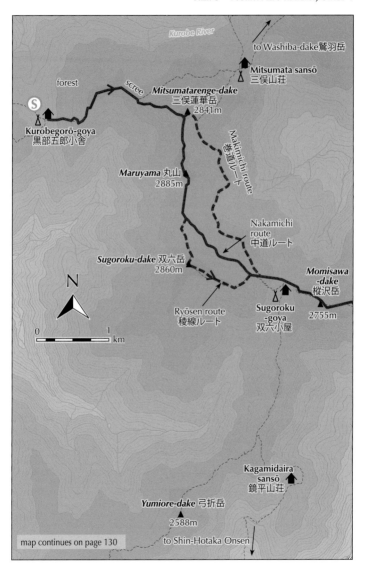

Kurobe River

to Washiba-dake 鷲羽岳

Mitsumata sansō
三俣山荘

forest

scree

Mitsumatarenge-dake
三俣蓮華岳
2841m

S

Kurobegorō-goya
黒部五郎小舍

Makimichi route
巻道ルート

Maruyama 丸山
2885m

Nakamichi
route
中道ルート

Sugoroku-dake 双六岳
2860m

*Momisawa
-dake* 樅沢岳

Ryōsen route
稜線ルート

**Sugoroku
-goya**
双六小屋

2755m

N

0   1
——————— km

**Kagamidaira
sansō**
鏡平山荘

Yumiore-dake 弓折岳

2588m

map continues on page 130

to Shin-Hotaka Onsen

Follow the path left around the back of **Kurobegorō-goya hut** 黒部五郎小舎 and start climbing steeply through birch forest, with occasional glimpses through the trees of the fine form of Mt Kurobegorō and its cirque. In less than 1hr you will emerge onto the open ridgeline; continue following the stony path up through low creeping pine.

Climb steadily as the trail veers right up along the ridge, skirting the top of a steep scree slope. Scramble over rocks to meet a trail branching down left; this is a short-cut to Mitsumata sansō hut 三俣山荘 if taking a detour to Mt Washiba-dake, although snow lingers late here so care should be taken. ◄

Mt Washiba-dake is a striking peak in the centre of the North Alps with a small crater lake below its summit. It's 2hr to the top of the peak from here.

Otherwise continue right up the ridge for 30min to a trail junction near the flat summit of **Mt Mitsumatarenge-dake** 三俣蓮華岳 (2841m). This point marks the boundary of three prefectures – Toyama, Gifu and Nagano – and you have a choice of trails from here; a lower-level alternative or the more direct route along the ridge.

Lower-level option

A popular and fairly easy path goes straight on and down steeply to a junction, turning right onto the **Makimichi route** 巻道ルート (turn left for the detour to Mitsumata sansō hut and Mt Washiba-dake). This is a lower-level 1hr 30min walk which gently winds through stunning alpine meadows with exceptional views of the nearby mountain ranges, joining up with the other ridge trails just before the short steep descent to Sugoroku-goya.

For the more direct route, turn right at Mt Mitsumatarenge-dake and walk south along the undulating ridgeline. Drop a little then climb again to reach the rounded **Mt Maruyama** 丸山 (2854m) in 25min. From here, meander through the creeping pine for a further 20min down to another saddle, and then climb briefly to find an innocuous-looking path branching left, marked by a small white arrow on a stone. This is for the **Nakamichi route** 中道ルート, a quick and direct 30min descent to the main path via a secluded alpine meadow. Alternatively, continue along the ridge for the longer **Ryōsen route** 稜線ルート, which climbs to the top of **Mt Sugoroku-dake** 双六岳 (2860m) for nice panoramic views before descending another 30min to meet the other trails.

A few more ups and downs before Sugoroku-dake

From the wooden signpost where all the trails join up again, proceed down a steep stony path through thick creeping pine for 10min to reach the bottom of a saddle and the often-bustling **Sugoroku-goya** 双六小屋. This large, well-equipped hut is directly across the valley from Mt Washiba-dake, and is a popular place to stay or rest. There is also a large campsite next to the hut, adjacent to a pond. ▶

From Sugoroku-goya carry on east straight up the other side of the saddle on a zigzagging trail up the ridge, reaching the top of **Mt Momisawa-dake** 樅沢岳 (2755m) in about 40min. The view of Mt Yari and the ridgeline ahead is exceptional. From the summit it is an undulating and enjoyable 2hr 30min clamber along the **Nishikama ridge** 西鎌尾根, which is a little exposed in places. The terrain becomes more challenging as you go along, with the odd fixed chain as you get closer to Yari, but the path is well marked and the views are stunning.

After a few exciting chain sections you'll arrive at a narrow shoulder where a path leads down into the valley to the right. It is now a steep and steady 300m climb up the rocky

A path heads south past the campsite for an escape route to Shin-Hotaka Onsen in about 5hr, via Kagamidaira sansō 鏡平山荘 (a hut near a mirror-like pond with wonderful reflections of Mt Yari).

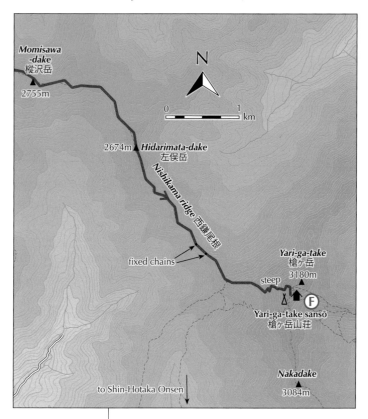

The campground at Sesshō Hut is somewhat less exposed than the one next to Yari-ga-take sansō, so it may be a better option if it is windy and/ or you don't have confidence in your tent's durability.

ridge, ascending scree and zigzags at the higher reaches. It should take 1–1hr 30min, depending on fitness. Near the top of the mountain, turn right to arrive at **Yari-ga-take sansō** 槍ヶ岳山荘, a huge hut perched on the narrow ridge directly below Mt Yari's pointy summit. There are exposed tent spots just south past the hut. There are also a couple of huts 20–30min further east of the summit (Ōyari Hut ヒュッテ大槍 and Sesshō Hut 殺生ヒュッテ), giving a range of accommodation options. ◄

Looking east along the Nishikama ridge towards Mt Yari-ga-take

STAGE 5
Yari-ga-take to Kamikōchi 槍ヶ岳~上高地

Start	Yari-ga-take sansō hut 槍ヶ岳山荘
Finish	Kamikōchi 上高地
Distance	18km (11 miles)
Total ascent	100m (330ft)
Total descent	1675m (5490ft)
Time	7hr
Terrain	A short and steep optional scramble to Yari's summit and a steep rocky descent, and then a steady rugged mountain path down a narrow river valley. The descent through forest ends on a long and mostly flat riverside track.
Accommodation	Huts and camping at regular intervals and at Kamikōchi
Note	For more on Kamikōchi (including access), see Hotaka chapter introduction

Catch the sunrise from the top of the spear-like Yari-ga-take (3180m) and then prepare for a long but fairly comfortable descent to the popular resort and transport hub of Kamikōchi. The second half of the stage is a very easy and pleasant walk along a flat, meandering riverside track, and there are plenty of huts and campsites along the way should you wish to break it up further.

This stage happens to be the exact reverse of Trek 5, Stage 1, so see that description if approaching from the opposite direction.

Purists may say that a true North Alps traverse can only be made by heading south from Mt Yari for the challenging and thrilling climb to Mt Oku-Hotaka-dake, via the notorious Daikiretto (see Trek 5, Stage 2). That route, however, can only be recommended for experienced and strong scramblers, and then only if the weather is good. The route described here is a much gentler descent along the Yarisawa and Azusa-gawa river valleys, and just as enjoyable in its own right.

If you have a head for heights it is worth making the 100m climb from **Yari-ga-take sansō** 槍ケ岳山荘 to the summit of **Mt Yari-ga-take** 槍ケ岳 (3180m). From the hut, head north over the flat saddle and bear right to start scrambling; the route is clearly marked with paint marks on the rock and there are fixed metal chains and ladders on the steeper parts. The path splits into ascending and descending one-way sections in places to alleviate congestion, and these are also clearly marked. If you are lucky and there are few people then the scramble up should take less than 20min, and poses no real problems although the final ladder below the summit is long and possibly scary for those with a fear of heights. Enjoy the magnificent views from the narrow and exposed peak before using the 'descent' ladder and returning to the hut. ◀

Early mornings can be busy with bottlenecks forming, as many people go up to see sunrise from the summit. At other times of day the peak is generally much quieter.

To start the long walk to Kamikōchi, descend the paved stone path leading from the terrace outside the hut. Go down a stretch of zigzags to reach a trail junction in 20min. For Sessho hut 殺生ヒュッテ and campground go left, otherwise carry on descending right over rocks and scree. You will pass a large boulder with a **cave**-like opening underneath it; this was used as shelter by the chanting priest Banryū during his many ascents of Mt Yari. A small metal plaque provides some information in English.

Soon pass a wooden signpost and carry on downhill, following the white paint marks. Meander down on stony ground, passing a few thickets of creeping pine and trickling water sources, and reach another signpost in less than 1hr. From this point, right leads up to Tenguhara 天狗原 in 40min. ▸ However, to continue on the main route, head downwards for 'Yoko-o and Kamikōchi'. The gradient eases; follow the stony path down the left side of a rocky and usually dry riverbed.

After about 35min you will reach another wooden signpost, from where it is straight on down a twisting path for another 20min to the **Yarisawa** campground 槍沢キャンプ地. There are toilets and water here, and there once also used to be a mountain hut but it was swept away in an avalanche. Continue down the Yarisawa valley, passing through mixed forest to reach **Yarisawa Lodge** 槍沢ロッヂ in a further 30min.

From the hut it is a steady descent through beautiful woodland, closely skirting alongside the river. After the path flattens, cross a couple of bridges and smaller footbridges to arrive in 1hr 20min at **Yoko-o sansō** 横尾山荘, a nice hut (with a bath for staying guests) and riverside campground. (For those with time and energy to spare, a popular trail heads right across the large suspension bridge for the walk

Tenguhara is a wonderfully secluded spot where beautiful reflections of Mt Yari can be seen in Tengu-ike pond.

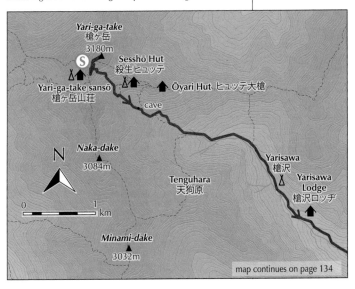

map continues on page 134

133

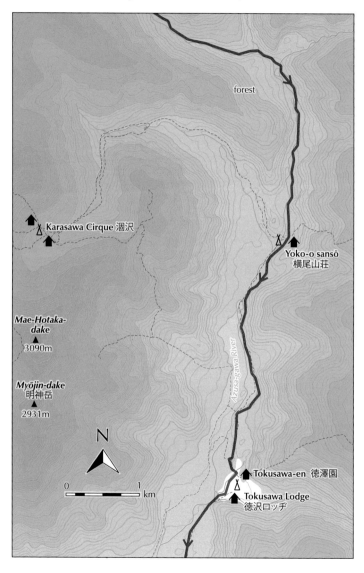

forest

Karasawa Cirque 涸沢

Yoko-o sansō
横尾山荘

Mae-Hotaka-dake
▲
3090m

Myōjin-dake
明神岳
▲
2931m

Azusa-gawa River

N

0   1
km

Tokusawa-en 徳澤園

Tokusawa Lodge
徳沢ロッヂ

up to Karasawa Cirque 涸沢 and beyond to the Mt Hotaka ridgeline (see Trek 4).)

From Yoko-o, maps indicate that it is a 3hr walk to Kamikōchi, but the track is gentle and flat so the 10km can be walked quicker than that. ▶ Pass the huts and grassy camping field at **Tokusawa** 徳沢 (1hr from Yoko-o), then continue on to another hut at **Myōjin** 明神 (2hr from Yoko-o). The path right here leads to Myōjin-ike Pond 明神池 and an alternative route to Kamikōchi on the other side of the river.

Otherwise carry straight on through the forest, passing through **Konashidaira** campground 小梨平 to soon arrive at the famous Kappa-bashi bridge at **Kamikōchi** 上高地. There are hotels, two hot spring baths (at Lemeiesta Hotel and the Onsen Hotel), restaurants, basic shops and hordes of tourists, and the bus terminal is a 5min walk downstream of the bridge.

The track between Yoko-o and Kamikōchi offers a good chance to see groups of wandering Japanese macaques.

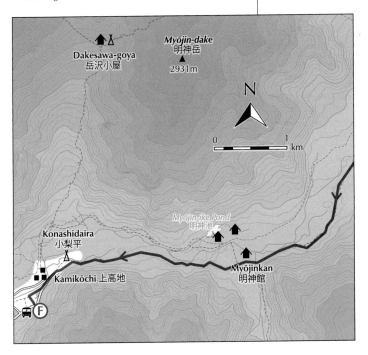

135

HOTAKA AREA – 穂高エリア

The Kappa-bashi Bridge, Kamikōchi's best-known landmark

The southern end of the North Alps is dominated by a huge mass of spectacularly jagged rock called Mt Hotaka. It's an imposing mountain of brutally serrated ridges and secluded glacial valleys, beautiful and intimidating in equal measure, with trails and approaches from almost every direction making for innumerable and varied route options. Steeped in Japanese mountaineering history, the Hotaka massif also happens to be surrounded by some of the Japan Alps' more distinctive and famous mountains, making the area something of a Mecca for serious outdoor enthusiasts. Aiding the area's popularity is its easy access from the two main cities in the region, Takayama and Matsumoto,

with shorter walks in the area easy to do as day-trips from either city.

BASES

Kamikōchi 上高地 is a small alpine resort village at 1500m elevation, tucked away in a beautiful highland valley on the southern side of Mt Hotaka, and is one of the main bases for exploring the region. The valley is so remote that it only used to be reached by an arduous trek over the Tokugō-tōge pass, but now there is a road tunnel providing easy access from either Takayama or Matsumoto. This road into Kamikōchi is closed to private vehicles, so all visitors must take a bus or taxi. The resort is completely buried in snow during the winter, and so only opens for business on the last Sunday in April until early November. Kamikōchi's most famous landmark is the Kappa-bashi, a small suspension bridge spanning the amazingly clear and blue Azusa River, from where there are magnificent views of towering Mt Hotaka and its jagged ridges, with the upper crags often holding snow until well into summer.

Taishō-ike and Myōjin-ike are two picturesque ponds at the western and eastern ends of Kamikōchi respectively; they are both gentle, well-signposted and short walks (1–2hr return) along flat forest paths from the Kappa-bashi and very popular with tourists and photographers.

Kamikōchi is accessed from Matsumoto (see below) by trains to Shin-shimashima Station on the small Kamikōchi Line, with connecting buses to Kamikochi (www.alpico.co.jp/en). Kamikōchi can also be reached by bus from Takayama (see below), with a change at Hirayū Onsen (www.nouhibus.co.jp/english).There are frequent buses from Shin-Shimashima Station (30min from Matsumoto) and Takayama, and the last returning bus of the day leaves Kamikōchi bus terminal at 6pm. The 'Alps Wide Free Passport' is a four-day bus and train pass covering most routes between Takayama, Matsumoto, Kamikōchi, Shin-Hotaka Onsen and the popular tourist spot of Shirakawa-go. It is available from bus stations and costs around 10,000 yen. The closest car parks to Kamikōchi are at Hirayu Onsen 平湯温泉 and Sawado 沢度, from where there are frequent shuttle buses to the resort.

Kamikōchi has many (rather expensive) hotels and lodges, most of which require reservations beforehand (especially on weekends and public holidays; details can be found at www.kamikochi.org – select 'Plan your visit'). Apart from a large visitor information centre near the bus terminal, a few small shops and a restaurant, there aren't all that many facilities in the village, and there is no ATM or convenience store. There is a luggage storage facility at the back of the bus terminal building. Two of the lodges (Lemeiesta Hotel and the Onsen Hotel) have hot spring baths open for non-staying customers, but they have quite limited opening hours, typically from mid morning until around 3pm.

The large Konashidaira campground 小梨平キャンプ場 is a pleasant spot in the forest with plenty of space for pitching tents. There are also cabins for those who prefer a little more comfort,

---

SHORT WALKS FROM KAMIKŌCHI

- **Taishō-ike:** 2hr return. Gentle stroll on flat paths, with choice of 'forest' or 'river' courses. Pass marshland to reach Taishō-ike, a pond famous for its beautiful reflections and with good views of Mt Yake-dake.

- **Myōjin-ike:** 2–3hr. Gentle walk through forest to the rustic Kamonji-goya hut and Myōjin-ike pond (small entry fee). Loop back along the other side of the river. Good chance of seeing Japanese macaques.

and it is possible to rent tents and basic equipment (not for use elsewhere). There is also a restaurant, a basic shop and bathhouse. See www.nihonalpskankou. com for information (English-language option).

Shin-Hotaka Onsen 新穂高温泉 is a small hot spring resort tucked away in a secluded valley to the west of the Hotaka mountain range. There are a cluster of hotels and guesthouses among the forests of white birch, and some of them have their own hot springs baths. Shinhotaka-no-yu 新穂高の湯 is a natural outdoor hot spring next to the Kamata River which is almost large enough to swim in (entry requires a donation, mixed bath so women can wear a costume, closed in the winter). Nearby there is a campground, but this hamlet has little in the way of shops or amenities so come prepared.

The main attraction in the area is the Shin-Hotaka Ropeway (www. shinhotaka-ropeway.jp; English-language option) with its double-decker gondola cars which carry people up to an elevation of 2156m on Mt Hotaka's western ridge and operate all year round (see Walk 5).

There are direct buses to Shin-Hotaka Onsen from Takayama (see below) and a small number from Matsumoto (see below) and Toyama in the summer. See www.nouhibus.co.jp/ english and www.alpico.co.jp/en, or ask at the bus stations in Takayama and Matsumoto for more information.

Takayama 高山 is a small, attractive city in Gifu Prefecture on the western side of the North Alps, situated about 35km from Kamikōchi. It is also sometimes known as Hida-Takayama, and is a good base for exploring the wider Hida region. The city retains a traditional and rural feel, with its quaint old quarter and famous festivals in spring and autumn, and there is plenty of accommodation on offer.

From the main bus terminal outside the station there are regular buses to Shin-Hotaka Onsen and Kamikōchi (change at Hirayu Onsen), and despite the distance it is perfectly viable to do some of the walks around Kamikōchi as a day-trip from Takayama.

JR Takayama Station is on the Takayama Line with trains running from Nagoya in the south and Toyama in the north. There are also occasional direct trains from Osaka and Kyoto. Highway buses also run from Tokyo, Osaka and Nagoya.

Matsumoto 松本 lies on the flat plains to the east of the North Alps in Nagano Prefecture. An historic old city, it is best known for its beautiful castle, which is one of the few remaining castle keeps in Japan almost in an original state. Notable local delicacies include *soba* noodles, *basashi* (horse *sashimi*) and juicy Azusagawa apples. The city has a fairly cosmopolitan feel despite its rural location, and there are lots of hotels, *ryokan* (traditional inns) and hostels for travellers. Like Takayama, with an early start it is possible to stay in Matsumoto and do some of the walks around Kamikōchi as a day-trip.

From Matsumoto, the main way into the Alps is via Shin-Shimashima Station which is just 30min away on the Kamikōchi Line. From there, buses regularly depart for Kamikōchi. There are also a small number of direct daily buses from Matsumoto to Shin-Hotaka

One of the most spectacular campsites in Japan (Trek 4, Stage 2)

Onsen in the summer; this route requires a change at Hirayu Onsen at other times.

Matsumoto is easy to reach from Tokyo, with JR Azusa and Super Azusa trains taking under 3hr from Shinjuku Station, and there are also trains from Nagoya and Nagano. Highway buses run from Tokyo, Osaka and Nagoya. See Appendix E for transport provider contact details.

MAPS

The walks and treks in this section are covered at 1:50,000 by the Yama-to-Kogen (No. 38) Yarigatake and Hotaka-dake 槍ヶ岳・穂高岳 sheet, which also includes most of the main routes at 1:25,000. The Yamakei – Yari/Hotaka renpō 槍・穂高連峰 sheet covers all the routes in this chapter, except Trek 7, at 1:25,000.

WALK 4
Mt Yake-dake 焼岳

Start/finish	Kappa-bashi Bridge 河童橋, Kamikōchi 上高地
Distance	10.5km (6½ miles)
Total ascent/descent	920m (3020ft)
Grade	2 **
Time	6–7hr
Terrain	Rugged forest path, with occasional ladders (one of which in particular may be intimidating to those with a fear of heights). Steep and stony slopes with a short scramble near the summit.
Access	See Hotaka chapter introduction
Accommodation	Hotels and camping at Kamikōchi; hut just below summit area
Facilities	Basic shops, restaurants and hot spring baths at Kamikōchi; drinks and snacks available at Yake-dake-goya hut
When to go	Trails should be mostly snow-free from June until late October. The large 8m ladder halfway along the route is removed at the end of October for winter storage, making this route impassable.

Clearly visible from the bus into Kamikōchi, Mt Yake-dake (2455m) is an instantly recognisable peak, its rocky and yellow sulphur-stained summit dominating the valley. One of the best day-hikes in the region, a walk to the top of Yake-dake can be done as a day-trip from Takayama or Matsumoto, and it offers more of a challenge than the other walks around Kamikōchi, with a satisfying ascent, multiple fixed ladders to climb, and a straightforward rocky scramble to the summit.

Yake-dake translates as 'burning peak', an apt name for the most active volcano in the entire North Alps, having erupted numerous times in the last century, most recently in 1995. Accordingly, the mountain is well monitored and it is important not to stray from the designated paths, as poisonous gas emissions are a known hazard. It does make for an interesting hike however, as the peak is peppered with fumaroles and the gassy-egg smell of sulphur can be quite strong in places. The summit itself is constantly steaming and has a crater lake, although a full loop of the crater is currently prohibited due to the badly eroded rock, meaning the true summit on the southern side is off-limits. But the designated summit is only 7m lower and offers fantastic panoramic views.

There are a number of approaches to the summit, but the one described here is the most direct route from Kamikōchi.

To save a bit of time when arriving by bus, you can get off at 'Taishō-ike' bus stop and then follow the path towards Kamikōchi, turning left at the access bridge for a more direct approach to the trailhead.

From the **Kappa-bashi bridge** 河童橋, follow either of the flat riverside paths heading downstream. The left-side (bus terminal side) path has marginally better views; the right-side path passes the famous Walter Weston relief. Both paths meet up after 20min at a bridge and tarmac access road. Turn right to reach a large information map. Ignore the blocked-off tarmac road heading north and instead follow the sign for 'Mt Yake-dake trailhead (800m)', heading along the gravel road and soon reaching the trailhead on the right.

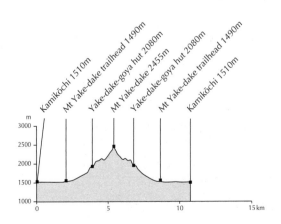

141

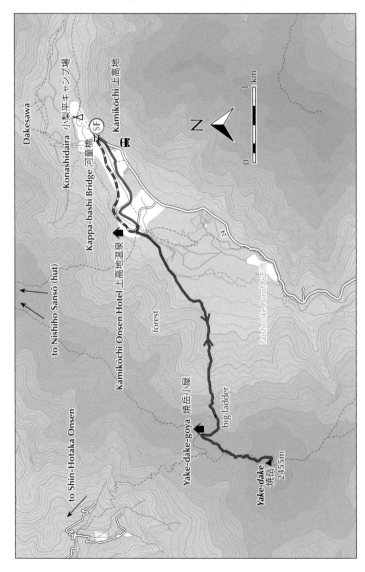

The path is narrow and muddy at first through thick forest-floor growth, then ascends over rocks and tree roots as the gradient gradually steepens. Note a dam through the trees to the left, then cross a small stream on a wooden bridge. The route now twists and turns up the mountainside, snaking through pine, birch and bamboo grass, with log steps in places and an occasional ladder on steeper sections. Pass to the right of some large boulders, looking out for a huge scree-filled ravine cutting spectacularly down the mountainside to the left, above which Yake-dake's bald peak can clearly be seen.

Continue to a clearing in the trees roughly 1hr in and arrive at some small cliffs, crossing a narrow chasm in the rocks on a sturdy metal footbridge. Head upwards using a succession of fixed metal ladders and enjoy the views of Mt Kasumisawa-dake 霞沢岳 across the valley. The trees begin to thin out and the path crosses an open hillside of *sasa* grass, with good views of Yake's rocky summit.

At the foot of some steep cliffs, climb an 8m-high fixed aluminium **ladder** (actually two regular ladders tied together). ▶ At the top of the ladder, scramble up a short,

This ladder is much longer and steeper than others on the route and somewhat nerve-wracking for those with a fear of heights.

The big ladder on Mt Yake-dake

143

steep rock section using a chain on the right, and head over the rocky lip as the nearby upper slopes of Mt Yake come into view. Follow the narrow path for 20min, zigzagging up through *sasa* grass, then drop into a shaded, pine-filled col to reach the ramshackle-looking but welcoming **Yake-dake-goya** 焼岳小屋. There are a couple of benches outside the hut and toilets here too.

Walk past the hut and turn left at the junction to climb up over a small grassy hill. On clear days there are fantastic views of the nearby mountains. ◄ Wander down the other side of the hill, and at the bottom pass some big rocks on the left and ignore the trail coming up from the right. Mt Yake's rocky summit looms overhead and is only about 1km away, but it's all uphill from here.

The small, gently steaming fumaroles along the path are a clear indication of the area's volcanic nature.

Ascend the lightly vegetated slope, passing a precarious rock-filled landslide gully on the left. The mountainside becomes much steeper and rockier, but the path is clearly marked with white circles and arrows painted on rocks. Proceed to a small saddle where yellow- and white-stained fumaroles steam incessantly and fill the air with a distinctive sulphurous smell. Continue upwards on loose rocks as

Mt Yake's crater lake

144

the path zigzags and steepens before veering left under the
summit cliffs, then scramble over boulders and follow yellow paint marks to the lip of the ridge, turning right for the
summit.

*Mt Yake-dake as seen
from the shores of
the Azusa River*

A path heading down to the left is another popular trail
leading to Naka-no-yu onsen 中の湯温泉 in 2hr. Instead,
carry on and scramble up right of some heavily stained yellow fumaroles to reach the summit of **Mt Yake-dake** 焼岳
(2455m) in a few minutes. The panoramic vistas are magnificent, with views into the crater which is home to a small blue
lake and some very active fumaroles billowing thick steam
from directly below. Return to **Kamikōchi** the same way in
about 2hr 30min.

WALK 5
Mt Nishiho-Doppyō 西穂独標

Start/finish	Shin-Hotaka Ropeway (top station) 新穂高ロープウェイ
Distance	7.5km (4¾ miles)
Total ascent/descent	545m (1790ft)
Grade	1 *
Time	4hr 30min
Terrain	Rugged forest path at first, then a stony and steady climb along the ridge, with a short scramble near summit
Access	Hourly buses all year round from Takayama (1hr 30min) and Hirayu Onsen (30min, for buses from Matsumoto or Shinjuku) to Shin-Hotaka Ropeway, which is the final stop. See www.nouhibus.co.jp/english (select 'Route Bus') for schedules. Lots of parking available around Shin-Hotaka Ropeway.
Accommodation	Comfortable but sometimes crowded lodgings at Nishiho sansō; small campsite next to hut. Hotels and ryokan (traditional inns) in Shin-Hotaka Onsen.
Facilities	Restaurants and shops at ropeway stations, and hot spring baths nearby. Food, refreshments and toilets at hut.
When to go	Ropeway and hut open all year, but be prepared for winter conditions from November until early June

A few different trails converge at the Nishiho hut, an hour's walk from the top ropeway station, including a challenging traverse all the way along the jagged and fractured ridge to Mt Oku-Hotaka, Japan's third highest peak – the most difficult and dangerous 'standard' route in the whole of the Japan Alps. The walk described here only goes as far as Nishiho-Doppyō (2701m), a small, rocky, flat-topped peak at the western end of the ridge which forms a natural cutting-off point where the terrain changes from mostly rolling ridgeline to increasingly steep and precipitous. It's an easy walk for most hikers, with only a tiny bit of scrambling required near the top, but it has a real alpine feel and the views are jaw-dropping.

To reach the start of the walk, ride the Shin-Hotaka ropeway (www.shinhotaka-ropeway.jp – English-language option) up to the top station. There are actually two ropeways; the first one climbs 200m to a small plateau called Nabedaira Kōgen where there is a free outdoor foot spa, an onsen and parking for cars. From there it is a short walk to the second ropeway, which ferries passengers up in large double-decker gondola cars – the first of its kind in Japan. A discount ticket including return bus fare, return ropeway ticket and free hot spring entry at Hirayu Onsen (all valid for three days) is available from Takayama bus station.

Leave the **Shin-Hotaka Ropeway** 新穂高ロープウェイ top station from the exit at the back of the restaurant. Go down steps and walk along the flat path, which splits in places and meanders through woodland, following signs for 登山道

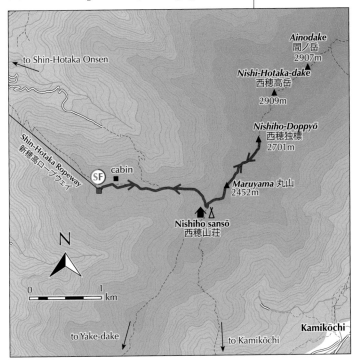

Nishiho sansō sits just on the tree line

(*tozandō*, meaning 'mountain trail'). Turn right at a wooden sign and small shrine, and after a few minutes arrive at a small **cabin** which houses a tozan (climbing) post box and marks the start of the trail proper.

Follow the narrow path to the right of the cabin, cutting through bamboo grass and pine trees. There is a little up-and-down and a few wooden boardwalks crossing muddy

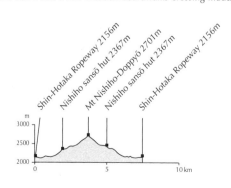

spots, but the path is always easy to follow, with occasional glimpses through the trees of the towering and jagged ridge-line up to the left.

After about 30min the path gets rougher and starts climbing more steadily. Cross a small bridge and ascend over rocks and up a few switchbacks. The path is uneven and moderately steep with steps in places, but it is not a particularly long climb. After passing a small shack you will arrive at **Nishiho sansō** 西穂山荘, a cosy hut on the edge of the tree line with room for tents out front, roughly 1hr from the ropeway. If staying the night and carrying big packs, you can leave them on the wooden shelves just outside the hut if you intend to come back this way. There are also toilets outside for non-staying walkers (requiring a small donation).

Take the trail marked 'Mt Nishihotaka-dake 2.4km' on a signpost adjacent to the hut, and clamber up a short distance over awkward large rocks to the top of a hill covered in waist-high creeping pine. ▶ A little further on is the minor summit of **Maruyama** 丸山 (2452m), marked by a wooden post. Carry on up a big rounded hill, with the flat, rocky top of Mt Nishiho-Doppyō visible just beyond it and reachable in about 1hr.

There are stone cairns and fantastic views of Mt Kasa-ga-dake to the left and the smouldering volcano Mt Yake-dake behind.

Drop to a small saddle and the begin the long, steady climb uphill. As you follow the stony path upwards the vegetation becomes thinner and the views ever more expansive. Near the top, navigate a few zigzags and roughly fashioned steps. The distinctive Nishiho-Doppyō homes into close view, and the aptly named Pyramid Peak looms large beyond that. Continue up to near the crest of the ridge, noting the Azusa river and the popular resort of Kamikōchi way down in the valley to the right.

Edge up the rocky path and skirt along the left side of the ridge, with a fairly steep drop to the left, and then follow paint marks on rocks as you scramble up and then down to a narrow saddle. It is now a fairly easy 5min scramble to the top of **Mt Nishiho-Doppyō** 西穂独標 (2701m), with plenty of paint marks and a chain near the top for assistance. ▶

From the summit there are great views of the rest of the Nishi-Hotaka ridgeline, including the Pyramid Peak, Mt Nishi-Hotaka, Mt Oku-Hotaka (Japan's third highest summit) and Mt Mae-Hotaka over to the right.

The peak's full name is **Nishihotaka-dake-Doppyō**, but is usually abbreviated to Nishiho-Doppyō, or even just Doppyō. The correct reading of the peak's *kanji* characters is actually 'Dokuhyō', but as an example of the vagaries of the Japanese language

Spectacular views southwest to the bald peak of Mt Yake-dake, and in the distance Mt Norikura

'Doppyō' is how most refer to it, presumably because this pronunciation rolls off the tongue a little easier.

A full traverse of the ridge over to Mt Oku-Hotaka takes another 5–8hr and is only for fit and experienced scramblers, as it is very rocky and exposed, including multiple steep climbs and menacing knife-edge sections (helmet advised, rope usually unnecessary). Instead, retrace your steps to **Nishiho sansō** hut in about 1hr. From the campground at the hut there are a number of trail options, including a path down to Kamikōchi in about 2hr 30min, or another quiet trail down the ridge towards Mt Yake-dake, also taking 2hr 30min. To return to the ropeway however, retrace your steps through the forest for 1hr.

TREK 4
Mt Oku-Hotaka-dake and Karasawa Cirque
奥穂高岳~涸沢カール

Start/finish	Kamikōchi 上高地
Distance	25km (15½ miles)
Total ascent/descent	1685m (5530ft)
Grade	3 **
Time	2 or 3 days
Terrain	A long, steep and rugged climb, with a steep descent into a spectacular cirque. Fixed ladders and chains at several points. Return via a steady walk down a river valley with an easy flat finish.
Access	See Hotaka chapter introduction
Accommodation	Hotels, huts and camping at Kamikōchi; huts and camping at intervals along the route
Facilities	Basic shops, restaurants and hot spring baths at Kamikōchi; drinks, refreshments and meals available at huts
When to go	Should not be attempted until July, and there is a chance of lingering snow around Dakesawa until the end of the month. Huts close and winter conditions can be expected at higher elevations by around late October.

A tough but incredibly rewarding short trek up and over the third highest mountain in Japan, Mt Oku-Hotaka-dake (3190m). With just under 1700m of altitude to gain in a day (and then lose again the following day), the climb can be a shock to the system if you're not fit, and trekkers must be comfortable climbing fixed ladders and chains which are liberally dotted along the route. If the weather is good then the views are wonderful and ever-changing, encompassing some of the most rugged mountain landscapes in the country.

The highlight of Stage 2 is the descent into the Karasawa Cirque (see dedicated text), a spectacular amphitheatre of rock and ice, where snow lingers virtually all year round. It is also famous for the 'tent city' that appears at busy times of the year, but even this doesn't detract from the majesty of the place.

151

Looking north from near the summit of Mt Oku-Hotaka-dake towards Mt Yari-ga-take (Stage 1)

This trek can be done in two days with an early start from Kamikōchi, but three days (perhaps staying at Yoko-o or Tokusawa on the return) will allow more time to admire

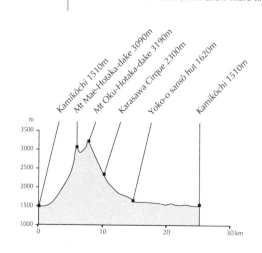

the surroundings. Aim to stay at Kamikōchi (or even further up the trail at Dakesawa) the night before to get a nice early start. Also check the last departure times for buses before heading out.

The route described here is also popular in reverse, but allow 5–6hr to reach Karasawa Cirque from Kamikōchi and then 2hr 30min to get up to Hotaka-dake sansō. The following day it will take over 6hr to go over the summit and drop back down to Kamikōchi via Dakesawa, on what is arguably one of the longest and most knee-knocking descents in the Japan Alps.

The descent into Karasawa (Stage 2) is one of the highlights of the trek, but Karasawa also makes a worthwhile destination in its own right if you have two days to spare and no desire to summit a large mountain. Most people do it as a there-and-back trek from Kamikōchi, walking up the Azusa river valley to Yoko-o (2–3hr), and then turning left for the steady climb to Karasawa (2hr). Stay the night in one of the huts or camp, and then retrace your steps back to Kamikōchi the following day (5–6hr). See Stage 2 for details. Even if the trail between Kamikōchi and Yoko-o is clear, the path onwards to Karasawa can still be covered in snow until mid July, so light crampons are advisable.

STAGE 1
Kamikōchi to Hotaka-dake sansō 上高地~穂高岳山荘

Start	Kamikōchi 上高地
Finish	Hotaka-dake sansō hut 穂高岳山荘
Distance	8km (5 miles)
Total ascent	1685m (5530ft)
Total descent	210m (690ft)
Time	8–9hr
Terrain	A steady walk through forest followed by a very steep ascent on a rugged path, with some short scrambles and fixed ladders. A traverse along a rocky ridgeline – exposed in places – and then a short, sharp descent from the summit.
Accommodation	Hotels near start; huts and camping at Kamikōchi, Dakesawa and Hotaka-dake sansō
Warning	If the weather is bad, consider changing plans as most of the route is potentially hazardous when wet

This is a long and steep climb, with almost 1700m of altitude to gain in a day, so it is imperative to get an early start. The path is well marked but very rugged and somewhat exposed in places, with plenty of enjoyable scrambling and a few vertigo-inducing ladders thrown in for good measure. If the weather is good the views are sensational though, and despite its precarious position, Hotaka-dake sansō is a very comfortable hut in which to recuperate.

For those with extra energy and a penchant for rocky scrambles there's the option of a visit to the 3090m summit of Mae-Hotaka-dake along the way.

It's hard to believe that you will (hopefully!) be standing at the top of that towering ridgeline in a few hours' time.

From the bus terminal at **Kamikōchi** 上高地, walk to Kappa-bashi Bridge, cross it, and take the gravel path leading right of the rustic-looking Hotel Shirakabasō. The path runs alongside the river and offers views of the mountains just as magnificent as those from the bridge, but with fewer crowds. ◄

Bear right when you meet a gravel track after 200m and continue on the path through thick *sasa* grass and forest, then cross a couple of small bridges and walk along narrow wooden boardwalks in an area of grassy marshland. Pass a

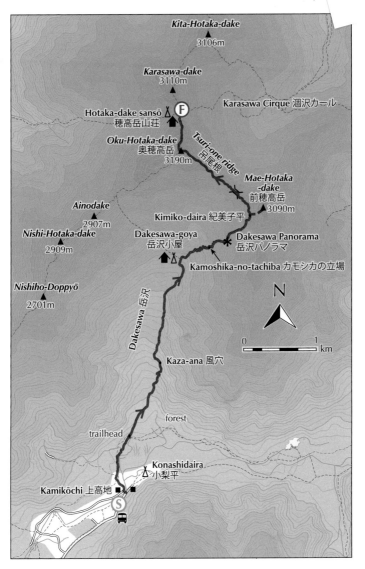

Kita-Hotaka-dake
3106m

Karasawa-dake
3110m

Karasawa Cirque 涸沢カール

Hotaka-dake sansō
穂高岳山荘

F

Oku-Hotaka-dake
奥穂高岳
3190m

Tsuri-one ridge
吊尾根

*Mae-Hotaka
-dake*
前穂高岳
3090m

Ainodake
2907m

Kimiko-daira 紀美子平

Nishi-Hotaka-dake
2909m

Dakesawa-goya
岳沢小屋

Dakesawa Panorama
岳沢パノラマ

Kamoshika-no-tachiba カモシカの立場

Nishiho-Doppyō
2701m

Dakesawa 岳沢

N

0   1
km

Kaza-ana 風穴

forest

trailhead

Konashidaira
小梨平

Kamikōchi 上高地

S

The classic view of Mt Hotaka and the Azusa-gawa river

wooden viewing platform to the right, and then at the end of the boardwalks turn left at a signpost for 'Dakesawa' 岳沢. Around 20min from the start you'll reach the trailhead, which is marked by a few large wooden signboards.

Follow the path as it first climbs gently through the woods, the ground muddy and knotted with tree roots in places. After about 35min pass an interesting feature called the **Kaza-ana** 風穴 – a curious spot where cool air blows out from holes in the ground. Carry on steadily uphill for 1hr 30min, as the path climbs up the forested edge of the **Dakesawa valley**. Just before the hut, emerge onto and cross the wide rocky gully and follow the markings to reach **Dakesawa-goya** 岳沢小屋.

> This **hut** sits at about 2200m and was completely destroyed by an avalanche in 2006, but was rebuilt and now has a nice veranda which makes for a comfortable place to rest. If you're tired or arrive after midday then consider staying here, as it is over 5hr and almost 1000m of altitude gain until the next refuge. Just beyond the hut there are spaces for pitching tents on rocky ground.

Continue to the right of the hut and through the camping area. There are impressive views all the way up the rock gully, ending in high and distant cliffs and a semi-permanent snow patch. ▶ Follow the markings across the gully as the path re-enters the undergrowth at the side of the valley. From here on things start to get much steeper.

Climb through a steep meadow of grasses and wildflowers, then zigzag up the mountainside. Scramble up a narrow rocky section and carry on up the rugged path, eventually reaching and ascending a steep 8m-long fixed ladder before arriving at a tan-coloured rocky prominence known as **Kamoshika-no-tachiba** カモシカの立場 at about 2500m.

Clamber on upwards, taking in two more fixed metal ladders in quick succession. Further on there is a straightforward rocky section, easily scrambled with the aid of a fixed chain. Continue up the rugged and steep path to emerge above the tree line at a splendid rocky viewpoint called **Dakesawa Panorama** 岳沢パノラマ. If the weather is good the views back down the valley are magnificent, while the granite turrets of the surrounding ridges still loom above but now feel much closer.

Carry on up the rocky shoulder, following the paint marks and scuff marks. The path is very rugged and rises steeply among swathes of green creeping pine. In about 25min reach a stony spot called Raichō-hiroba 雷鳥広場 (indicated by Japanese characters painted on the rocks), named after the ptarmigan – a bird that can frequently be seen on these slopes.

Continue scrambling up the rugged, steep and rocky mountainside, the route always clearly marked by white spots of paint. Skirt up and around a small peak, drop down a short ladder and then ascend rock slabs with the help of metal chains. You will soon arrive at **Kimiko-daira** 紀美子平, a junction marked by a wooden signpost.

Optional ascent of Mt Mae-Hotaka-dake

A paint-marked path leads almost directly upwards for an optional and steep 30min rock scramble to the summit of **Mt Mae-Hotaka-dake** 前穂高岳. If you have the time and energy then it is well worth doing, as the views down into the Karasawa Cirque from the 3090m summit are quite special. You can leave your rucksack at the junction to make the climb a little easier. Take care on the way down; the descent can be somewhat vertigo-inducing.

There can be lingering patches of snow in the gully as far down as the hut in early July.

To continue on the main route, bear left (or right if you descended from Mae-Hotaka) in the direction of Mt Oku-Hotaka-dake. Traverse the steep and exposed slopes on a narrow rocky path, and after 30min arrive on the ridgeline at **Saitei Col** 最低コル (written in Japanese on the rocks and on a signpost), the lowest point along the **Tsuri-one ridge** 吊尾根 which runs between Mae-Hotaka and Oku-Hotaka.

From here follow the path for over 1hr as it creeps along the ridge, mostly well below the crest, with some big drops and exposure to the left-hand side. Traverse carefully and climb steadily, using fixed chains in places. Climb a substantial steep section of rusty-coloured slabby rocks to a signpost at Nanryō-no-kashira 南稜ノ頭. A long metal chain is bolted into place, but take extra special care if it is wet as it is an exposed scramble and can get slippery. The gradient eases a bit and it is then only 15min to the summit of **Mt Oku-Hotaka-dake** 奥穂高岳, the third highest mountain in Japan at 3190m. ◄

The summit is marked by a small shrine on top of a plinth of rocks. A faint path leads southwest along the spectacular Nishi-Hotaka ridge, but it is a long and exposed route only for very experienced scramblers. After admiring the panoramic views, head north following the sign for

Oku-Hotaka (sometimes abbreviated again to 'Oku-Ho') is the highest peak in the North Japan Alps.

The summit of Oku-Hotaka, Japan's third highest peak

Hotaka-dake sansō commands a startling position

Hotaka-dake sansō 穂高岳山荘. It is only about 30min to the hut from here.

Trace the scuff-marked path over jumbles of rocks and then carefully descend steep, stony ground via a short series of zigzags. Almost directly above the hut, climb down two metal ladders and then scramble down to the safety of **Hotaka-dake sansō** 穂高岳山荘, a hut which almost defies belief, perched as it is on a narrow and exposed col. ▶

The terrace outside **Hotaka-dake sansō** offers tremendous views down into Karasawa Cirque, and just north of the hut narrow terraces chiselled into the mountainside serve as exposed camping spots. There is also a helicopter landing pad here.

On particularly busy days there can be bottlenecks on the narrow trail and ladders above the hut, so be prepared to wait in line.

STAGE 2
Hotaka-dake sansō to Kamikōchi 穂高岳山荘~上高地

Start	Hotaka-dake sansō hut 穂高岳山荘
Finish	Kamikōchi 上高地
Distance	17km (10½ miles)
Total ascent	Negligible
Total descent	1475m (4840ft)
Time	6–7hr
Terrain	A steep, stony drop to Karasawa (with occasional chains and ladders), followed by a rugged but steady descent through forest, ending with a long walk along a flat and easy valley track. The Panorama Course (optional) is very rugged and awkward in places, only for those with scrambling experience.
Accommodation	Huts and camping in Karasawa Cirque, along the Azusa river and at Kamikōchi
Note	The cirque holds snow until late in the year, so be prepared for snow covering parts of the trail, sometimes to the end of July. Light crampons may be useful.

In contrast to the relentlessly steep climb of the previous day, this stage is almost entirely downhill (although an optional ascent of Mt Karasawa-dake provides some ascent, should it be longed for), descending first into the magnificent Karasawa Cirque (see below), and then winding down to the Azusa river valley before the last flat stretch back to Kamikōchi. An alternative route between Karasawa and Tokusawa provides a more challenging return, but it is only recommended for experienced hikers.

Optional ascent of Mt Karasawa-dake
The steps up past the tent spots at Hotaka-dake sansō lead to the 3110m summit of **Mt Karasawa-dake** 涸沢岳, an optional 20min climb of 130m on steep, stony ground for more fine views. A path continues north from the summit all the way to Kita-Hotaka-dake along a savagely jagged and exposed ridge, and is no place for the inexperienced (see 'Daikiretto and Hotaka ridgeline traverse', Trek 5). Retrace your steps to the hut.

Gazing down into Karasawa Cirque from the north

The descent into Karasawa Cirque takes around 1hr 30min and starts at **Hotaka-dake sansō hut** 穂高岳山荘, by going down the stone steps directly beneath the tent spots. ▶ Follow the clear path as it twists and turns downwards over steep ground and scree, with white paint marks dotted for guidance in places. This route is known as the 'Seitengrat' ザイテングラート and is very rugged, with a few simple rock scrambles and the odd ladder or chain to navigate. Take care as the loose stones are easy to slip on and dislodge, and accidents on this stretch of path are common in the high season. Note also that snow can linger in the cirque until late in the year.

After 50min reach a jutting rocky spur called 'Seitengrattoritsuketen' ザイテングラート取付点 – a nice spot to rest with grand views of the cirque. Below this the path drifts left for a steady descent down the scree slope. About 20min later the path splits, with the left branch being the more direct path for Karasawa-goya hut 涸沢小屋 while the other one heads more directly to Karasawa Hut 涸沢ヒュッテ. Both ways lead to the bottom of the cirque, so take your pick.

Continue down either path for 20min to reach the base of the spectacular **Karasawa Cirque** 涸沢カール, where you

A steep path also descends west from the hut, but this leads down the other side of the mountain to Shin-Hotaka Onsen in around 5hr.

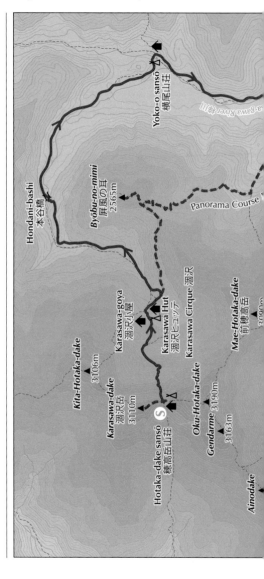

162

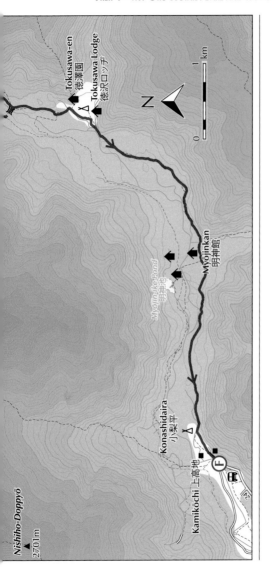

can find the two aforementioned huts and a sprawling, extremely popular campground, often likened to a 'tent city'.

To carry on to Kamikōchi, walk through the outdoor terrace and seating area at **Karasawa Hut** 涸沢ヒュッテ (the

KARASAWA CIRQUE 涸沢カール

The Karasawa Cirque is one of the most famous spots in the whole of the Japan Alps; a massive bowl-shaped amphitheatre carved out by long-gone glaciers at the head of a high valley. Entering the cirque for the first time is a genuine 'wow' moment, and there is no finer alpine setting in Japan for the two huts and extensive campground nestling in its lower reaches at 2300m.

Encircled on three sides by the steep walls and serrated spires of the Hotaka massif, Karasawa's shaded inner recesses hold snow almost all year round. In the summer, alpine wildflowers (*Trollius japonicus*) grow in abundance, while in the autumn the more vegetated slopes are a riot of vivid colour.

Karasawa is popular throughout the hiking season; when Kamikōchi officially opens at the end of April, well-equipped hikers traipse through the snow to camp in full winter conditions, while at busy times later in the year (particularly national holidays in the summer, and early to mid October when people come to view the autumn leaves) the famous Karasawa 'tent city' can accommodate over 1000 tents! While camping in close proximity to hundreds of other people may

The expansive campground in the bowl of the Karasawa Cirque

not be to everyone's liking, most campers are a like-minded and friendly bunch, and combined with the stunning surroundings it makes for one of those 'only in Japan' experiences.

If you don't have a tent but want to camp then it is possible to rent a tent and sleeping bags/mats from Karasawa Hut between mid July and early October. Supplies are limited and must be booked by telephone in advance; see www.karasawa-hyutte.com (Japanese link).

lower of the two huts) and go down the stone steps just past the main entrance. A path called the Panorama Course パノラマコース branches right, but it is a longer, wilder and more arduous high route back to the river valley.

Tokusawa via the Panorama Course パノラマコース
Also known as the Panorama Shindō パノラマ新道, this is an alternative high-altitude route (around 130m ascent/800m descent) between Karasawa and Tokusawa, and is far more challenging than the main trail down in the valley. It follows a narrow, rugged, up-and-down trail along the mountainside, with plenty of fixed chains and awkward sections and so is only for experienced scramblers. Partway along the route (about 1hr from Karasawa) an optional dead-end path branches left at a wooden signpost and leads up to a great viewpoint called **Byōbu-no-mimi** 屏風の耳 (2565m) in 30min. The Panorama Course should be avoided altogether if there is any remaining snow. Allow around 3hr 30min from Karasawa Hut to Tokusawa, and about 4hr 30min in the other direction.

For the valley route, follow the main path down the narrowing Karasawa valley, passing thickets of trees. ▶ Traverse across a loose and stony scree slope, then descend steadily on a rugged path through woods of birch and maple. Drift right as the valley curves east and drop down to the rocky riverbed to reach **Hondani-bashi** 本谷橋, a small wooden bridge which must be crossed. About 1hr after leaving the hut, this is a good place to rest.

The path carries on down the other side of the river and follows a much flatter course through beech forest and thick *sasa* bamboo grass. Stroll along for 50min to reach

Snow can remain here until late July.

Azusa-gawa River 梓川, and cross a large suspension bridge to reach Yoko-o 横尾, a major trail junction on the path between Kamikōchi and Mt Yari-ga-take. **Yoko-o sansō** 横尾 山荘 is a friendly hut with a bath (only for staying guests) and a grassy campsite next to the river.

Turn right on the main trail and follow the signs for Kamikōchi 上高地. Maps suggest that it is a 10km, 3hr walk, but the path is mostly flat so it can be done much quicker than that if you are a brisk walker. Continue down the wide gravel trail, closely following the Azusa river downstream. After 3km there is a **bridge** to the right which leads to the other end of the Panorama Course パノラマコース, but carry on straight for another 1km to reach **Tokusawa** 徳沢 – another major trail junction. Here there is a hut, benches, toilets and a huge grassy field for camping. ◄

Continue along the flat meandering track, which leaves the riverside to pass through woods full of ferns and pink wintergreen flowers. After skirting past a boggy patch of forest to the right, rise and fall gently before fording a shallow stream to soon arrive at **Myōjin** 明神, the last major junction before Kamikōchi. There is a hut and some toilets here, and the path heading right leads to Myōjin Pond and an alternative route to Kamikōchi on the other side of the river.

Otherwise carry on down the main trail, through more pristine forest and along some very gentle ups and downs to reach the wooded **Konashidaira** campground 小梨平 after 2.5km. The path winds through the campsite, past some toilets, and soon emerges back where you started at the Kappabashi Bridge in **Kamikōchi** 上高地. ◄

This field was used as pasture for grazing cattle in the past, and the early mountaineer Walter Weston documented run-ins with angry bovines in this valley.

The splendid view of Mt Hotaka will be seen in a new light, having climbed all the way up and over it.

TREK 5
Mt Yari-ga-take 槍ヶ岳

Start	Kamikōchi 上高地
Finish	Shin-Hotaka Onsen 新穂高温泉
Distance	34km (21 miles)
Total ascent	1675m (5500ft)
Total descent	2090m (6860ft)
Grade	2+ **
Time	2 or 3 days
Terrain	Gentle riverside track, followed by a steady and rugged climb up the valley. A short but steep rocky scramble to the summit, with some ladders and fixed chains. Stony descent, becoming flatter and forested.
Access	See Hotaka chapter introduction
Accommodation	Hotels, huts and camping at Kamikōchi, with huts and camping thereafter
Facilities	Basic shops, restaurants and hot spring baths at Kamikōchi; drinks, snacks and meals available at huts
When to go	Snow often remains in the Yarisawa valley until rainy season (June to mid July), so the best time to go is from July until the end of October

The iconic pointy spire of Mt Yari-ga-take (3180m) makes it one of the most instantly recognisable mountains in Japan, and also one of the most popular in the North Alps. Its remote location means that all approaches to the summit are long with considerable altitude gain, so most people choose to climb it over two days or more, staying at one of the huts near the top.

Yari (abbreviations are common in Japan) was first climbed by a hardy Buddhist monk called Banryū who, after many failed attempts, finally reached the summit in 1828. He went on to climb the mountain multiple times, and once spent 50 consecutive days chanting in a cave near the summit. The first foreigner to climb it was an English engineer called William Gowland in 1878 (he was also the first person to coin the name 'Japan Alps'), and this was followed in

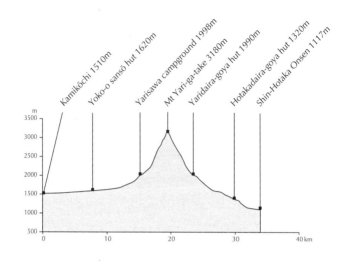

Kamikōchi 1510m
Yoko-o sansō hut 1620m
Yarisawa campground 1998m
Mt Yari-ga-take 3180m
Yaridaira-goya hut 1990m
Hotakadaira-goya hut 1320m
Shin-Hotaka Onsen 1117m

Yari-ga-take and the large summit hut

1891 with an ascent by another Englishman and the 'father of mountaineering in Japan', Walter Weston. Native climbers soon began to make their mark on the mountain, pioneering alternative routes and winter ascents, and these days Mt Yari is a highly sought-after goal for many Japanese hikers.

The route here is an up-and-over hike, starting at the resort hub of Kamikōchi and looping towards the summit from the southeast before descending west to Shin-Hotaka Onsen. The final 100m scramble to the summit is rocky and steep, with a number of fixed chains and ladders in place to make it easier and a few one-way sections to ease congestion at busy times. Stage 2 starts with a steep descent on scree to below the tree line, then follows a rugged forest path down the valley to Shin-Hotaka Onsen. Those looking for more excitement could try the Daikiretto and Hotaka ridge-line route, a thrilling and challenging trail for experienced scramblers only.

STAGE 1
Kamikōchi to Yari-ga-take 上高地~槍ヶ岳

Start	Kamikōchi 上高地
Finish	Yari-ga-take sansō hut 槍ヶ岳山荘
Distance	20km (12½ miles)
Total ascent	1575m (5170ft)
Total descent	Negligible
Time	8hr
Terrain	The first half is an easy walk along a flat forest track; the second half is continually more rugged, rocky and steep
Accommodation	Hotels, huts and camping at Kamikōchi, and then at regular intervals along the route, with hut and campground just below the summit
Note	From Yoko-o sansō hut onwards there can be lingering snow right up until July; crampons advised before then

A long but popular and relatively easy route from Kamikōchi all the way to the hut below the summit of Mt Yari. The first couple of hours are along a flat river valley, with the path gradually becoming steeper and rockier as it climbs towards the huge hut just below the summit. If you can't get an early start from Kamikōchi, then consider splitting this stage by staying at one of the huts or campsites along the way.

Arriving at the bus terminal in **Kamikōchi** 上高地 there is a large visitor centre on the left and an array of small shops, restaurants and the bus ticket counter to the right. Taps near the picnic benches can be used to fill up water bottles. Walk past the benches and follow the path through the trees, soon joining a wide paved road. In a few minutes you'll reach the famous Kappa-bashi Bridge 河童橋, with its classic views of Mt Hotaka. Don't cross the bridge, but instead continue following the road, passing toilets to the left, before meandering through the **Konashidaira** campground 小梨平 – a pleasant forest campsite that's a good place to stay for an early start the next morning.

Japanese macaques frequent this area; they are accustomed to humans but should not be fed.

Follow the gravel road into the forest, leaving most of the tourist crowds behind. ◄ The path is very easy going, rising and falling gently, arriving at a junction for Myōjin-ike Pond

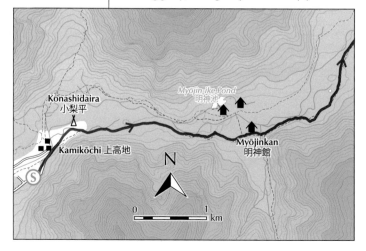

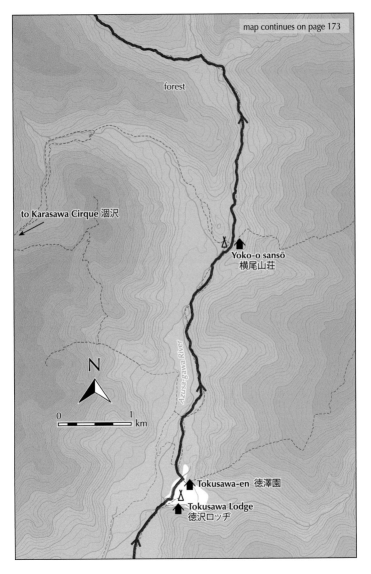

map continues on page 173

forest

to Karasawa Cirque 涸沢

Yoko-o sansō
横尾山荘

Azusa-gawa River

N

0   1
km

Tokusawa-en 徳澤園

Tokusawa Lodge
徳沢ロッヂ

The views open up in the Yarisawa valley

The map says it is 70min from Tokusawa-en to Yokō sansō, but it is doable in half that time.

明神池 after a couple of kilometres. There are huts and toilets here, but continue straight on following signs for Tokusawa 徳沢. Views of the wide river valley open up left, followed by more gentle ups and downs, and a small stream needs fording. Pass the murky **Furuike Pond** 古池 on the left, and then cut through a peaceful glade of ferns and dense foliage.

Skirt close to the river again for more sweeping views down the valley as the path bypasses some slopes prone to landslides. After a large information sign and map, branch left at a fork, passing some toilets on your left and a grassy field for camping on your right. At the far end of the field reach **Tokusawa-en** hut 徳澤園 and some benches, 2hr from Kamikōchi. Cross the bridge left of the hut and follow the main track, ignoring any turnoffs to the left. Continue north up the valley, with occasional views of the wide stony river-bed and one or two very gentle ups and downs. ◄

The **Yoko-o sansō** hut 横尾山荘 is at the meeting point of a few trails, and can be a good place to stay with a camp-ground and hot baths. It is also almost exactly halfway between Kamikōchi and Mt Yari, although the next part is much more strenuous and almost all uphill. Don't cross the bridge over the river, as that trail leads to the ever-popular Karasawa Cirque 涸沢 (see Trek 4). Instead take the trail heading north, signposted 11km 槍ヶ岳 (Yari-ga-take).

The real hike now begins, the narrow path starting off level but gradually rising as it climbs up the Yarisawa 槍沢 river valley. Cross a couple of small footbridges over gurgling streams, then two more substantial bridges in quick succession. After the second bridge the path hugs the river closely and begins to climb more steeply over rocks and tree roots. **Yarisawa Lodge** 槍沢ロッヂ is soon reached and may be a good place to stay as the next hut is a few hours away (pay the camping fee here if you intend to stay at Yarisawa campground).

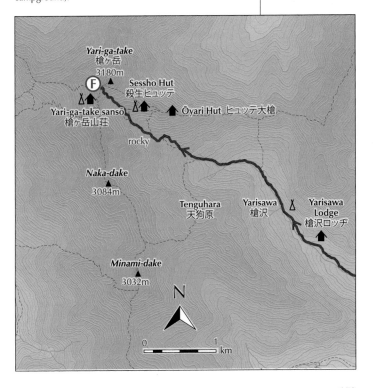

There used to be a
mountain hut here
but it was destroyed
by an avalanche.

The path left leads up
to Tenguhara 天狗原
in 40min – a scenic
and secretive spot
where you can see
beautiful reflections
of Mt Yari in Tengu-
ike pond 天狗池.

Climb steadily onwards, passing through an area of yel-
lowish rocks, and cross a footbridge near a huge dark boulder marked with the character 槍 (Yari) in white paint. The
trees begin to thin out and views of the spectacular valley
walls open up. About 30min from the lodge you'll reach
a flat stony area called Babadaira ババ平, home to the
Yarisawa campground 槍沢キャンプ地, which has water and
a toilet. ◄

Meander steadily up the stony path, staying close to the
mostly dry riverbed. At a junction and sign, bear west for
'Yari-ga-take', ignoring the path right (for Minamata-no-koshi
水俣乗越). The trail becomes steeper and rockier but is clear
and easy to follow. The trees thin out completely. At another
signpost continue on towards Yari-ga-take. ◄ The path
becomes steeper still, passing some trickling water sources
and traversing grey scree. Up ahead the pointy summit of
Mt Yari looms into close view for the first time, but it is still
a long slog away.

Climb the rocky scree slope (the cliffs up to the left may
be concealing a late-season snow patch) and follow white
paint marks to another sign. The right-hand option climbs to
Ōyari Hut ヒュッテ大槍 in about 30min, but continue left for
Yari-ga-take 槍ヶ岳 1.25km. You will pass a small cave-like
opening under a large boulder, with a plaque indicating that
this was used as shelter by Banryū, the chanting priest and
first ever climber of Mt Yari.

Boulder-hop over large rocks and scree to another
wooden signpost, this one for Sessho Hut 殺生ヒュッテ,
150m above and to the right. This hut has a campground
which offers better protection from the wind than the more
exposed one at the summit.

Push on from the signpost towards the pointy spire of Mt
Yari looming large and imperiously above, the path becoming even steeper. A last stretch of zigzags leads upwards
along a section that can be breath-sapping. About 4–5hr from
Yarisawa Lodge you will finally emerge in front of **Yari-ga-
take sansō** 槍ヶ岳山荘, a huge hut built on the narrow ridge
below the summit with spaces for pitching tents to the south.
If the weather is good, the stone benches out front command
splendid sweeping views of the valley just climbed.

STAGE 2

Yari-ga-take to Shin-Hotaka Onsen 槍ヶ岳~新穂高温泉

Start	Yari-ga-take sansō hut 槍ヶ岳山荘
Finish	Shin-Hotaka Ropeway 新穂高ロープウェイ
Distance	14km (8½ miles)
Total ascent	100m (330ft)
Total descent	2090m (6860ft)
Time	7hr
Terrain	A short exposed scramble with fixed chains and ladders (one of which in particular requires a head for heights), followed by a steep and rugged descent, ending on a gentle forest track
Access	See Hotaka chapter introduction
Accommodation	Hut and camping at Mt Yari-ga-take summit; huts and campground on the descent

A short and steep scramble to the summit, followed by a relatively straightforward but long descent down to the wooded valley floor on a rugged path, then onwards to the hot spring resort of Shin-Hotaka Onsen.

Yari-ga-take's summit can only accommodate about 20 people, so if you want to miss the worst of the crowds, avoid weekends and aim to climb it later in the day. This being 'The Land of the Rising Sun' there can be bottlenecks as people climb to the top for sunrise, but afternoons are usually quieter in comparison.

From **Yari-ga-take sansō hut** 槍ヶ岳山荘, head north along the flat saddle for the short but steep climb to the summit of Mt Yari-ga-take 槍ヶ岳 (3180m). ▶ The path is very clearly marked with paint marks on the rock and metal chains and ladders on the steeper parts. The route splits into ascending or descending one-way sections in places to alleviate congestion, and these are also clearly marked. If you're lucky and there are few people then the scramble up should take less than 20min and it poses no real problems, although the final ladder below the summit is long and may be a challenge for those with a fear of heights. Enjoy the magnificent views from the small, exposed **summit** before returning down the 'descent' ladder and back to the **hut**.

Yari means 'spear' in Japanese.

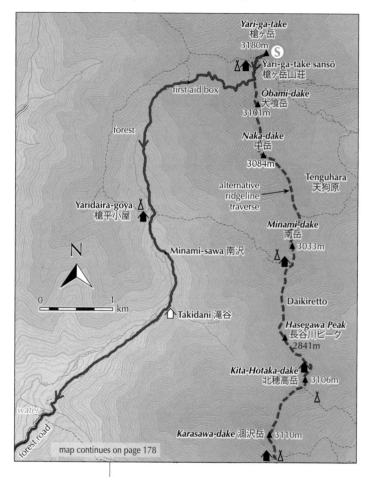

The infamous and remote **Kitakama Ridge** on Yari's north face poses many attractions for serious mountaineers. It gained notoriety, however, after a number of high-profile incidents, including the deaths of several well-known climbers in the early days of Japanese alpinism.

Scrambling up Yari's summit

Head south from the hut, past small spaces used for pitching tents, and descend the winding gravely path down to a small saddle. ▶ Follow the sign pointing right for 槍平 (Yaridaira, 4.3km) and immediately lose altitude down the long and steady rocky scree slope, enjoying splendid views of Mt Kasa-ga-take far across the valley. After zigzagging downwards for about 1hr you will reach a small trail junction where there is a first-aid box.

The hump-shaped peak of Ōbami-dake 大喰岳 rises directly ahead (see below), but there is no need to climb it here.

Continue down the valley and below the tree line, passing a few trickling water sources and clambering over boulders as the rugged path gradually descends. After a further 1hr 30min you will arrive at **Yaridaira-goya** 槍平小屋, a nice hut with plenty of room for tents and an emergency hut for use in the winter. A couple of other trails lead off east and west, but carry on following the river downstream.

After crossing some wooden boardwalks, descend ruggedly through forest. About 20min from Yaridaira-goya, cross a rocky gully called **Minami-sawa** 南沢 and follow the trail through forest, hopping over big rocks. In another 20min ford a small stream and reach a large rock gully called **Takidani** 滝谷. Follow the markings to work your way across, fording

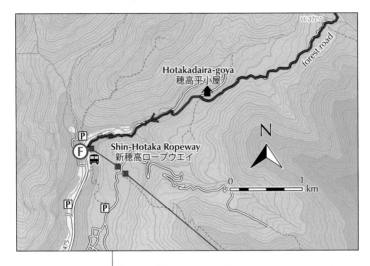

the river if log bridges have been washed away, and take special care after heavy rains. There is a small emergency shelter tucked away among the trees here.

Continue down the valley for about 1hr on a still rugged and slightly undulating forest path to reach another large gully, this one blocked with concrete dams. Cross to the other side of the gully to find a water source and the start of a gravel forest track, and follow the road down the valley for 50min to arrive at **Hotakadaira-goya** 穂高平小屋, a rustic hut next to some fenced alpine pastures. Just past the hut, take

The small and rustic Hotakadaira-goya

the shortcut (easily missed) before the forest track turns back on itself, and go down through the forest (or simply continue following the main forest track). In 35min arrive at the rope-way bus terminal at **Shin-Hotaka Onsen** 新穂高温泉.

DAIKIRETTO AND HOTAKA RIDGELINE TRAVERSE

One of the most exciting and challenging routes in the Japan Alps is the 6km ridge trail between Mt Yari-ga-take and Mt Oku-Hotaka. It includes a traverse of the notorious Daikiretto 大キレット or 'big cut', a huge gap in the ridgeline notable for its steep and exposed terrain, before climbing up to Kita-Hotaka and then clambering along the rocky ridgeline to Hotaka sansō, which is arguably even more challenging and exposed than the Daikiretto. At grade 3+ ***, the route is definitely not for the inexperienced and should not be considered by anyone who is the least bit nervous about heights and exposure; but it should be doable for those who enjoy committed, thrilling scrambling sometimes bordering on rock climbing. No specialist equipment is required as there are plenty of metal chains and ladders bolted along the steepest sections, but it should only be attempted in fine weather.

Allow 3 or 4 days for the full classic loop hike starting and ending at Kamikōchi (40km, 2885m ascent/descent). A good, sensible itinerary is to walk from Kamikōchi and stay at either Yoko-o or Yarisawa on day one, then climb up to Yari-ga-take and walk as far as Minami-dake on day two. You will then have plenty of time to traverse the Daikiretto and Hotaka ridgeline, staying at Hotaka-dake sansō (or even dropping down to the Karasawa Cirque) at the end of day three, before heading back to Kamikōchi via Mt Oku-Hotaka on day four.

The route starts at Kamikōchi and heads up to the summit of Mt Yari-ga-take (Trek 5, Stage 1). After climbing to the summit walk south from Yari-ga-take sansō hut, past the spaces for tents. Go down to the saddle, ignore the path right and head straight to climb to the stony summit of Mt Ōbami-dake 大喰岳 (3101m). In another 30min reach Mt Naka-dake 中岳 (3084m) and follow the stony and undulating ridge for 1hr to Mt Minami-dake 南岳 (3033m), then continue down to Minami-dake-goya 南岳小屋, a red-roofed hut with tent spots about 2hr 30min from Yari. This is a good place to stay for a nice early start the next day.

Just south beyond the hut lies the infamous Daikiretto 大キレット; allow around 3hr to reach Kita-hotaka-goya at the other end. The path drops steeply down splintered cliffs, with chains and ladders in places, but the way is always clearly marked. You will eventually reach lower and flatter terrain, with easy scrambling along the rocky and narrowing crest. Pass a small saddle (the lowest point on the ridge at 2748m), then scramble up to the small and very exposed summit of Hasegawa Peak 長谷川ピーク (2841m), marked with white paint as Hピーク. It is then an extremely exposed traverse along a perilously narrow knife-edge ridge, but the holds are good and there are chains and metal bolts in places. Descend a steep slab using a long chain, cross a wooden platform and drop to a flat saddle and good resting spot called A-sawa Col (A沢コル).Next scramble up the steep rock face following the paint marks, contending with chains, awkward ledges and sometimes loose rocks to eventually reach the safety of Kita-Hotaka-goya 北穂高小屋. This hut lies in a spectacularly rugged position, and around 15min beyond it is Mt Kita-Hotaka-dake 北穂高岳 (3106m), from where a path descends left to Kita-Hotaka's basic campsite and then down for 1hr 30min into the huge Karasawa Cirque 涸沢, home to a couple of huts, a large campground and an easy path back to Kamikōchi (allow 5hr). If the Daikiretto seemed overly intimidating then it's best to head this way.

Otherwise turn right at the signpost for 'Mt. Oku-Hotaka-dake 2.3km' to begin the traverse of the Hotaka ridgeline, bearing in mind that this section is even more exposed than the Daikiretto in places. Allow 2hr 30min to reach Hotaka-dake sansō at the other end. Follow the rugged rocky path along the ridge, past plummeting cliffs to the right and up to a craggy tower called Takidani Dome 滝谷ドーム. Cross shattered rocks and clamber down steeply to a prominent jutting tongue of rock, followed by more scrambling. Halfway along the ridge is a low saddle, with chains, ladders and some precarious, steep and exposed scrambling afterwards, passing close to the minor summit of Karasawa-yari 涸沢槍. *This pointy peak resembles the bigger and more famous Mt Yari from Stage 2, especially when viewed from the floor of Karasawa Cirque.* Continue up

The last stop before the big drop into the Daikiretto; Mt Hotaka looms beyond

a steep rock face for a final exposed climb to the scree-covered summit ridge of Mt Karasawa-dake 涸沢岳 (3110m), then descend steeply for 10min over loose stones to reach Hotaka-dake sansō 穂高岳山荘, a large hut built on an incredibly narrow and exposed col.

From here you can descend left (east) into the Karasawa Cirque (1hr 30min), head right (west) down a very steep path for Shin-Hotaka Onsen (5hr 30min), or climb the ladders next to the hut for a short, sharp ascent to the 3190m summit of Mt Oku-Hotaka-dake 奥穂高岳 in 40min. *Rumour has it that rocks were piled up on Oku-Hotaka's summit to increase its height so that it could be crowned the 'third highest mountain in Japan', instead of 3189m Mt Aino-dake in the Minami Alps.* To complete the 'classic' loop back to Kamikōchi, ascend to the summit of Mt Oku-Hotaka-dake and then follow the sign near the summit for 前穂高岳・岳沢 (Mae-Hotaka-dake and Dakesawa). The path heads southeast along the rugged Tsuri-one ridge 吊尾根 to reach Kimiko-daira 紀美子平 in around 1hr 30min. From here there is an optional 30min scramble up to the summit of Mt Mae-Hotaka-dake 前穂高岳 (3090m); otherwise head right for the very steep 4hr descent to Kamikōchi via Dakesawa (see Trek 4).

It is also viable to do this route in reverse, although the traverse of the exposed ridgeline between Oku-Hotaka and Kita-Hotaka and then the drop into the Daikiretto are arguably even more challenging and hazardous than the north-to-south route described here, featuring more in the way of awkward down-climbs.

TREK 6
Mt Chō-ga-take and Mt Jōnen-dake 蝶ケ岳~常念岳

Start/finish	Kamikōchi 上高地
Distance	34km (21 miles)
Total ascent/descent	1970m (6460ft)
Grade	2 *
Time	2 or 3 days
Terrain	Starts with an easy walk down a flat riverside track but soon climbs steeply through forest, passing above the tree line, then follows a well-trodden undulating path along a broad ridge, with a final rocky scramble to the summit
Access	See Hotaka chapter introduction
Accommodation	Hotels, huts and camping at Kamikōchi and along the valley; hut and camping at Chō-ga-take
Facilities	Basic shops, restaurants and hot spring baths at Kamikōchi; drinks, snacks and meals available at huts
When to go	Trails mostly free of snow from mid June to late October

A magnificent peak visible from Matsumoto city, Jōnen-dake (2857m) is one of the more accessible and easy 'big' climbs in the North Alps. The long, flat approach from Kamikōchi

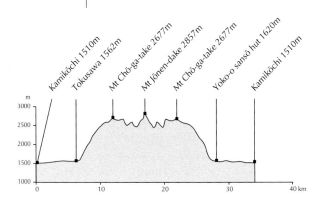

makes for a good warm-up before the steady ascent to Chō-ga-take Hut, and Stage 2 is mostly above the tree line, with fantastic vistas of the Hotaka massif and iconic Yari-ga-take, followed by a simple scramble to Mt Jōnen's summit. Consider splitting the second stage over two days (returning to Chō-ga-take Hut or staying at one of the huts in the valley).

From Mt Jōnen an alternative route leads north via Mt Tsubakuro-dake to Nakabusa Onsen. Although not included in the main itinerary, an overview of Tsubakuro is provided as it is one of the most popular and distinctive peaks in the North Alps.

STAGE 1
Kamikōchi to Chō-ga-take Hut 上高地~蝶ヶ岳ヒュッテ

Start	Kamikōchi 上高地
Finish	Chō-ga-take Hut 蝶ヶ岳ヒュッテ
Distance	12km (7½ miles)
Total ascent	1170m (3840ft)
Total descent	Negligible
Time	7hr
Terrain	Easy walking on a flat forest track. Fairly steep and long ascent on a rugged dirt and stony path through woodland.
Accommodation	Hotels, huts and camping at Kamikōchi, hut and campground at the summit of Mt Chō-ga-take

Starting at the bustling Kamikōchi bus terminal, the crowds are soon left behind with a pleasant walk along a flat forest road for 7km, followed by a rigorous and long climb through quiet woodland to the summit of Mt Chō-ga-take. The forest eventually thins out, revealing spectacular alpine views of the neighbouring mountains.

Leaving the bus at the terminal at Kamikōchi 上高地, you will see a large visitor centre on your left and an array of small shops, restaurants and the bus ticket counter on your right. Near the picnic benches are taps which you can use to fill up water bottles. Walk beyond the benches and through some trees to join a wide paved road, soon reaching the

famous Kappa-bashi Bridge 河童橋 with its fantastic views
of Mt Hotaka. Don't cross the bridge, but continue along the
road, soon passing some toilets on your left, before meandering through the **Konashidaira** campground 小梨平キャン
プ場.

Walk through the forest, keeping a lookout for Japanese
macaques. ◄ The path is very easy going, rising and falling
gently, arriving at a junction for **Myōjin Pond** 明神池 after
a couple of kilometres. There are huts and toilets here, but
continue straight following signs for Tokusawa. Views of the
river open up to the left, followed by more gentle ups and
downs, and then you'll need to ford a small stream. After
passing a murky pond called **Furuike** 古池 on the left, stroll
through quiet woodland of ferns and dense undergrowth.

Skirt close to the river again with sweeping views down
the valley, passing evidence of landslides to the right. Just
after a large map and information board, branch left past
some toilets and the grassy camping field at Tokusawa 徳沢.
Walk to **Tokusawa-en** hut 徳澤園 at the far end of the field
where there are also some benches.

The main forest track continues across a small bridge left
of the hut, but turn right in front of the hut instead. Walk
past the entrance to the hut and look for a small sign 蝶ヶ岳・長塀
山 indicating an easy-to-miss and narrow path branching off
to the left, running adjacent to a fence. Take this path. From

These Japanese
macaques are
accustomed to
humans and are
frequently found on
the trail itself, but
should not be fed.

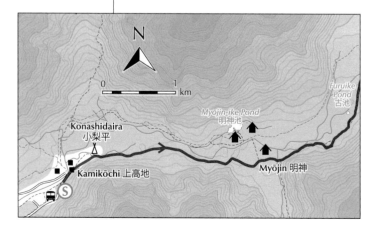

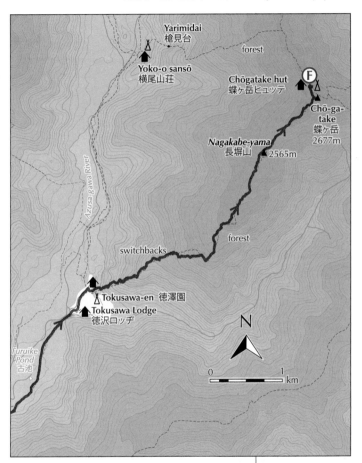

here on, the easy walking along the flat of the valley floor ends and the real hiking begins.

Rise steadily through the woods, twisting and turning steeply over exposed tree roots on a well-marked path. After a long series of switchbacks reach a small plateau with a few places to rest, then continue the steep climb through forest, the path becoming rockier underfoot. Halfway up, a sign on

Chō-ga-take Hut boasts splendid views

a tree stump signals 3km to go, and soon the gradient eases and the temperate greenery of the valley gives way to high alpine forest.

The trail flattens out and is muddy in places, passing by a brownish pond where early in the season patches of snow may linger. Follow red paint marks on trees to reach a sign indicating 1.8km to go in a slight clearing on a minor peak called **Nagakabe-yama** 長壁山 (2565m), around 3hr from Tokusawa. From here, drop into a shaded hollow and pass a small pool to the right. The forest thins out, and the path skirts past a much bigger pond.

Continue up a short slope from where magnificent views of Mt Hotaka and Mt Yari will open up. ◄ Follow the path up through alpine brush to gradually level out just below the 2677m summit of **Mt Chō-ga-take**. Clamber up the path to the right to reach the summit and enjoy the views. Afterwards, return to the main route and walk a few metres north to find a rocky campground and **Chō-ga-take** Hut 蝶ヶ岳ヒュッテ, about 1hr from Nagakabe-yama.

The 'big cut' in the ridgeline between Hotaka and Yari, known as the Daikiretto (see Trek 5), is clearly visible across the valley.

186

STAGE 2

Chō-ga-take Hut to Kamikōchi via Jōnen-dake
蝶ヶ岳ヒュッテ~常念岳~上高地

Start	Chō-ga-take Hut 蝶ヶ岳ヒュッテ
Finish	Kamikōchi 上高地
Distance	22km (13½ miles)
Total ascent	800m (2630ft)
Total descent	1970m (6460ft)
Time	11hr
Terrain	Rugged and rocky underfoot, sometimes muddy in shaded areas. Mostly short ascents/descents, a few more substantial. Flat gravel track down the river valley.
Accommodation	Hut and camping at Mt Cho-ga-take; huts and campgrounds en route to Kamikōchi

A walk along a broad undulating alpine ridge, with invigorating panoramic views for most of the way. The final ascent of Mt Jōnen is an easy scramble over large rocks. Consider spreading this stage over two days for a more leisurely return to Kamikōchi.

Head north from **Chō-ga-take Hut** 蝶ヶ岳ヒュッテ and walk up a short way to an exposed plinth and lightning conductor. Mt Jōnen is visible in the distance, along with much of the undulating ridge that comprises the traverse there. Follow the well-worn path between rocks and low brush, and descend to a three-way junction. Here, ignore the sign pointing left for 'Yokoo' and push onwards towards 'Mt Jonen-dake', climbing back up the wide ridge. The path rises and falls a little on mostly stony ground, but the going is easy. ▸

A large stone with 'TOP' scrawled in yellow paint marks a minor highpoint.

After scrambling over some rocks, continue along the ridge and then drop down suddenly through a forest of fir and birch. Descend further, and hop down a four-rung ladder to a muddy saddle. From here, climb a grassy knoll into mossy pine forest, and then continue rising steadily. A small pond is crossed via a crude log bridge, and then the route traverses a section of muddy ground.

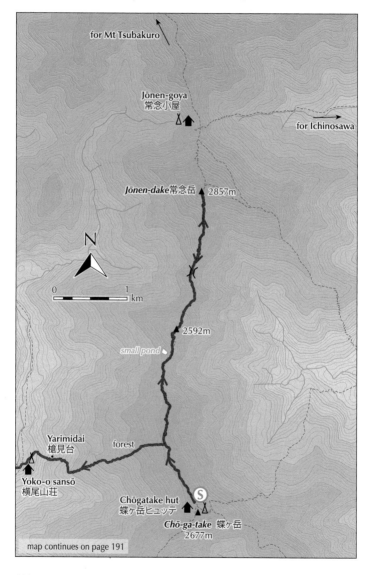

for Mt Tsubakuro

Jōnen-goya
常念小屋

for Ichinosawa

Jōnen-dake 常念岳 ▲ 2857m

N

0 1
km

▲ 2592m

small pond

Yarimidai
槍見台

forest

Yoko-o sansō
横尾山荘

Chōgatake hut
蝶ヶ岳ヒュッテ

Ⓢ

Chō-ga-take 蝶ヶ岳
2677m

map continues on page 191

188

Forest sections on the way to Mt Jōnen

Around 2hr from the start ascend a small grassy peak with a sign marking the altitude '**2592m**', and then descend into the forest once again, the route soon flattening out to follow a boulder-strewn but well-defined path. Trees give way to shoulder-high bushes as the path hugs the left side of a rounded hill, climbing gently. Emerge onto a small rocky peak, with the final steep climb looming ahead.

Drop to the rocky saddle and then start the final ascent, sticking close to the ridgeline. It should take less than 1hr to reach the top, with paint marks showing the way. As the summit gets nearer it becomes an enjoyable scramble over large boulders. There are some very steep drops on the east face, so stick left of the ridge if in doubt. At the summit of **Mt Jōnen-dake** 常念岳 (2857m) there is a small shrine and great views across the valley towards Mt Yari.

The path leading north down the other side of the summit makes for a steep 40min descent to Jōnen-goya hut, from where it is possible carry on along the ridge towards Mt Tsubakuro-dake (see below). From the hut there is also another trail east to Ichinosawa, a 9hr hike for those with their own transport.

To return to Kamikōchi however, retrace your steps towards Chō-ga-take Hut. Around 3hr 30min from Mt Jōnen, at the three-way junction, turn right for 'Yokoo' and drop abruptly down scree into the trees below. Descend steeply through the dense forest for over 1hr 30min to reach a

The ridgeline between Chō-ga-take Hut and Mt Jōnen (far right)

small clearing called **Yarimidai** 槍見台, where there are log benches and clear views of pointy Mt Yari.

Continue winding down, cutting through trees and thick bamboo brush, to reach another bench, from where it is a 20min descent to **Yoko-o sansō** 横尾山荘 hut and

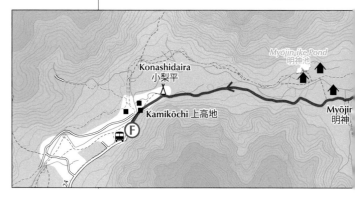

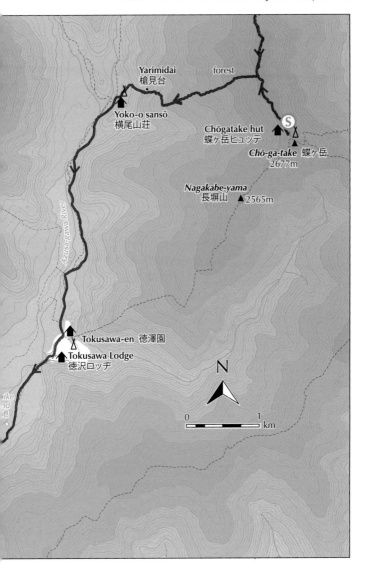

forest

Yarimidai
槍見台

Yoko-o sansō
横尾山荘

Chōgatake hut
蝶ヶ岳ヒュッテ Ⓢ ▲

Chō-ga-take 蝶ヶ岳
2677m

Nagakabe-yama
長塀山 ▲ 2565m

Azusagawa River

Tokusawa-en 徳澤園

Tokusawa Lodge
徳沢ロッヂ

ike
nd 池

N

0　　　　　1
└─────────┘ km

191

campground. Turn left and walk south along the flat forest road for 2–3hr all the way back to **Kamikōchi**, passing the huts at **Tokusawa** and **Myōjin** from Stage 1.

MT TSUBAKURO-DAKE

Mt Tsubakuro-dake 燕岳 (2763m) is a popular and distinctive mountain about 9km due north of Mt Jōnen. Its summit is peppered with shards and fins of grey/white granite (the most famous of which is shaped like a dolphin), creating the illusion of snow from a distance, while the attractive Enzansō hut 燕山荘 is just a 30min walk from the top and is one of the oldest mountain huts in Japan (open late April to late November, and for two weeks around New Year).

Many people climb Mt Tsubakuro-dake as a one- or two-day return hike from Nakabusa Onsen 中房温泉, a small rustic hot spring to the east of the peak. It's a 5hr climb and 3hr 30min descent, with one section said to be one of the three steepest paths in the North Alps – but this doesn't detract from the mountain's popularity.

Nakabusa Onsen could also be used as an alternative start or finish point for Trek 6, avoiding the need to cover the same ground twice. In total this route would be 33km (20½ miles), with 2750m (9020ft) of ascent/descent, taking three or four days. Nakabusa Onsen can be reached from Hotaka Station on the JR Oito Line by bus (60min, late April to early November, weekends only in May/June, otherwise daily) or taxi (40min). There is also parking for private vehicles.

Those heading to Mt Tsubakuro-dake from Mt Jōnen-dake should allow 7 or 8hr to reach the Enzansō hut from Jōnen-goya hut. From the summit of Mt Jōnen, drop to Jōnen-goya 常念小屋 in 45min. It is then a 3hr 30min walk along the ridge to the Daitensō hut 大天荘 and campground, which sit below the summit of Mt Otenshō-dake 大天井岳 (2922m). Follow the path north along the undualting ridge for another 3hr 30min on a popular stretch of trail known as 'Omote-Ginza' – a tongue-in-cheek reference to the busy Tokyo neighbourhood. From the Enzansō hut it is 30min to the top of Mt Tsubakuro-dake 燕岳 (2763m), or otherwise head east following the steep but well-used trail down to Nakabusa Onsen in 3hr 15min.

For those starting at Nakabusa Onsen, the trail to the summit of Mt Jōnen-dake is about 16km and usually takes two days. Having summited Mt Tsubakuro-dake and dropped to the Enzansō hut, the undulating 'Omote-Ginza' path leads south along the ridge to Mt Otenshō-dake in 3hr. The path splits below Otenshō-dake's summit, with the western branch heading to the Otenshō hut 大天井ヒュッテ in 45min and then on to the famous Mt Yari-ga-take in another 6 or 7hr. Trekkers heading to Jōnen-dake should follow the other branch up to the Daitensō hut and campground in 40min, then continue south along the ridge for 3hr to Jōnen-goya hut, before the steep 1hr climb up to Mt Jōnen-dake's summit.

TREK 7
Mt Kasa-ga-take 笠ヶ岳

Start/finish	Shin-Hotaka Onsen 新穂高温泉
Distance	18km (11 miles)
Total ascent	2010m (6600ft)
Total descent	1910m (6260ft)
Grade	2+
Time	2 days
Terrain	A narrow and sometimes muddy forest trail, with a few river crossings followed by a long climb on a frequently overgrown path. Rough stony ground at higher elevations and a long, rugged descent, ending on a gravel track.
Access	Buses from/to Takayama take about 1hr 30min and run hourly from 7am year-round. There are a few buses daily from/to Matsumoto and Toyama in summer. The Nakao-kōgen-guchi start point is 10min before the bus terminal at Shin-Hotaka Ropeway. Parking available near the trailhead and near the ropeway.
Accommodation	Hotels and ryokan (traditional inns) near the trailhead and ropeway; hut and camping at the summit and at Wasabidaira-goya (off route)
Facilities	Hot spring baths near the start and finish points, and a shop and restaurant at Shin-Hotaka Ropeway. Drinks, snacks and meals available at the huts.
When to go	Accessible year-round but best climbed mid July to late October. Crampons may be necessary before/after this.

Shin-Hotaka Onsen is a small hot spring resort in a secluded narrow valley, wedged between the massive Hotaka ridge-line on one side and the towering Mt Kasa-ga-take (2898m) on the other. It is barely a village at all, rather a clutter of *ryokan* and homesteads dotted along the river, but the abundance of tranquil hot springs among wonderful natural settings has attracted visitors for years.

Hikers have long been drawn to the area and Mt Kasa-ga-take is considered one of the tougher day-hikes in this part of the North Alps, with many people setting off before

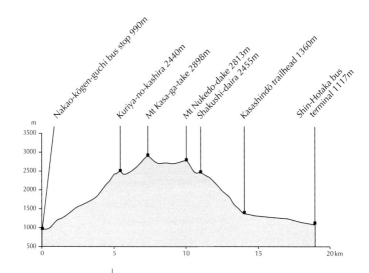

sunrise and ascending and descending the same day via the gruellingly steep Kasashindō path (see Stage 2). It is more enjoyable, however, to split the hike into two, either camping or spending the night at the hut near the summit. This can be followed by a leisurely return on day two, perhaps finishing with a relaxing soak at one of the many hot springs at Shin-Hotaka Onsen.

The route here follows a less frequented path through forest up a quiet river valley, before a long and unrelenting climb all the way to the summit, with just under 2000m of vertical ascent in a day! The second stage is somewhat less strenuous, with an easy ridge walk among spectacular alpine scenery, and then a long knee-knocking descent into the beautiful valley below.

STAGE 1
Nakao-kōgen-guchi to Kasa-ga-take sansō
中尾高原口~笠ヶ岳山荘

Start	Nakao-kōgen-guchi bus stop 中尾高原口
Finish	Kasa-ga-take sansō hut 笠ヶ岳山荘
Distance	8km (5 miles)
Total ascent	1910m (6270ft)
Total descent	100m (330ft)
Time	8–9hr
Terrain	Rough forest trail with shallow river crossings (the first of these is usually knee-height), giving way to a narrow and long mountain path, rugged and steep in places
Accommodation	Hotels and inns near the trailhead; hut and campground just past the summit of Mt Kasa-ga-take
Warning	The river crossing near the beginning of the trek can be treacherous and impassable when the river is high after heavy rains, so get a Japanese speaker to call Kasa-ga-take sansō (tel 090-7020-5666) or the 'tozan-shidō (mountain advice) centre' 登山指導センター (tel 0578-89-3610) at Shin-Hotaka Onsen to enquire about conditions if in doubt.

A long, remote and interesting route up the mountain, this trail sees much less foot traffic than the more popular Kasashindō path (used on the return leg, see Stage 2). The gradient is unrelenting and involves a huge gain in altitude, so good fitness is key. It can be a long day, so it is imperative to get an early start, either by taking the first bus in the morning from Takayama or by staying at one of the *ryokan* (inns) near the trailhead.

From the **Nakao-kōgen-guchi bus stop** 中尾高原口, cross the road and walk across the pedestrian foot bridge over the river (upstream of the main road bridge which crosses the river before a tunnel). At the other side of the bridge is an outdoor hot spring called Shin-hotaka-no-yu 新穂高の湯. Follow the path left then turn right onto a small road which climbs gently. After a few minutes turn left onto a gravel track, passing a ryokan called Yarimikan 槍見館 on the right. (This traditional

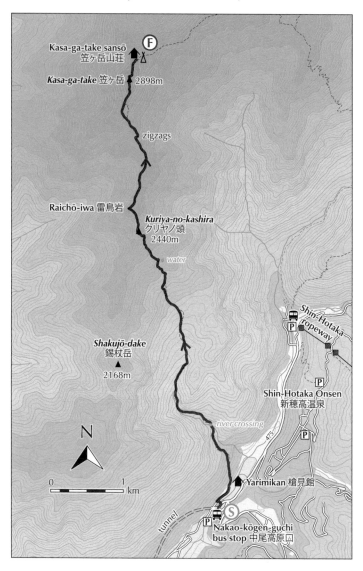

Kasa-ga-take sansō
笠ヶ岳山荘 Ⓕ

Kasa-ga-take 笠ヶ岳 2898m

zigzags

Raichō-iwa 雷鳥岩
Kuriya-no-kashira
クリヤノ頭
2440m

water

Shakujō-dake
錫杖岳
▲
2168m

N

Shin-Hotaka
ropeway P

Shin-Hotaka Onsen
新穂高温泉 P

0   1
km

river crossing

475

P

Yarimikan 槍見館

tunnel

P Ⓢ

Nakao-kōgen-guchi
bus stop 中尾高原口

inn has its own private indoor and outdoor baths, and would make a great place to stay for the start of this hike.) You will soon reach a large information board and tozan post box for registering your hike plan; from here follow the narrow trail left up into the forest.

Climb gently for 30min, hopping over some boulders, to arrive at a **river crossing**. The river can flow dangerously high after typhoons, but is usually no deeper than knee-height. Wade across, bear left and continue to climb steadily through the forest.

This valley is called **Kuriya-dani** クリヤ谷 and through gaps in the trees there are tantalising glimpses up ahead of the towering cliffs and buttresses of Mt Shakujō-dake 錫杖岳, a peak popular with rock climbers.

The narrow path rises high above the river and can be muddy with some steep drops to the left. Gradually bear right and meet the river again, crossing it at shallow rocky places a few times. ▶

The water is beautifully clear and there are some nice rest spots along this stretch.

The cliffs of Mt Shakujō-dake, visible through the trees

A resting spot next to the rock at Raichō-iwa

Climb out of the forest and follow the path through thick swathes of shoulder-high foliage, with the bald rocky peak of Mt Yake-dake 焼岳 in clear view directly behind. Continue steadily on up the narrow and rough path for about 1hr, thick vegetation almost engulfing the trail in places. As you meander upwards there are splendid views of the jagged Hotaka ridgeline on the other side of the valley, and you will pass a few trickling streams which can be used for drinking water. Keep following the rocky path up steep, grassy slopes.

As you twist and turn uphill the grass becomes shorter and patches of bare rock are increasingly visible, with the mountain taking a more alpine feel. Clamber over rocks and finally gain the ridgeline among short pine and fir trees. Angle right below a rocky prominence known as **Kuriya-no-kashira** クリヤノ頭, passing a steep gully on the right, and gradually ascend the rocky path through thick low-growing trees. Near a distinctive rock called **Raichō-iwa** 雷鳥岩 ('ptarmigan rock', about 6hr from start) you'll catch first sight of Mt Kasa's elegant peak, still some 2hr 30min away.

Follow the rugged and winding trail down through thick undergrowth, passing beneath a minor peak on the right, to reach a narrow saddle where you'll need to edge past a steep drop on the right. There is a bit of up-and-down as the trail snakes along the ridge, with expansive views into the remote valley to the west. Climb a series of wide zigzags to reach a lofty shoulder covered in shin-high creeping pine, and pass a rocky cleft on the right.

Continue steadily upwards on a stony path (look back for great aerial views of the ridge just traversed), bearing right to briefly leave the creeping pine and ascend stony ground on barren grassy slopes that are home to alpine flowers. Rise steadily over piles of rocks among more patches of creeping pine, following paint marks to eventually gain the main ridge below the summit.

The ridge has a couple of small ups and downs, so follow the twisting and undulating path over jumbles of rocks and through alpine brush. Scramble up shattered rocks for a few minutes to arrive at the stony summit of **Mt Kasa-ga-take** 笠ヶ岳 (2898m), which is marked by a wooden post. ▸

Take the narrow path north along the summit. There is a small wooden shrine protected by a wall, and a path leads down right for a short stony descent to **Kasa-ga-take sansō** 笠ヶ岳山荘, a comfortable hut with spaces for tents just a little further on.

If the weather is clear there are fantastic panoramic views in all directions.

STAGE 2
Kasa-ga-take sansō to Shin-Hotaka Ropeway
笠ヶ岳山荘~新穂高ロープウェイ

Start	Kasa-ga-take sansō hut 笠ヶ岳山荘
Finish	Shin-Hotaka Ropeway 新穂高ロープウェイ
Distance	10km (6 miles)
Total ascent	100m (330ft)
Total descent	1810m (5930ft)
Time	5–6hr
Terrain	A stony undulating path along the ridge, then a long, steep and rugged descent (with short laddered sections), ending on a flat gravel track
Accommodation	Hut and camping at Wasabidaira-goya (off route); many ryokan (inns) around Shin-Hotaka Onsen

The trail from Mt Kasa-ga-dake to Nukedo-dake is an enjoyable hour-long walk along a rolling ridge taking in fine mountain scenery, before a long steep descent on a path called the Kasashindō 笠新道 to the valley floor. It is then an easy walk on a forest track to the bus stop at Shin-Hotaka Ropeway.

There are superb views of pointy Mt Yari and the entire Hotaka ridgeline across the valley.

Leave **Kasa-ga-take sansō hut** 笠ヶ岳山荘 and follow the path down over rocks, reaching the campground in a few minutes to pick your way across flat stony ground. ◄ Carry on descending the ridge; where it narrows a little you will pass some rocky outcrops perched above a green and wonderfully secluded cirque down to the right. Rise and fall very gently for a while, sticking close to the top of the ridge along an enjoyable stretch.

At a place called **Nukedo-iwa** 抜戸岩, walk through a cleft in the rocks that almost looks like it has been carved out by people, and continue along the ridge on a twisting stony path through low creeping pine with a few more gentle ups and downs.

The Kasa-ga-take campground affords great views

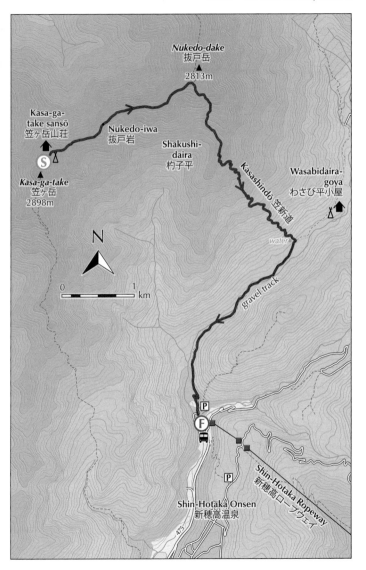

Nukedo-dake
抜戸岳
2813m

Kasa-ga-
take sansō
笠ヶ岳山荘

Nukedo-iwa
抜戸岩

Shakushi-
daira
杓子平

Kasashindō 笠新道

Wasabidaira-
goya
わさび平小屋

S

Kasa-ga-take
笠ヶ岳
2898m

water

N

0 — 1 km

gravel track

P

F

P

Shin-Hotaka Ropeway
新穂高ロープウェイ

Shin-Hotaka Onsen
新穂高温泉

475

Pass some rocky crags falling away to the right, and climb steadily to reach just below the summit of **Mt Nukedo-dake** 抜戸岳 (2813m) about 1hr from the hut. The trail continues north along the ridge, but turn right at a weathered signpost and ascend the stony path for a few minutes to arrive near the top of the peak for more magnificent views. The true summit lies a little way over to the left, but start walking downhill on a meandering path, taking care on the loose stones.

Steadily descend the rocky and grassy slope, which is peppered with yellow wildflowers, to reach a relatively flat plateau called **Shakushi-daira** 杓子平. Follow the rough, rocky path through grassy meadows, with Mt Kasa's shapely and now quite distant and towering peak visible up to the right. Then proceed over flatter and bushier ground and follow a sign for 新穂高温泉 (Shin-Hotaka Onsen). This leads to the brow of the plateau where you begin the 2–3hr descent to the valley floor on the notoriously steep **Kasashindō** 笠新道 path.

Bear left along the narrow path and enter mostly deciduous forest. Snake over rocks and occasionally use short metal ladders to descend steep sections. After crossing an open, grassy patch of hillside, carefully traverse a narrow, muddy rocky section which seems prone to landslides. Then head back into the trees and continue descending the rough and narrow trail, sparing a thought for those climbing up this way. You will pass a few simple benches fashioned from bits of metal or planks of wood.

There is a wooden sign at 1800m where leafy ferns litter the forest floor; continue the steady rugged descent, passing another sign at 1450m with the forest at these lower elevations now mostly comprising beech and oak. You will soon emerge onto a wide and mercifully flat **gravel track** next to a large signboard and a water source. Wasabidaira-goya わさび平小屋, a nice hut in the forest with spots for camping, is 10min to the left; otherwise turn right and walk down the track, following close to the river for about 40min to reach the trailhead.

Pass a gate and meander down the paved road for a few minutes, then turn left onto a path just before the road crosses a bridge to arrive at **Shin-Hotaka** ropeway and bus terminal. ◄

Bus tickets can be bought from a machine just inside the ropeway building.

NORIKURA AREA – 乗鞍エリア

Roads and trails crisscross Norikura's summit area (Walk 6)

Just south of Kamikōchi and the main peaks of the Japan Alps sits Mt Norikura-dake, a huge 3026m volcano which, although technically part of the North Alps, feels distinctly separate and solitary. While the lower elevations are thickly forested, the summit plateau is made up of rocky minor peaks, crater lakes and vegetated slopes of alpine flowers home to black bear and ptarmigan. Owing to the high altitude, pockets of snow remain late into the year, with one big patch on the mountain's east face a popular spot for summer skiing.

Despite being one of the tallest mountains in Japan, Mt Norikura is one of the easiest to climb, as a road winds all the way up the mountain to the 2700m bus terminal at Tatamidaira, and from there it is only a short hike up to the main summit of Ken-ga-mine. This means it is a good walk for those who want to climb to the top of a +3000m mountain without using too much time or energy, and can be done as a day-trip from either Takayama or Matsumoto.

BASES

Takayama 高山 and **Matsumoto** 松本 both make good bases for visiting Norikura as a day-trip. From Takayama just take a Hirayu Onsen-bound bus and change at Hōnokidaira ほおのき平 (1hr 30min total). If approaching from Matsumoto, take a train to

Shin-Shimashima Station (30min on the Kamikōchi Line), from where buses regularly depart for Norikura Kōgen (50min), then change to a bus for Mt Norikura.

JR Takayama Station is on the Takayama Line with trains running from Nagoya in the south and Toyama in the north. There are also occasional direct trains from Osaka and Kyoto. Highway buses also run from Tokyo, Osaka and Nagoya. Matsumoto is easy to reach from Tokyo, with JR Azusa and Super Azusa trains taking under 3hr from Shinjuku Station, and there are also trains from Nagoya and Nagano. Highway buses run from Tokyo, Osaka and Nagoya.

Norikura Kōgen 乗鞍高原 is a highland plateau at 1450m on the eastern side of Mt Norikura. It is home to a spread-out resort village full of *ryokan* (traditional inns), hot springs and hiking courses, with many natural attractions such as Ushidome Pond and Zengoro Waterfall, and a small ski resort operates in the winter months. The Kankō Centre (tourist centre) serves as the main transportation hub, with multiple bus connections and free parking. There are regular buses from Kankō Centre-mae bus stop 観光センター前 to Mt Norikura bus terminal (50min) between July and late October.

Hirayu Onsen 平湯温泉 is a small and secluded hot spring resort at an elevation of 1250m on the northern side of Mt Norikura. There are a number of places to stay (and a campground) and a few souvenir shops, but most people pass through briefly as it is a fairly busy hub for bus connections from Takayama (1hr), Shin-Hotaka (35min), Kamikochi (30min) and Mt Norikura (1hr).

Shirahone Onsen 白骨温泉 nestles on the eastern slopes of Mt Norikura. It is a tiny hot spring village famed for its milky opaque waters infused with magnesium and calcium said to cure many ailments. There are a handful of *ryokan* with their own baths, and the most famous hot spring, Awa-no-yu, has a picturesque gender-mixed outdoor bath (and some smaller segregated ones too).

There are only three or four buses a day to Shirahone Onsen from Shin-Shimashima Station (passing through Norikura Kōgen), so it is not the most convenient base if using public transport.

The road up to Tatamidaira is closed to private vehicles, but there is parking at Hōnokidaira, Hirayu Onsen and Norikura Kōgen.

MAPS

Walk 6 is covered at 1:50,000 by the Yama-to-Kōgen 山と高原 (No. 39) Norikura-kōgen 乗鞍高原 sheet.

WALK 6
Mt Norikura-dake 乗鞍岳

Start/finish	Norikura bus terminal 乗鞍バスターミナル, Tatamidaira 畳平
Distance	6.5km (4 miles)
Total ascent/descent	330m (1080ft)
Grade	1
Time	2hr 30min
Terrain	Gentle gravel track as far as Kata-no-koya hut, then a steeper climb on a rough rocky path to the summit
Access	There are regular buses to Norikura bus terminal at Tatamidaira from Norikura Kōgen between July and late October (www.alpico.co.jp/en/timetable/norikura). Or, from Takayama, take a bus bound for Hirayu Onsen and change at Hōnokidaira. Buses run from mid May until late October; see www.nouhibus.co.jp/english (select 'Route Bus') for schedules. Note that the road to Tatamidaira is closed to private vehicles.
Accommodation	Huts near bus terminal and at Kata-no-koya
Facilities	Water, food and toilets at huts and visitor centre
When to go	Buses to Tatamidaira run from mid May until mid October. In late May and June expect lots of snow on the paths to the summit, so good boots and crampons are advisable.

A short and easy hike from the bus terminal in a beautiful landscape of rocky summits, blue lakes, alpine flowers and occasional long-lasting snow patches. There are longer and more demanding courses starting at the foot of the mountain, but the route here to Mt Ken-ga-mine 剣ヶ峰 (3026m), Norikura's highest point, is suitable for all abilities and is an easily accessible taste of Japan's high alpine terrain.

From Norikura bus terminal at **Tatamidaira** 畳平 you have two initial choices. For the direct route go down the stairs on a well-made path between the large visitor centre and the pointy-roofed hut, and descend gently to a flat meadow. A path to the right makes a small loop around a field of black lilies, yellow cinquefoils and other alpine flowers. Having

The bus terminal at Tatamidaira

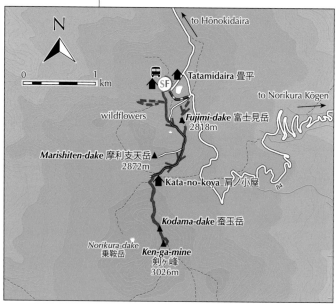

N

0   1 km

to Hōnokidaira

Tatamidaira 畳平

to Norikura Kōgen →

wildflowers

Fujimi-dake 富士見岳
2818m

Marishiten-dake 摩利支天岳
2872m

Kata-no-koya 肩ノ小屋

Kodama-dake 蚕玉岳

Norikura-dake
乗鞍岳

Ken-ga-mine
剣ヶ峰
3026m

visited the wildflowers, continue straight on and up a gradual incline, and turn right onto a wide and flat gravel track.

Optional variant via Mt Fujimi-dake

The other option involves a short climb to the minor summit of Mt Fujimi-dake (2818m). From the bus terminal walk past the small hut with a pointy red roof, and turn right onto a track swinging south of Tsuru-ga-ike pond 鶴ヶ池. Leave the track where it turns sharply right, join a narrow stony path and climb for 15min to reach the rocky summit of **Fujimi-dake** 富士見岳, a name meaning 'peak from where Mt Fuji can be seen'. ▶ Continue onwards down the stony path to soon rejoin the gravel track.

The tip of Fuji-san's conical peak can indeed be glimpsed on very clear days.

Both routes merge onto the same track, which climbs very gently following the contours of the hillside, looping around a pond down to the right which is used for drinking water. At a small brow another track branches off to the right and leads to another minor summit, Mt Marishiten-dake 摩利支天岳 (2872m) in 15min (not typically visited). ▶

This peak is crowned by a large solar observatory with a distinctive white dome.

Continue along the main track with great views of the summer snowfield (people can often be spotted skiing), and descend very gently towards **Kata-no-koya** hut 肩ノ小屋, 35min from the start. Just before the hut, a trail comes in from the left, providing a possible 20min descent to the winding road and Kata-no-goya-guchi bus stop 肩の小屋口 (a convenient alternative start/finish point if taking the bus to or from Norikura Kōgen). It is even possible to follow the trail all the way down to Norikura Kōgen in around 3hr.

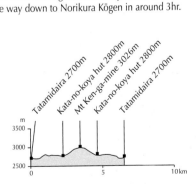

Norikura in its winter garb

There are views down to a nearby summit basin containing a blue lake, just below the west side of the ridge.

For Norikura-dake, however, continue beyond the hut, passing some red buildings to the right used by the University of Tokyo for cosmic ray research. Follow the rocky but clearly marked trail uphill, climbing gently at first but gradually steepening. It is rough underfoot, going over boulders and rocks. You will reach **Mt Kodama-dake** 蚕玉岳 on the barren and stony summit ridge after about 40min; from here continue a short way towards the true summit. ◄

Partway up the final peak the path splits for ascent and descent. Take the left branch, passing the small Norikura-chōjō-goya 乗鞍岳頂上小屋, a hut selling only snacks and souvenirs. It is then a short distance to the rocky summit of **Mt Ken-ga-mine** 剣ケ峰, Norikura's highest point and home to a tiny summit shrine. Return via the descent branch and retrace your steps to the bus terminal at **Tatamidaira** in 1hr 15min.

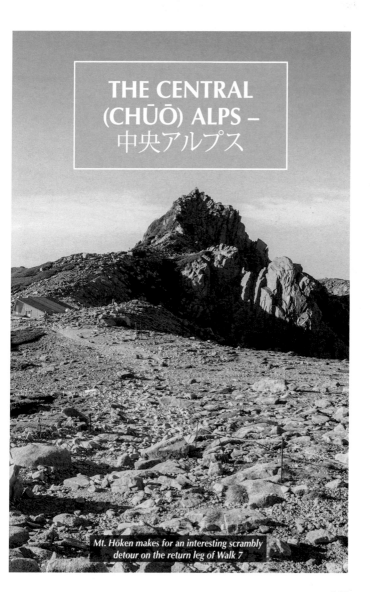

THE CENTRAL (CHŪŌ) ALPS – 中央アルプス

Mt. Hōken makes for an interesting scrambly detour on the return leg of Walk 7

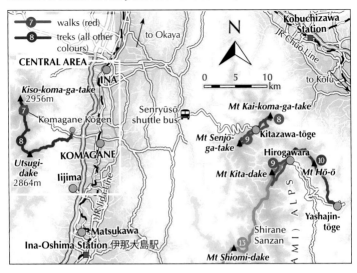

The Central Alps are the smallest of the three regions that comprise the Japan Alps, but they have a lot to offer with easy access, rewarding walks and spectacular alpine views. The Central Alps are sandwiched between the other two big ranges, directly south of the North Alps and just west of the sprawling South Alps. Also known as (but rarely called) the Kiso Sanmyaku (Kiso Range), they form a spine of high granite peaks all under 3000m in height running neatly from north to south, with Mt Kiso-koma-ga-take the tallest at 2956m. Koma-ga-take – meaning 'horse' or 'pony' peak –is one of many mountains in Japan with that name (Mt Kai-koma-ga-take in the South Alps is another example). Glacial features and late-lying snow patches can be found around the summits, most notably at Senjōjiki Cirque, which is also famed

for abundant alpine flowers in the summer and dazzling autumn colours from late September. The Komagatake Ropeway hauls day-trippers up to 2612m at the base of the cirque from the Komagane side of the mountain. The sight of crowds of people queuing for the ropeway can be alarming, but most of them don't make it much further than the immediate vicinity of the upper ropeway station (Senjōjiki Station) and adjoining hotel, meaning the trails are much quieter.

The walk through Senjōjiki Cirque to Mt Kiso-koma (Walk 7) is popular with hikers as it is relatively short and undemanding, yet it offers rugged mountain vistas and a taste of the alpine. Mt Hōken (2931m) is a distinctive peak which looms over Senjōjiki Cirque and has gained notoriety as an accident hotspot over the years, so care

The summit sign on Mt Hinokio (Trek 8, Stage 1)

should certainly be taken when navigating its rocky and chain-laden contours. It makes for an interesting detour if you enjoy scrambling (see Walk 7, alternative descent). Further south the ridge becomes quieter as only dedicated trekkers follow the long and undulating path to Mt Utsugi (2864m), an impressive peak in a remote setting (Trek 8).

Many trails crisscross these mountains, and as the valleys on both sides of the Chūō Alps have JR train lines there are plenty of possible variations. In the past Mt Kiso-koma was most commonly tackled from the west on a long and tiring route taking a full day, still sometimes climbed now. However, since the building of the ropeway the vast majority of visitors approach from Komagane city to the east, and this ease of access makes these mountains a good option for those without the time or inclination to attempt some of the bigger peaks found elsewhere in the Japan Alps.

OVERVIEW

Location: Chūbu region of central Honshu, Nagano Prefecture.

Information: Lots of good English information, including ropeway and bus timetables, can be found at www.chuo-alps.com (English-language option).

For **access**, **bases** and **maps** see below.

Komagane 駒ヶ根市 is a small city with
a few hotels, restaurants and supermar-
kets. Komagane Station is on the JR Iida
Line running between Okaya Station and
Toyohashi Station. If approaching from
Nagoya it is quicker to take the JR Chuo
Line and change at Shiojiri Station.

There are also regular highway
buses from Tokyo Shinjuku Nagoya and
Osaka (use https://highway-buses.jp
or www.highwaybus.com/gp/index to
make bus reservations in English). There
is a round-trip ticket from Shinjuku
which also includes the local bus and
ropeway fares for 10,000 yen (in 2018),
available from Shinjuku Expressway Bus
Terminal (located at JR Shinjuku Station
New South Gate).

Komagane Kōgen 駒ヶ根高原 is
a small outdoorsy area just west of
Komagane City, home to a small ski
resort, nature trails and scenic ponds.
It is the access point for the mountains
for those with cars, as there is plenty of
parking and regular buses to the ropeway from the Suganodai bus station 菅
の台バスセンター. There are a number
of basic restaurants and shops, an outdoor gear store, hotels, a campsite and a
couple of hot springs nearby. Komagane
Youth Hostel is a cheap accommodation
option.

Walk 7 and Trek 8 are covered at
1:50,000 by the 1:50,000 Yama-to-
Kogen (No. 41) Kiso-koma and Utsugi-
dake 木曽駒・空木岳 sheet. A 1:50,000
Central Alps guide map, covering both
routes, is also available for free at the
ropeway station.

WALK 7
Mt Kiso-koma-ga-take 木曽駒ヶ岳

Start/finish	Senjōjiki Station 千畳敷駅 (upper station, Komagatake Ropeway)
Distance	4km (2½ miles)
Total ascent/descent	380m (1250ft)
Grade	1+ (descent via Mt Hōken 2 *)
Time	3hr
Terrain	Rough path and a brief, steep climb out of the cirque. Stony underfoot on the summit plateau and small peaks. Exposed scrambling on the Mt Hōken alternative return.
Access	Regular buses from Komagane Station to Komagane Ropeway
Accommodation	Hotel, huts and camping
Facilities	Restaurant and basic shop at ropeway station
When to go	Komagatake Ropeway and Senjōjiki Hotel are open all year; the walk is best done from July until late November. Lots of snow (winter equipment needed) from December until mid June. The ropeway can be busy, especially in midsummer and autumn (late Sept—early Oct), so arrive early or late in the day to avoid long waiting times and large crowds.

A short hike across and then up the rim of a glacial cirque, followed by an easy walk on rocky paths to the peak of Mt Kiso-koma-ga-take (2956m). There's a return option of exciting and at times exposed scrambling up and over Mt Hōken – this could also be used to combine the walk with Trek 8 (Central Alps traverse) which continues south along the ridge.

Exit the **Komagatake Ropeway** at the upper station (Senjōjiki Station), turn left to find a small wooden shrine at a trail junction, then turn right into the cirque and follow the path across the bowl-shaped valley. In early summer there may still be patches of snow to traverse. ▶

The path rises and falls gently, meeting another trail coming up from the bottom of the cirque in 15min. (This trail

By midsummer the valley is lush with greenery and alpine flowers, and later in the year people come to see the autumn colours.

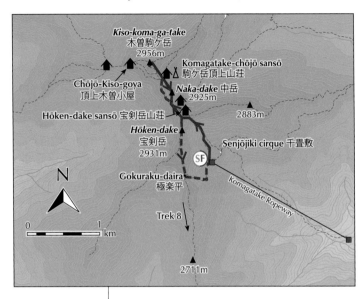

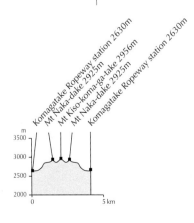

leads back to the ropeway station via a small pond noted for wildflowers – a short loop hike that is popular with day-trippers.) Turn left here and follow the rocky path upwards to climb towards the rim of the cirque.

After 30min emerge onto the lip of the cirque, turn left and wander over to **Hōken-dake sansō** hut 宝剣岳山荘 with its distinctive blue roof. Then walk left of the hut to a small sign among the jumble of rocks. The pointy promontory of Mt Hōken-dake 宝剣岳 is to the left (see alternative descent), but follow the path right behind the hut onto flatter stony ground.

Tengu-sō 天狗荘 hut comes into view on the right and the path splits a little further on. Both branches lead to the same place; the right-hand path is an easy climb up and over the summit of **Mt Naka-dake** (2925m) 中岳, while the left-hand path is a more awkward scramble along the peak's western face (closed off when there is snow). Both paths join up in 20min at a wide and rocky saddle below the main peak of Mt Kiso-koma-ga-take 木曽駒ケ岳, where you will find **Komagatake-chōjō sansō** 駒ケ岳頂上山荘, a hut with campground. From the hut it is a 15min walk to the 2956m **summit**. ▶

There are a few small shrines on the summit and startling views in every direction.

For the return, go back the same way to the blue-roofed **Hōken sansō hut**, turning left to retrace your steps through the cirque to the **Komagatake Ropeway**.

Alternative descent via Mt Hōken

For an exciting rocky scramble, and for those continuing on to Trek 8, carry straight on at Hōken sansō hut, following the path upwards over rocks towards the spire-like peak of Mt Hōken-dake 宝劍岳 (2931m). Allow 1hr 30min for the 1.5km (1 mile) route back to the ropeway. The trail is marked as dangerous on maps, but there are fixed chains and paint marks in places, making it easy for experienced scramblers.

Climb for 15min to arrive at the summit and a prominent summit stone which can be mounted for dizzying views into the cirque. From here, follow chains and paint marks

The path leads left of Tengu-sō hut

A view of Koma-ga-take from the top of Mt Hōken

The views west across to the shapely Mt San-no-sawa-dake 三ノ沢岳 are fantastic.

southwards over a series of secondary peaks, with frequent short, steep scrambles over exposed terrain. At one point, pass under a large rock and descend to a saddle, then climb a 5m wall with the aid of a fixed chain.

Scramble up and over a crest to reach a relatively flat section of ridge and a large cairn with a plaque. Ignore the path heading right and instead wander southwards down a mostly flat stony path, with low-growing creeping pine blanketing the gentle slopes falling to the right. ◄

At a shallow col called **Gokuraku-daira** 極楽平 there is a signpost and a path branching down to the left into the cirque; turn left and follow this trail to reach the ropeway station in about 20min. (Those attempting the Central Alps traverse (see Trek 8) should carry on along the ridge.)

TREK 8
Central Alps traverse 中央アルプス縦走

Start	Senjōjiki Station 千畳敷駅 (upper station, Komagatake Ropeway)
Finish	Komagane Kōgen 駒ヶ根高原
Distance	17km (10½ miles)
Total ascent	755m (2480ft)
Total descent	2520m (8270ft)
Grade	2 *
Time	2 or 3 days
Terrain	A long and open ridge walk with plenty of ups and downs, scrambling sections and relatively steep ascents/descents. Access by ropeway means there is no big initial climb, but the descent from Utsugi-dake is a long one.
Access	Regular buses from Komagane Station (via Komagane Kōgen) to Komagatake Ropeway at Shirabi-daira; see www.chuo-alps.com (English-language option)
Accommodation	Hotel, huts and camping
Facilities	Restaurant and basic shop at ropeway station; snacks at huts
When to go	Komagatake Ropeway and Hotel Senjōjiki are open all year; a traverse of the ridge all the way to Utsugi-dake is best done from July to mid October
Note	Aside from at the huts, there are few water sources along the way, so plan accordingly

This trek follows the Chūō Alps ridgeline along its most interesting stretch, taking in one of the range's most famous mountains, Mt Utsugi-dake (2864m). Ropeway access means there is no big climb at the start, but there are many ups and downs along the length of the ridge, staying above the tree line all the way and barely dropping below 2500m. As such, it feels like a proper mountain route, with plenty of broad alpine vistas and some straightforward scrambles in places.

Kisodono sansō 木曽殿山荘 is a hut just before the climb up Mt Utsugi-dake and the place most people stay when attempting this trek over two days. Unlike most huts in the region, the map stipulates that reservations are necessary,

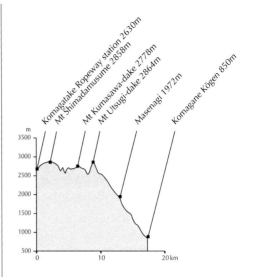

so get a Japanese speaker to call if you have trouble doing so. Alternatively, taking your own food and sleeping equipment gives you the option of staying in the emergency huts around Mt Utsugi.

To make the first stage easier it is advisable to take the ropeway up the day before, staying at Hotel Senjōjiki (or huts/campground – see Walk 7) in order to get an early start the following day. This also has the advantage of avoiding the early-morning queues for the ropeway, which can sometimes be hours long, particularly around public holidays.

Many people opt to combine the route described here with that of Walk 7 in order to make a full traverse of the ridge, starting the trek with Mt Koma-ga-take and including the scramble over Mt Hōken-dake for a three-day, 20km outing that is both challenging and rewarding.

STAGE 1

Senjōjiki Station to Kisodono sansō
千畳敷駅~木曽殿山荘

Start	Senjōjiki Station 千畳敷駅 (upper station, Komagatake Ropeway)
Finish	Kisodono sansō hut 木曽殿山荘
Distance	7km (4¼ miles)
Total ascent	390m (1280ft)
Total descent	520m (1710ft)
Time	5–6hr
Terrain	Stony paths along the ridge, lots of short ascents and descents, occasional easy scrambling
Accommodation	Hotel, huts and camping (reservation required if staying at Kisodono sansō hut)

After an easy climb out of Senjōjiki Cirque to the main ridgeline, the route towards Mt Utsugi is straightforward but somewhat strenuous with lots of up-and-down, offering great alpine scenery with a surprisingly remote feel.

Those combining this trek with Walk 7 to make the classic (and more demanding) full ridge traverse will go north from Senjōjiki Station (the upper ropeway station) to climb Mt Kiso-koma-ga-take and then Mt Hōken, and later rejoin the route described here at the Gokuraku-daira trail junction. See Walk 7 for details.

After exiting the upper station on the **Komagatake Ropeway** (Senjōjiki Station), take a left at the shrine junction and ascend a rugged path for 30min to gain the ridgeline. This is where the trail from Mt Kiso-koma and Mt Hōken comes in from the right at a place called **Gokuraku-daira** 極楽平, so turn left to continue following the ridgeline southwards.

Walk south and immediately ascend over a small rocky knoll, then meander very gently over a broad and barren ridge where the ground is stony and sandy and peppered with tufts of grass. Climb easily to a minor peak called **Shimadamusume** 島田娘 (2858m). ▶

There are fine views over to Mt Utsugi on a clear day, and the full scale and undulating nature of the ridgeline is visible ahead.

219

Carry on over boulder-strewn ground and descend gradually to an area of thick shin-high creeping pine. Weave through the vegetation, first dropping then climbing among large outcrops of granite. The ridge narrows slightly and drops to a bushy saddle. After a short, steep climb, arrive on a rocky promontory with a wooden post wedged between the rocks, and follow the uneven path just below the crest of the ridge, clambering over rocks painted with red arrows and avoiding red crosses.

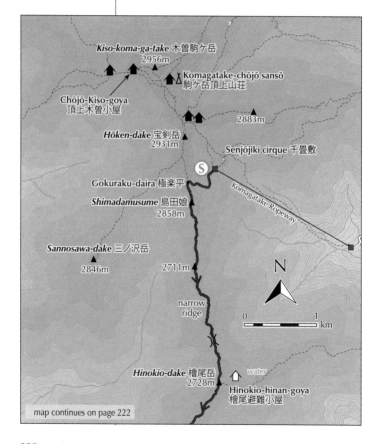

Kiso-koma-ga-take 木曽駒ケ岳
2956m

Komagatake-chōjō sansō
駒ケ岳頂上山荘

Chōjō-Kiso-goya
頂上木曽小屋

2883m

Hōken-dake 宝剣岳
2931m

Senjōjiki cirque 千畳敷

Gokuraku-daira 極楽平

Komagatake Ropeway

Shimadamusume 島田娘
2858m

Sannosawa-dake 三ノ沢岳
2846m

2711m

N

0   1 km

narrow
ridge

Hinokio-dake 檜尾岳
2728m

water

Hinokio-hinan-goya
檜尾避難小屋

map continues on page 222

Push through head-high bushes to reach a narrow and mildly exposed section of ridge, then scramble along the rocky spine and drop down a ledge with the aid of a fixed chain and metal handholds. Continue steadily downwards, briefly traversing the left side of the ridge to reach the bottom of a saddle and one of the lowest points of the day at 2536m.

From the saddle, climb towards the summit of Mt Hinokio-dake 檜尾岳 (2728m) on a winding path which is steep at first, passing through creeping pine which thins out on rockier ground. Emerge on the rocky and bald **summit** about 2hr after leaving Gokuraku-daira. The peak offers the best views yet of Mt Utsugi if the cloud isn't in. ▶

Press on southwards, descending past some large rocks and then on a stony path. Reach a broad saddle, and then a short climb up a twisting trail leads to a spur of jumbled rocks and sandy, pebbly ground. Wind over and around another bushy crest, hop over rocks and then level out among thickets of alpine brush. After skirting along the right side of the ridge, drop down to another saddle and push through tall and dense undergrowth, then follow the path up a small spine of rocks and slip through a patch of head-high conifers.

The path follows the ridgeline all the way to Mt Utsugi-dake in the far distance

A trail peels off to the east down another ridge, leading in 10min to Hinokio-hinan-goya 檜尾避難小屋 – an exposed and unmanned emergency hut with a toilet and water source.

221

HIKING AND TREKKING IN THE JAPAN ALPS AND MOUNT FUJI

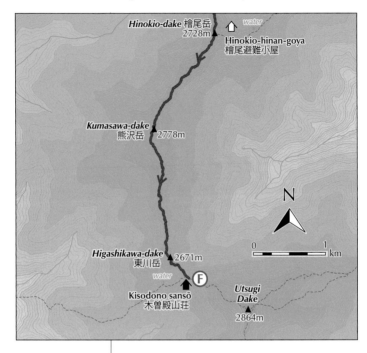

Escape the foliage by scrambling up some rocks to the left, then cross a narrow path at the top of a landslip.

There is another climb up a clear but rough path to the foot of some impressive tooth-shaped rocks and jumbles of large boulders. This marks the relatively flat summit of **Mt Kumasawa-dake** 熊沢岳 (2778m) – a good place to rest. From here, pass over relatively flat hummocky ground, and for the next 1hr hug the right side of the ridge just below the crest. The ridge falls away steeply to the east, while the gentle verdant slopes on the west side offer sweeping views of the lowlands.

Continue along the rocky path as the ridgeline descends gradually. There is a simple scramble over rocks followed by a short ascent to the top of **Mt Higashikawa-dake** 東川岳 (2671m), around 1hr 30min from Kumasawa-dake. Cross the stony summit and descend a steep path to reach **Kisodono**

Kisodono sansō is one of the few huts that stipulates reservations

sansō 木曽殿山荘 in about 15min. This hut lies in a narrow saddle and unlike most, requires a reservation (although they will likely provide accommodation if you are really desperate). There is a water source 10min down a spur trail to the west. ▶

If you started early in the day then you could make the steep climb to Mt Utsugi to stay at one of the huts there instead (allow 2hr).

STAGE 2
Kisodono sansō to Komagane Kōgen
木曽殿山荘~駒ケ根高原

Start	Kisodono sansō hut 木曽殿山荘
Finish	Komagane Kōgen 駒ケ根高原
Distance	10km (6¼ miles)
Total ascent	365m (1200ft)
Total descent	2000m (6560ft)
Time	7hr 30min
Terrain	A steep, stony ascent with scrambling sections; a long and rugged descent ending on forest trails
Accommodation	Huts; tent space next to Utsugi-daira emergency hut

An initial steep climb to the summit of Mt Utsugi offers wonderful views of the entire Chūō Alps ridgeline and to mountains far beyond. The descent to Komagane Kōgen is long and unrelenting, with interesting rock formations near the peak and ever-changing vegetation as you pass through the various altitude zones.

The summit of Mt Utsugi is a 1hr 30min climb from Kisodono sansō.

◄ From **Kisodono sansō hut** 木曽殿山荘 continue along the trail which immediately begins climbing steeply out of the saddle. Small trees cling to the sheer eastern face of the ridge, but the path mostly sticks to the slightly less

Komahō Hut is a small and basic shelter

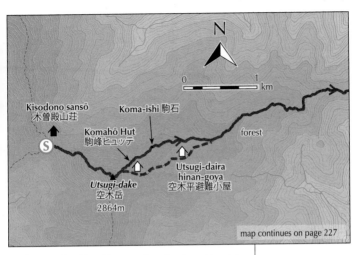

map continues on page 227

precipitous right side, with a covering of rocks and low-lying alpine scrub. Climb to a small rocky flat shoulder offering brief respite and a glimpse of the crumbling crags to the left, then continue upwards on a steep path of loose stones and boulders, paying attention to the red paint marks. Eventually reach a rocky spur marked with red paint as 第1ピーク ('peak no.1') around 45min from the start and roughly halfway to the summit.

Huge craggy rocks jut out from the now narrow ridge and a well-worn path weaves around and over them, with plenty of rock-hopping and simple scrambling required. Follow the winding trail and red arrow marks, passing to the right of some towering rocks that dominate the ridge. A small and sturdy four-rung wooden ladder leads to a short scramble, followed by a more prolonged traverse up over rocks, furnished in a few places with metal handholds. Clamber up to arrive on a secondary peak thick with creeping pine and a view of the final climb, and then ascend timber steps to a section of loose, sandy earth to gain the ridgeline. After passing over scuffed rocks you will arrive at the sandy summit of **Mt Utsugi-dake** 空木岳 (2864m).

A promising-looking ridge curves away southwards with a path leading in 2hr to Mt Minami-koma-ga-take 南駒ケ岳 and on to the even less-travelled southern end of the Chūō

225

The veranda outside the hut clings to the side of the mountain and is a great place to enjoy the scenery.

Alps. Instead, follow the summit sign pointing towards Mt Ike-yama 池山, descending a sandy and eroded path for 5min to reach a fork in the track just before **Komahō Hut** 駒峰ヒュッテ. This small hut is only open from mid July to mid October and has futons, a toilet and sells snacks but no hot meals (there is an honesty box if there are no staff). ◄

From the fork, both paths lead to the same place in 2km, so take your pick. The left branch is arguably the more scenic choice, slipping past the hut and down an easy winding path with mild ups and downs, snaking through creeping pine to a huge rock called **Koma-ishi** 駒石, which begs to be climbed. Beyond the rock, continue descending the open ridge which is covered with low creeping pine, later giving way to birch trees at the top of the tree line.

Alternative route via Utsugi-daira hinan-goya

Koma-ishi is a well-known landmark and fun to climb

Alternatively, the right-hand fork drops down rough stone steps into a small secluded basin, joining a rocky and mostly dry riverbed. (Early in the season there can be a bit of remaining snow here.) Follow the vague path for 30min, sometimes marked by pink ribbons on tree branches, to

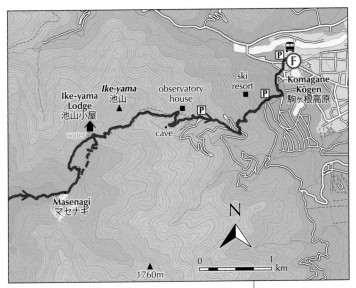

reach a grassy meadow and an emergency hut called the **Utsugi-daira hinan-goya** 空木平避難小屋. The hut is in good condition and has a toilet but no other facilities, so you will need your own sleeping equipment and food. ▶ No water source is marked here on maps, but there is a river (the one you've been following) next to the hut, although this may only flow when there is snowmelt or after rain and so can't be relied upon. Near the river there is some flat ground with room to pitch a couple of tents. Otherwise continue along the twisting trail, gradually climbing through forest to meet the other path in 10min.

Continue meandering down the ridge through alpine forest. Ascend metal stairs and walk along a dirt path, sometimes stony and lined with tree roots. Wooden walkways, ladders and stairs aid progress over steep, eroded sections. After 1hr, reach a sign with warnings in English about the narrow ridge ahead, and proceed with caution along a narrow, earthy trail with steep drops to the side and a fair number of minor ups and downs. There are some easy scrambles over rocks, and fixed metal chains help descend a steep rocky section,

There is an honesty box to receive donations for using the hut.

227

leading to a rough path over exposed tree roots. This is followed by a short climb up and over a rocky knoll, and then a steep descent through more open forest. Pass through an eroded notch, then go down a wooden ladder and cross a slope of beech and pine to arrive at **Masenagi** マセナギ – a flat, wooded area blanketed with thick *sasa* grass – in a further 1hr.

Walk down the gentle forest path for 10min to reach a fork. The right 'access trail' climbs a small hill and then drops down through forest; the left 'mountain trail' descends steeply and then levels out in a glade of *sasa* and ferns. Both trails meet up at a four-way junction after 1.7km. From the junction, **Ike-yama Lodge** 池山小屋 lies up one trail 100m north, but follow the path labelled 'start of the trail (Suganodai)', and reach a water source and rest spot in a few minutes.

There are short detours along the way to a wildlife hide (labelled an observatory house on the sign) and further on, Komorigasawa Cave 篭ヶ沢の岩窟.

Continue down an easy forest path and follow signs for 'the start of the trail'. ◀ In about 35min you will reach the trailhead, where there is a gravel car park and basic toilets. Don't follow the road, but re-enter the forest down some steps next to a wooden signpost for the start of the trail. After passing what looks like a grave and a stone *jizō* statue (these statues of Bodhisattva Ksitigarbha are often seen at temples and along tracks and roadsides in Japan and are believed to protect travellers) on the left, descend for about 2km, crossing the road a couple of times and always following the signs.

The route passes through ferns and cedar; ignore any other minor trails that appear, and carry on downhill to reach a ski resort. You will emerge at a large car park where you need to head left to rejoin the path into the forest, leading to a tarmac road. The path appears to continue straight ahead through a gap in the fence, but turn left and walk down the road for 500 metres to soon reach Suganodai bus station菅 の台バスセンター at **Komagane Kōgen**, from where there are regular buses to Komagane Station.

THE SOUTH (MINAMI) ALPS –
南アルプス

The vast boulder field below Hakuhō pass (Trek 10, Stage 2)

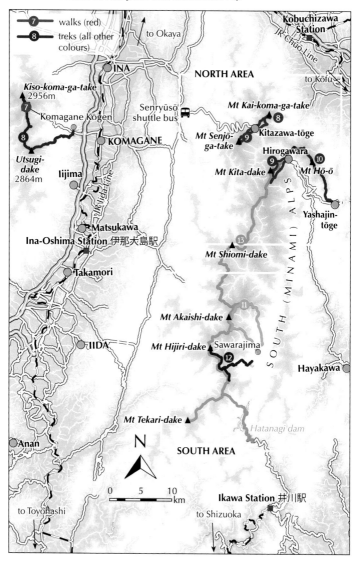

7 — walks (red)

8 — treks (all other colours)

to Okaya

Kobuchizawa Station

JR Chūō Line

NORTH AREA

to Kōfu

INA

Kiso-koma-ga-take 2956m

Komagane Kōgen

Senryūsō shuttle bus

Mt Kai-koma-ga-take

KOMAGANE

Mt Senjō-ga-take

Kitazawa-tōge

9

Hirogawara

Utsugi-dake 2864m

Iijima

JR Iida Line

9

Mt Kita-dake

Mt Hō-ō

10

Yashajin-tōge

Matsukawa

Ina-Ōshima Station 伊那大島駅

Takamori

Mt Shiomi-dake

13

SOUTH (MINAMI) ALPS

IIDA

11

Mt Akaishi-dake

Mt Hijiri-dake

Sawarajima

12

Hayakawa

Mt Tekari-dake

Hatanagi dam

N

SOUTH AREA

Anan

0   5   10
km

Ikawa Station 井川駅

to Toyohashi

to Shizuoka

Mt Akaishi, with Mt Kamikōchi behind (Trek 11, Stage 2)

There is a healthy north/south rivalry when talking about the Minami Alps, with this southern range often taking a back seat while the North Alps bask in the tourist limelight. The South Alps have just one-third the number of campsites and a fraction of the mountain huts, and while the North Alps generally receive around half a million yearly visitors, the lack of tourist facilities and difficult access means that only around 120,000 hikers make the journey to the South Alps annually, the majority concentrated around Mt Kita-dake. The crowds thin greatly the further south you trek from the main access hub of Hirogawara, and even on weekends the summit of Mt Shiomi in the centre of the range attracts only the most dedicated mountaineers.

Formed by seismic uplift around 100 million years ago, the South Alps consist of sedimentary red chert and limestone deposits with the exception of the white sandy granite covering Mt Hō-ō and Mt Kai-koma-ga-take. The South Alps are the fastest-growing mountain range in Japan, rising vertically at an annual rate of 3–4mm. For that reason, the local people often refer to Mt Ai-no-dake as Japan's third tallest peak, even though it is officially 50cm shorter than Mt Oku-Hotaka in the North Alps. That doesn't stop the locals from claiming it's possible to see the three tallest mountains in Japan from many vantage points throughout Yamanashi Prefecture!

The South Alps were designated a national park in 1964 and have recently been named a UNESCO Biosphere Reserve (or 'Eco Park'). The park ranger office and visitor centre at Hirogawara was completed in 2010, but this popular base for exploring the South Alps lacks other touristy amenities – the main attraction is the hiking.

OVERVIEW	
Location:	The border of Yamanashi, Shizuoka and Nagano prefectures in the Chūbu region of central Honshu.
Information:	Pick up a copy of the excellent English-language pamphlet *Road to the Minami-Alps* at either Hirogawara or the tourist information counter at Kōfu Station.
	For **bases**, **access** and **maps** see North Area and South Area.

The official name of the South Alps is the Akaishi Mountains, and they stretch in a north-south direction for nearly 80km along the border of Yamanashi, Shizuoka and Nagano prefectures. A full north-south traverse (Trek 13) can be completed in 7–8 days, crossing six separate 3000m peaks with large losses of altitude between each summit. The mountains run parallel to Mt Fuji and offer outstanding views of Japan's highest mountain in the clear-weather windows of early morning. With double the average annual precipitation of the rest of Japan, the South Alps have earned the nickname the 'Rainy Minami Alps', due to the almost daily deluges that arrive like clockwork on summer afternoons.

Unlike the North Alps, many of the mountain huts require advanced booking if you want meals, so prior planning is essential. Campers do not need to book but it's best to arrive early in the day before the best sites get taken. The tree line in the South Alps is around 2700m and most huts are located below it near water sources, but lack panoramic views.

Mt Senjō-ga-take, the Queen of the South Alps (Walk 9)

Kita-dake, the highest alpine summit in Japan (Trek 9)

Perhaps the best place to start your exploration of the South Alps is at the northern end of the range for the climb up Mt Hō-ō (Trek 10), which offers incredible panoramic views and, at 2840m, less altitude acclimatisation issues. The trek finishes at Hirogawara, the starting point for the full South Alps traverse (Trek 13), as well as the Mt Kita-dake loop (Trek 9) and the Shirane Sanzan traverse (see Trek 9). Kita-dake is arguably the second most popular 'big mountain' hike in Japan after Mt Fuji, so avoid going on weekends during the busy summer months.

Other options involve boarding a shuttle bus from Hirogawara to Kitazawa-tōge, the base camp for the day-hikes up Mt Kai-koma-ga-take (Walk 8) and Mt Senjō-ga-take (Walk 9).

Mt Senjō is the easiest 3000m peak in the South Alps, offering a close-up view of a glacial cirque and a good chance of spotting ptarmigan. Mt Kai-koma-ga-take, on the other hand, is the most treacherous of the peaks in the South Alps, with a steep rock-scramble and a thrilling traverse on a knife-edge ridge.

BASES

Kōfu 甲府 is the capital city of Yamanashi Prefecture and a good place to pick up supplies. Budget accommodation is available at Guesthouse Bacchas (http://bacchus-kofu.net). Kōfu Station is just 1hr 30min by limited express train from Tokyo, and can also be reached by highway bus from Shinjuku and Nagoya. Those coming from Kyoto or Osaka may find the overnight bus more conveni-ent, as it arrives at Kōfu Station at 4am in time for the first bus to Hirogawara. Advanced booking is required; see http://willerexpress.com/en.

Hirogawara 広河原 is the starting point for the South Alps traverse and the Kita-dake hike and has a campground, mountain hut and visitor centre (but no ATMs). The hut serves a curry lunch and sells basic supplies.

Seasonal buses (late June to early November) depart from Kōfu Station via Yashajin-tōge to Hirogawara (2hr, seven buses daily during the main summer season, three buses daily on weekdays and early summer and autumn).

There are also shuttle buses to Hirogawara from Narada (45min, four buses daily during the main summer season, two buses daily on weekdays and early summer and autumn). Narada is accessible from Minobu Station, from where there are three buses a day (1hr 30min). The waiting time between con-nections is long, so it's faster and easier to head to Hirogawara from Kōfu; see http://yamanashikotsu.co.jp (Japanese link). The road between Yashajin-tōge and Hirogawara is closed to private vehicles.

Kitazawa-tōge 北沢峠 sits in a nar-row valley between Mt Senjō and Mt Kai-koma-ga-take and is home to three different mountain huts and a large campground. Reservations are essential as the huts are often fully booked on weekends and holidays.

Daily shuttle buses run from Hirogawara to Kitazawa-tōge (25min, four buses daily from late June to early November; http://yamanashikotsu.co.jp). There's also a shuttle bus from Senryūsō (55min, five buses daily from mid June to mid November). Senryūsō can be reached by bus from Chino Station (45min, one bus on weekends from mid June to early November, daily bus from late July to mid August) and by local bus from Ina-shi Station via Takato (1hr, buses daily but with a transfer at Takato, so check the connection times beforehand; www.inacity.jp/kankojoho). The road between Senryūsō and Kitazawa-tōge is closed to private vehicles.

MAPS

The routes in this chapter are covered at 1:50,000 by the 1:50,000 Yama-to-Kogen (No. 42) Kita-dake and Kaikoma 北岳・甲斐駒 sheet. The 1:25,000 Yamakei – Kita-dake, Kai-koma-ga-take, and Senjo-dake 北岳・甲斐駒・仙丈 sheet covers all the routes except Trek 10 at 1:25,000.

WALK 8
Mt Kai-koma-ga-take 甲斐駒ヶ岳

Start/finish	Kitazawa-tōge 北沢峠
Alternative start/finish	Chikuu-komagatake Jinja (shrine) 竹字駒ヶ岳神社
Distance	8.5km (5¼ miles) or 16km (10 miles) on the Kuroto-One
Total ascent/descent	935m (3070ft) or 2200m (7220ft) on the Kuroto-One
Grade	2 * or 2+ ** on the Kuroto-One
Time	7hr 30min or 15hr (return) on the Kuroto-One
Terrain	A steady forest walk to a large boulder field, followed by a steep climb over tree roots and a knife-edge traverse with an exposed rock scramble to the summit. The descent loops back through forest.
Access	See North Area chapter introduction (35min taxi ride from Nirasaki Station for Kuroto-One)
Accommodation	Huts and camping at the trailhead (Shichijō-goya hut on the Kuroto-One)
Facilities	Water, food and toilets at huts. Lunch served at Komorebi sansō hut from 9am to 3pm.
When to go	Late June to early November, when the shuttle bus to Kitazawa-tōge is operating. Avoid Kuroto-One in winter and during wet conditions.

Mt Kai-koma-ga-take (2967m), better known as 'Kai koma' to the locals, is a sacred pyramidal peak rising above the Kōfu basin on the northern edge of the South Alps. It has been worshipped since ancient times and the first documented ascent was two centuries ago by a mountain ascetic along the northeastern flank. The main route from Kitazawa-tōge was created by mountain guide Takezawa Chōei in the early 20th century and the walk described here follows that path, passing a mountain hut that still bears his name. In sharp contrast to neighbouring Mt Senjō (Walk 9), Kai-koma is a strenuous and exposed hike up a western face of gritty sand granite, offering unobstructed views of the main South Alps ridge to the southwest.

From the **Kitazawa-tōge** bus stop, walk southeast down the gravel road in the direction of Hirogawara. Soon turn left at the signpost 仙水峠 2.5km and follow the road down to the campsite and **Chōei-goya** hut 長衛小屋. Cross the metal bridge and turn left on the path marked for Sensui-tōge 仙水峠, heading upstream past a couple of dams before crossing a log bridge. Continue following the river bank and cross another log bridge to reach **Sensui-goya** 仙水小屋 in 30min.

You can fill up on water at the hut, then continue left through a gentle forest dotted with seasonal broomrape and false lily-of-the-valley flowers. The track soon leaves the forest and enters a vast field of rough boulders. Go north for 30min along the scuffed rocks towards the mountain pass directly ahead and reach the pass at **Sensui-tōge** 仙水峠, then turn left at the Japanese signpost 駒津峰を経て甲斐駒ヶ岳 3時間 (3hr to Kai-koma-ga-take via Komatsu-mine).

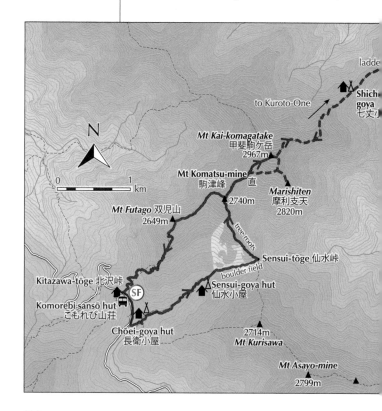

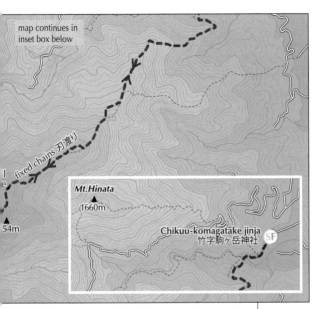

map continues in
inset box below

fixed chains 刃渡り

54m

Mt.Hinata
▲
1660m

Chikuu-komagatake jinja
竹字駒ヶ岳神社 SF

Mt Kai-koma-ga-take floats above a sea of clouds

237

It gets steeper now along a spur of exposed **tree roots** and rocks for nearly 500 vertical metres to the 2740m summit of **Mt Komatsu-mine** 駒津峰. With luck you will rise above the fog here on misty mornings to enjoy magical panoramic vistas. ◄

Mt Komatsu-mine often sits snugly above a sea of clouds.

From the top of Mt Komatsu-mine, turn right and head northeast along the undulating knife-edge ridge directly towards the summit plateau, following a mix of painted arrows, pink tape and scuff marks on the sandy granite rock formations. Take care in wet weather of the near-vertical drops on your left. After 20min arrive at a junction with red paint marks and follow the sign pointing up marked 'rock climbing course' (or head right for the standard and most popular route to the summit). ◄

Make a note of this point as you will return here later.

Proceed straight ahead through a minefield of exposed rock formations leading to the summit, carefully following the red arrows and circles as the correct line can be difficult to pick up in foggy conditions. After about 40min of ascent you will reach the summit of **Mt Kai-koma-ga-take** 甲斐駒ケ岳 (2967m), marked by a large rock temple and old Buddhist statues. There are panoramic views of the rest of the Minami Alps and the upper half of Mt Fuji (partially obstructed by Mt Hō-ō).

From the summit, head southeast for 5min to reach 竹宇登山口 (Chikuu-tozanguchi) junction. This is the trail for the alternative Kuroto-One route described below. Ignore this

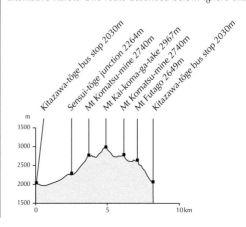

and go down a gritty sandstone trail to the right at a Japanese signpost for 駒津峰を経て北沢峠, then switchback through an area of sandy gravel with poor footholds and green ropes. There are red metal stakes bolted to the rocks. After a few minutes you'll reach a junction for 摩利支天 (**Marishiten**) on your left. This is an optional 20min detour to a small 2820m summit lined with Buddhist statues and splendid views of Kai-koma's summit. Ignore this in poor visibility and traverse west to complete the loop.

Red metal stakes mark the standard route

On returning to the junction from earlier, turn left and retrace your steps to **Komatsu-mine**. From the summit, take the trail heading west signposted 双児山を経て北沢峠 and descend to the tree line before climbing a short way to the summit of **Mt Futago** 双児山 (2649m). Now follow the pink tape through Veitch's silver-fir forest; the route loses roughly 600m of altitude to reach **Kitazawa-tōge** in 1hr 30min.

Alternative approach along the Kuroto-One 黒戸尾根

The Kuroto-One (pronounced 'oh-nay') route is included on the Nihon Dai-san Kyūtō (Japan's Three Steepest Climbing Routes). The trail starts at the Chikuu-komagatake Jinja shrine 駒ヶ岳神社 (770m) and follows a spur for 8km via Mt Kuroto (2554m) to the summit of Mt Kai-koma-ga-take. ▶ Access is

Walter Weston climbed this route in 1902 and for many years it was the only path up Kai-koma.

239

35min by taxi from Nirasaki Station 韮崎駅 to the trailhead at the shrine.

Walk through the shrine grounds and cross a wooden suspension bridge over the river. Ignore the trail to the right and head straight up through the forest, turning left for 甲斐駒ヶ岳 at the first junction. Climbing through bamboo grass with intermittent views of Mt Fuji, you will pass a variety of Buddhist statues which line this historic route. Follow the waymarks for 登山道 along the well-used track.

After 2hr, navigate the fixed chains of 刃渡り (literally 'sword blade crossing') at 2000m. The narrow path continues along chains and ladders through the forest past a small shrine dotted with Buddhist artwork, flattens briefly, then steeply climbs a minor peak lined with stone stupas under a rock formation. This is the halfway point; there used to be a mountain hut here but now there is just a small flat area to pitch tents.

A tricky climb begins along a series of exposed wooden ladders, bridges and chain sections for another 1hr, reaching a new wooden mountain hut (Shichijō-goya 七丈小屋) offering accommodation. Most visitors break up the hike by staying here before continuing on to the summit the following morning.

Take the wooden ladder just to the right of the newer hut and ascend above the tree line for 2hr, via more fixed chains, to reach a large boulder embedded with two iron sword-like projections. Follow the red metal stakes that line the route for another 1hr to arrive on the summit plateau of **Mt Kai-koma-ga-take** 甲斐駒ヶ岳. Turn right to reach the top (2967m), around 8hr after starting your hike. Return via the same route in 7hr or continue down to Kitazawa-tōge in 4hr.

WALK 9
Mt Senjō-ga-take 仙丈ヶ岳

Start/finish	Kitazawa-tōge 北沢峠
Distance	9km (5¾ miles)
Total ascent/descent	1175m (3850ft)
Grade	1+
Time	6hr 30min
Terrain	Virgin forest on the lower slopes; rocky ridge above the tree line
Access	See North Area chapter introduction
Accommodation	Mountain huts and camping at Kitazawa-tōge, and at huts near the summit
Facilities	Water and other drinks available at huts. Lunch available at Komorebi sansō hut.
When to go	Late June to early November, when the shuttle bus to Kitazawa-tōge is operating
Note	Snow tends to linger in the gully below Uma-no-se hut early in the season and the track is sometimes closed due to landslides. Ask locally or check https://inashi-kankoukyoukai.jp (Japanese link) for updates.

Known as the 'Queen of the Minami Alps', Mt Senjō (3033m) is perhaps the easiest 3000m hike in the South Alps, with lush woodlands, breathtaking panoramic views, and a good chance of spotting an elusive ptarmigan. The path traverses through verdant forests of fir, beech, and other hardwoods before ascending to an alpine area of glacial cirques. The panoramic vistas are incredible, with the whole of the South Alps spread out before you, and unobstructed views of the Central Alps stretching across the western horizon. The route is split into 10 stages called *gōme* (合目) in Japanese; they can be used to measure your progress.

▶ Just behind the restroom at **Kitazawa-tōge** 北沢峠, take the trail right waymarked in English for Senjō-ga-take and follow the pink tape along long switchbacks for 1hr through a mossy forest. As the gradient eases at the **second stage** 二合目, ignore the trail on your left and continue straight on a meandering rocky section with a small wooden ladder. After

The route is incorrectly signposted for Senjyo. Don't worry – Senjō and Senjyo are the same mountain!

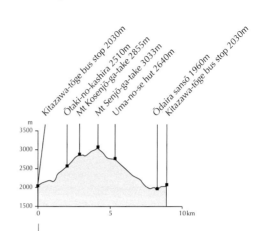

another 1hr of steady climbing through fir and birch trees, the trail splits at a junction called **Ōtaki-no-kashira** 大滝頭: this is the fifth stage 五合目.

The initial ascent is through a beautiful forest.

◀ Follow the sign for 'Kosenjyo-ga-take' north through thinning tree cover and into creeping pine. The vistas open up towards Mt Kai-koma behind you and Mt Kita-dake

Enchanting forests along the ascent route

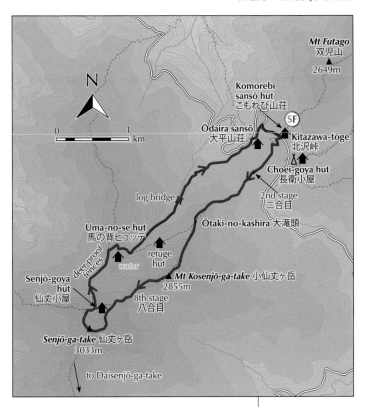

and Mt Fuji on your left. Navigate the switchbacks, paying close attention to the red paint arrows in poor visibility, and keep a lookout for ptarmigan and stoats on the ascent to **Mt Kosenjō-ga-take** 小仙丈ヶ岳 (2855m), the first peak on the alpine ridge and the seventh stage 七合目.

From the summit, follow the undulating track which drops to a saddle at the **eighth stage** 八合目, then navigate tight switchbacks along the edge of a large cirque. At the top of a long rise, ignore the trail on the right for Senjō-goya and keep to the ridge, following painted red arrows and circles. Go past a junction to the left marked for 'Daisenjo-ga-take'

The weather-beaten summit marker on Mt Senjō-ga-take

There are remnants of glacial activity in cols below the summit.

and climb a short way for panoramic views from **Mt Senjō-ga-take** 仙丈ヶ岳 (3033m). ◄

Drop north down the far side of the summit, veering right at the Jizō-one 地蔵尾根 junction for Kitazawa-tōge. Drop to a col and reach **Senjō-goya** hut 仙丈小屋 in 10min, then turn left at the junction next to the hut, marked for Kitazawa-tōge. Descend back below the tree line and amble through an area with **deer-proof fences**, veering right at the next junction for 'Yabusawa・Kitazawa-tōge' to soon reach the water source at **Uma-no-se** hut 馬の背ヒュッテ.

From the hut continue straight towards 北沢峠 (Kitazawa-tōge). Turn left at a mountain stream and signpost (Yabusawa・Shigoyuki Shindō) and follow the left bank downstream, using the fixed ropes on the steeper sections. After passing a small waterfall to the right, cross a **log bridge**. The exact route of the trail varies from year to year depending on land-slide and avalanche damage, so follow the painted arrows and coloured tape marks. Finally leave the river after 1hr and climb to the top of a pass before starting the steep descent to the valley.

Zigzag through the forest, past a clearing on the left with pleasant vistas, and onto a trail with an easier gradient. After crossing a small stream with a signpost (大平山荘), continue through the forest and over a couple of rotting wooden bridges to reach **Ōdaira sansō** hut 大平山荘, 1hr after leaving the river. ◄ Continue past the hut and veer right, zigzagging through the forest to meet up with the road. Turn right here to return to the starting point at **Kitazawa-tōge** 北沢峠.

Ōdaira sansō is family-run and serves a great cup of fresh coffee.

TREK 9
Mt Kita-dake 北岳

Start/finish	Hirogawara 広河原
Distance	13.5km (8½ miles)
Total ascent/descent	1705m (5595ft)
Grade	2 *
Time	2 or 3 days
Terrain	A steady climb through forest, then steeply up and along a rocky ridge to the summit. Wooden stairs and ladders on the descent.
Access	See North Area chapter introduction
Accommodation	Mountain huts and camping at Hirogawara, Shirane-oike, Kata-no-goya and Kitadake sansō
Facilities	Water, drinks, lunch and snacks available at most huts
When to go	Buses operate between late June and early November, with the prime hiking season from July to mid October
Note	Trail closures along the Happonba col route sometimes occur after heavy rains. Confirm trail information at the visitor centre on arrival at Hirogawara bus stop.

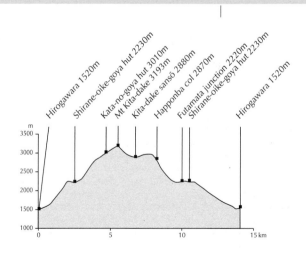

245

The summit of Kita-dake looms near (Stage 2)

If Mt Senjō is the Queen of the South Alps, then Mt Kita-dake (3193m) must be the King, as Japan's second highest mountain is at the top of the 'must-climb' list of every budding alpinist. On weekends you'll share the trail with half of Tokyo, so aim for a quieter weekday when the crowds are more manageable.

The loop hike described here climbs steadily on a steep spur to Shirane-oike base camp, where a meandering trail leads to the summit ridge. From there it's an exciting walk along a narrow track of weather-beaten boulders to the top before dropping to Kita-dake sansō hut to loop back to Shirane-oike through a landscape of wildflowers

and lingering snowfields. Some people climb Kita-dake as
a tough 10hr day-hike, but it's much more enjoyable to take
your time and savour the views.

STAGE 1
Hirogawara to Shirane-oike 広河原~白根御池

Start	Hirogawara bus stop 広河原
Finish	Shirane-oike-goya hut 白根御池小屋
Distance	4km (2½ miles)
Total ascent	715m (2350ft)
Total descent	Negligible
Time	3hr
Terrain	A steady climb through a wonderful deciduous forest followed by a steep climb along a root-infested spur lined with tight switchbacks and wooden log stairs
Accommodation	Camping and accommodation at the start and at Shirane-oike-goya. Note that advanced booking is required at Shirane-oike hut if you plan on staying with meals. Campers do not need to make a booking but should try to show up early, as the best sites tend to fill up quickly. Plan on arriving at the hut by 3pm, in time for dinner (usually served at 4.30pm).

A short stage involving a climb through forest to Shirane-oike hut and campground
at 2230m. On arrival at Hirogawara, pick up a free copy of the English-language
Road to the Minami-Alps pamphlet at the visitor centre. Inside you'll find a basic
map as well as information about the surrounding peaks.

From the bus stop at **Hirogawara**, head northwest on the
paved road between the river and information centre. Turn
left at the fork in the road and pass a log building and a gate
across the road. Just past the gate, drop left to a suspension
bridge, cross it and turn right to reach **Hirogawara sansō** 広
河原山荘. The hut serves lunch from 11am to 2pm and also
sells basic snacks and provisions.

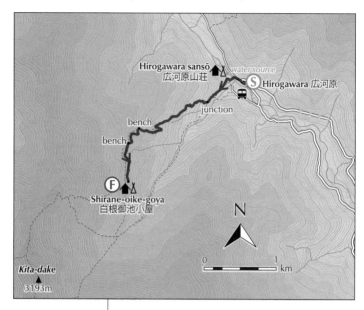

One of the many wooden ladders lining the forested route

Shirane-oike-goya hut

Take the trail to the left of the hut, marked for Ōkanbasawa 大樺沢. After passing a sign for Shiraneoike 白根御池, reach another sign at a junction pointing the way to Mt Kita-dake. Head straight and climb steadily through a forest of towering hardwoods, soon passing by an electronic people counter and then crossing a couple of log bridges over gently flowing streams.

The path steepens, climbing over exposed tree roots for 15min to reach a **junction**. This is the start of the loop hike, so take the right fork marked for 白根御池 (Shirane-oike) and climb the steep switchbacks along the narrow spur of moss-covered rocks and tree roots. The route is well marked with red circles and arrows, and wooden ladders and stairs help on the steeper sections.

In about 1hr reach the first rest bench, marked by a sign reading 北岳 白根御池, then continue up the spur past a second bench to an unmarked shoulder. The path veers left and flattens out, heading south towards Shirane-oike. Cross a wooden bridge and emerge into a small meadow to find **Shirane-oike-goya** 白根御池小屋, a hut and campground with nice views. ▶

If you started early and still have plenty of time, consider carrying on to the next hut in Stage 2 about 3hr away.

STAGE 2
Shirane-oike and Kita-dake loop 白根御池~北岳

Start/finish	Shirane-oike-goya hut 白根御池小屋
Distance	6.5km (4 miles)
Total ascent/descent	990m (3250ft)
Time	7hr 30min
Terrain	A steady and steep climb to the tree line, then along a rocky alpine ridge to the summit. The steep descent has many wooden ladders and stairs.
Accommodation	Huts and camping at start/end of stage, and at Kitadake Kata-no-goya and Kita-dake sansō

Starting and ending at Shirane-oike hut, this stage involves an ascent of Mt Kita-dake, returning to the hut via steep slopes, fields of wildflowers and late-season snow gullies. It is possible to carry on down to Hirogawara if you don't want to spend another night at Shirane-oike, but be wary of missing the final return bus to Kōfu (ask hut staff for the timetable).

Leave **Shirane-oike-goya hut** 白根御池小屋 and turn right to soon reach a junction near 白根御池 (Shirane-oike) pond. Take the right fork, marked Kata-no-goya 肩の小屋・北岳山頂. The trail climbs steeply through a field of wild plants and purple flowers with views of the pond and Mt Hō-ō directly behind.

After 1hr 30min, pass through an open area of rocks at the edge of the tree line, then veer right to a vast field of wild-flowers lined with deer-proof fencing. Just above this clearing, turn right at the junction and climb for 20min to the **ridgeline** for the first of many views of Mt Fuji to the southeast.

Turn left on the ridge and follow the well-trodden path towards the summit massif, skirting over a small pinnacle aided by fixed rope and painted red arrows before reaching **Kitadake Kata-no-goya** 北岳肩ノ小屋 in a further 20min.

The path to the summit continues left just behind the hut and immediately enters a vast boulder field with yellow paint marks showing the way. ◄ The top of the first rise is marked by a junction with plenty of stone cairns; keep left, following

The path can be tricky to pick up when the cloud is in, so follow the other hikers.

the signs to 北岳山頂 (Kita-dake summit) for the final steep scramble to the top.

Arrive at a false summit on the ridge after about 20min, then drop down to a small saddle and follow the paint marks to the top of **Mt Kita-dake** 北岳 (3193m) – the highest peak in the Japan Alps.

After admiring the panoramic views, continue south along the ridge towards the red-roofed hut sitting 1hr away on a saddle far below. The path drops abruptly with chain-link handrails in places, before reaching a junction for Happonba col. If you're short of time you can turn left here for a shortcut back to base camp and Hirogawara. Otherwise stick to the

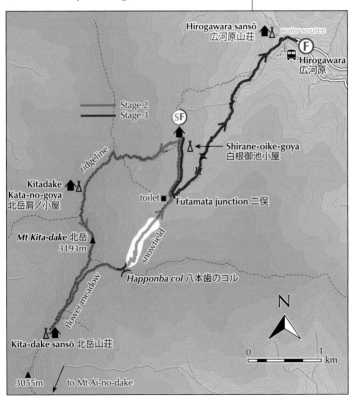

The narrow traverse to Happonba col

trail on the ridge and drop down wooden stairs to a gentler path leading to **Kita-dake sansō** 北岳山荘. This hut is actually on a side-track just off the main ridge, and there you'll find a water source just outside the entrance along with a row of benches offering fantastic views of Mt Fuji across the valley.

Take the trail in front of the hut leading left back towards Kita-dake. The track soon forks, so follow the signpost トラバース道 parallel to the main ridge through a vast **flower meadow** with signs pointing the way to Happonba col 八本歯のコル.

There are several staircases along the exposed path, so watch your footing if wet.

Pass deer-proof netting and scramble over a series of wooden boardwalks and stairways perched on the eastern face of the mountain. Reach a junction below the summit in 45min; turn right and negotiate a large boulder field, heading towards the narrow col. ◄

Turn left at **Happonba col** 八本歯のコル, following the sign for 広河原. This is the steepest part of the descent, with seemingly endless wooden staircases and ladders taking you down below the tree line.

Happonba col is just under the **Kita-dake Buttress**, a popular alpine rock-climbing destination. Look up to spot rock pitons and climbers scaling the near-vertical rock face.

The path terminates at a snow gully, so turn left and follow the coloured tape marks on the left edge of the snowfield, crossing a couple of gullies to reach **Futamata junction** 二俣 in about 1hr. (There are portable toilets here in the summer months.) Continue down the snowfield if returning to Hirogawara today; otherwise head left at the junction for the gentle 30min up-and-down route back to the **Shirane-oike-goya** hut 白根御池小屋.

STAGE 3
Shirane-oike to Hirogawara 白根御池~広河原

Start	Shirane-oike-goya hut 白根御池小屋
Finish	Hirogawara bus stop 広河原
Distance	3km (2 miles)
Total ascent	Negligible
Total descent	715m (2350ft)
Time	3hr
Terrain	A long, rugged descent through forest following a mountain stream
Accommodation	Hut and camping at Hirogawara
Note	Double-check the bus times with the staff before leaving Shirane-oike hut. The first bus usually departs around 8am, so you'll need an early start if you plan on catching it.

From **Shirane-oike-goya hut** 白根御池小屋, retrace your steps back to **Futamata junction** 二俣 by following the trail past the pond. At the junction, turn left and follow the left bank of the river, passing through a field of wildflowers before dropping down a dry river gully to a metal **bridge** spanning the river.

For map, see Stage 2.

Cross the bridge and follow the trail between the main river and a small shallow stream flowing on the right. The track crosses this smaller stream several times before dropping back to another metal **bridge** further downstream. Cross back over to the left bank and walk through an area of slippery wooden and metal planks. After about 20min you'll reach a people counter, then a series of concrete dams, before returning to the junction that was passed on Stage 1. Turn right and retrace your steps back to **Hirogawara sansō** hut and the bus stop across the river.

SHIRANE-SANZAN TRAVERSE

Those hikers with a bit more time on their hands may consider continuing along the ridge past Kita-dake to Mt Ai-no-dake and Mt Nōtori-dake – collectively known as The Shirane Sanzan or 'Three Peaks of the Shirane Mountains'. The tough 18km traverse requires an extra night of accommodation at either 'notorious' Nōtori-goya hut (with its short-tempered hut owner) or Daimonsawa-goya hut located in a lush valley framed by views of Mt Fuji, before terminating at the lovely hot spring baths of Narada.

Instead of doubling back on reaching Kita-dake sansō, continue southwest along the alpine ridge for a steady climb to the summit of Naka-shirane 中白根山 (3055m), followed by a rock scramble and a series of ups and downs to reach Mt Ai-no-dake 間ノ岳 (3189m), Japan's fourth highest mountain.

Take the left fork on the summit, heading south (towards Mt Fuji) for Mt Nōtori 農鳥岳, and drop steeply to a saddle (ignore the trail heading right) before climbing a short distance to Nōtori-goya 農鳥小屋. From the hut, switchback through the dwarf pine for 50min to the summit plateau and sweep left to arrive at Mt Nishi-nōtori-dake 西農鳥岳 (3050m), the highest point on the Nōtori ridge. *If you look left here you can visually retrace your route from Kita-dake and Ai-no-dake.*

Drop down the other side of the summit and continue along the ridge to Mt Nōtori-dake 農鳥岳 (3025m), and then further south to a junction marked by a large yellow tripod structure. Turn left here and drop steeply off the ridge through switchbacks to the tree line. It's a 2hr descent to Daimonsawa-goya hut 大門沢小屋. From here the route follows the river along unstable walkways and log ladders before crossing a series of suspension bridges about 2hr downstream.

Turn left on reaching a forest road and follow it to reach 第一発電所 (Daiichi-hatsudensho) bus stop on the main road. Turn right on the main road for the 40min walk to Narada bus stop. The hot spring bath (open from 8.30am in summer) is a short climb up a hill behind the bus stop.

TREK 10
Mt Hō-ō 鳳凰山

Start	Yashajin-tōge 夜叉神峠
Finish	Hirogawara 広河原
Distance	17km (10½ miles)
Total ascent	1450m (4760ft)
Total descent	1320m (4330ft)
Grade	2 *
Time	2 days
Terrain	A long climb through forest, followed by a tough ridge walk above the tree line over four peaks before dropping to a mountain pass and then a steep descent (some fixed ladders and ropes) to Hirogawara
Access	Bus from Kōfu to Yashajin-tōge. For Hirogawara, see North Alps chapter introduction.
Accommodation	Hut and camping at Minami-omuro (prior booking required for hut). No camping allowed at Yakushi-dake-goya.
Facilities	Water available at Minami-omuro hut. No water at Yakushi-dake-goya or anywhere else on the route.
When to go	Buses operate between late June and early November, with the prime hiking season from July to mid October

Mt Hō-ō (2840m), or the 'Phoenix Mountain', is a scenic ridge of three white sandy granite peaks named after Buddhist deities. There's Mt Yakushi (god of healing), Mt Kannon (goddess of mercy) and Mt Jizō (protector of travellers and children), and each bouldery summit makes a great backdrop for photos.

The mountain is situated on the northeastern edge of the South Alps, nestled up against the Kōfu basin and directly opposite Mt Kita-dake (the second tallest mountain in Japan). Hō-ō's unique location affords unobstructed panoramic views of the entire South Alps, as well as fantastic clear-weather views of Mt Fuji, Yatsu-ga-take, and the North Alps.

The trek described here starts at the Yashajin-tōge trailhead, climbing to the Yashajin pass and then following the ridgeline north. Beyond the hut and campground at Minami-omuro the route ascends rapidly above the tree line to

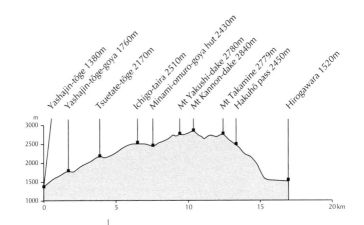

2700m, with plenty of up-and-down across the three summits before turning west to Mt Takamine, from where it's a
knee-knocking descent back below the tree line to the bus
stop at Hirogawara. The rugged landscape is the perfect test-
ing ground for fitness and endurance before attempting some
of the tougher multi-day treks in the area.

STAGE 1
Yashajin-tōge to Minami-omuro-goya
夜叉神峠~南御室小屋

Start	Yashajin-tōge trailhead 夜叉神峠登山口
Finish	Minami-omuro-goya hut 南御室小屋
Distance	7.5km (4¾ miles)
Total ascent	1050m (3445ft)
Total descent	Negligible
Time	5hr 30min
Terrain	A zigzag climb to the Yashajin pass, then a long steady ascent to 2500m with a short optional climb to Tsujiyama, followed by a descent to the hut
Accommodation	Hut and camping at Minami-omuro-goya

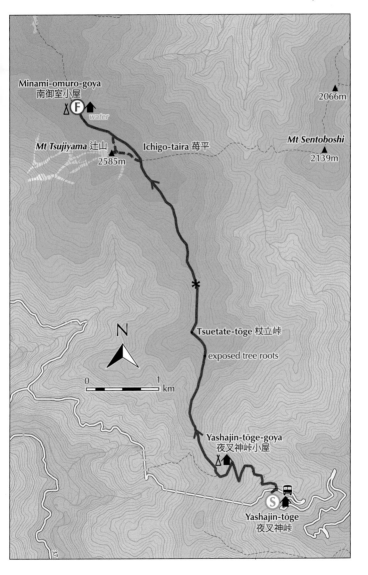

Minami-omuro-goya
南御室小屋
water

Mt Tsujiyama 辻山
2585m

Ichigo-taira 苺平

2066m

Mt Sentoboshi
2139m

N

0   1 km

Tsuetate-tōge 杖立峠

exposed tree roots

Yashajin-tōge-goya
夜叉神峠小屋

Yashajin-tōge
夜叉神峠

A steady climb up the mountain, with wonderful views in places. Prior booking is required if staying at Minami-omuro-goya hut. Campers do not need a reservation.

Exit the bus at **Yashajin-tōge** 夜叉神峠 and walk downhill for a few meters to the trail entrance on the left. Signs point the way to 夜叉神峠 (Yashajin-tōge) through a forest of oak, birch, alder, larch and fir. Climb gentle switchbacks for 1hr to a junction on the ridge and turn right for the short walk to **Yashajin-tōge-goya** 夜叉神峠小屋. The grassy field in front of the mountain hut affords views of the Shirane Sanzan (see Trek 9) in perfect alignment.

Head north away from the hut on the signposted path (Itigotaira•Mt Hō-ō). After 20 metres a trail branches right and ends at two small stone shrines housing the mountain gods of Yashajin; ignore this side-trail and continue north, dropping to a narrow ridge marked with pink tape. The route steepens and passes ancient trees clinging to the crumbly ridge. The wide path is easy to follow, with the grade easing after 30min, and brief views of Mt Fuji to the right. Walk over **exposed tree roots** for a 1hr climb through hardwood forests to the first major mountain pass, **Tsuetate-tōge** 杖立峠

Tolkienesque forests of silver fir

One of the numerous oversized trail markers

(2100m), where there is a large, rusting trail marker resembling a funeral pyre. ▶

Take the path marked for 苺平 (辻山), dropping then climbing gradually over exposed tree roots and moss. The trail steepens in a forest of silver fir, and after 1hr reaches a small clearing with fantastic views of the Shirane Sanzan.

Beyond the clearing, follow the steep trail for 1hr along a dry rocky riverbed. Red paint marks guide you to a junction at the top of a long rise. A trail branches right to Mt Amari 甘利山, but ignore this and carry on for 5min to the pass at **Ichigo-taira** 苺平 (2500m). There is no view here, but there is the option of heading left for 10min on a side-trail (marked by red tape for 辻山) up to Mt Tsujiyama 辻山 (2585m), where there are fantastic vistas of the South Alps. Backtrack and turn left at an unmarked junction just below the peak for a shortcut down to the main trail.

Otherwise simply continue north for a 30min descent to **Minami-omuro-goya** hut 南御室小屋. Just before reaching the hut there is a clearing on the right where people often stand checking their phones. The hut has incredibly low ceilings so take care if you're tall. There is a small campground and plenty of fresh water just right of the hut; this is the only water source on the entire trek.

These mysterious markers can be found throughout the Hō-ō range and were seemingly put up by someone with a lot of money and free time.

STAGE 2

Minami-omuro-goya to Hirogawara 南御室小屋~広河原

Start	Minami-omuro-goya hut 南御室小屋
Finish	Hirogawara bus stop 広河原
Distance	9.5km (5¾ miles)
Total ascent	400m (1310ft)
Total descent	1320m (4330ft)
Time	8hr
Terrain	A steep climb above the tree line and a slippery scramble along a sandy granite ridge before descending through forest (some sections with fixed ladders and ropes) to Hirogawara
Accommodation	Hut and camping at Hirogawara and Hō-ō goya; hut at Yakushi-dake-goya (no camping)

This stage comprises a steep ramble over the multiple distinctive grey-white granite peaks of Mt Hō-ō and then a long descent back to the tree line and Hirogawara. The ridge is one of the most impressive in the entire South Alps, so take your time and enjoy the scenery.

Turn right when heading out of **Minami-omuro-goya hut** 南御室小屋 at the sign for 薬師岳. The well-worn path is heavily eroded and several side-trails run parallel to the main route up the spur. Veer left at a sign that reads 無雪期登山道; this is the snow-free summer route and it meets up with the eroded trail on the crest of the ridge.

The path flattens out in 40min and traverses towards the eastern side of the mountain before reaching a series of **head-high boulders** on the edge of the main summit plateau. Views open up as the path broadens to a wide sandy track of gritty rock. Follow red paint marks and occasional fixed ropes to the unmarked summit of Mt Sunabarai-dake 砂払岳 and the first of many unobstructed views of Mt Fuji to the southeast. Drop quickly on a series of wooden planks to reach a broad saddle and the bright-red roofed hut of **Yakushi-dake-goya** 薬師岳小屋, 1hr from the start. ◄

The hut serves hot drinks and would be a fantastic place to stay if not for the lack of drinking water.

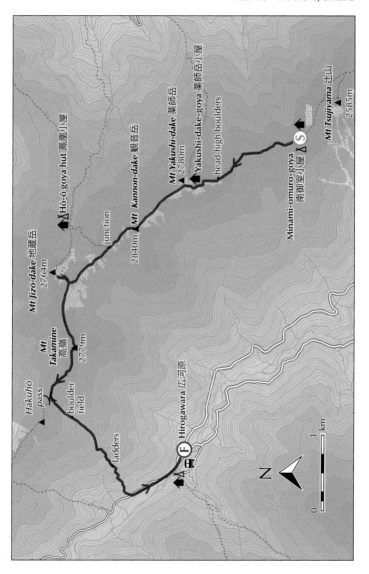

Mt Tsujiyama 辻山
2585m

water S

Minami-omuro-goya 南御室小屋

Yakushi-dake-goya 薬師岳小屋

head-high boulders

Mt Yakushi-dake 薬師岳
2780m

Mt Kannon-dake 観音岳

Hō-ō goya hut 鳳凰小屋

2840m

junction

Mt Jizō-dake 地蔵岳
2764m

Mt Takamine 高嶺
2779m

Hakuhō pass

boulder field

ladders

Hirogawara 広河原

N

0 ____ 1 km

Mt Jizō-dake's obelisk

Just beyond the hut the route broadens out with incredible panoramic views. It's a short climb to **Mt Yakushi-dake** 薬師岳 (2780m), followed by a gentle 40min ascent to the top of **Mt Kannon-dake** 観音岳 (2840m), the highest point on Mt Hō-ō. The summit itself is a rock scramble just off the main ridge and it's best to leave your rucksack at the junction as the top is quite narrow. Look northwest from the summit for views of the whitish pyramid of Mt Kai-koma-ga-take (Walk 8).

Retrace your steps to the junction and continue north between head-high boulders scattered across the ridge, then descend steeply for 30min on slippery sand granite to a broad saddle and **junction** in the forest. Ignore the trail heading right to Hō-ō goya hut, marked with a rusty sign reading 小屋, and stick to the main trail straight ahead.

This rock formation is the unofficial symbol of Mt Hō-ō and is known as the 'obelisk'.

Climb steeply back above the trees and along a narrow, exposed ridge for another 30min. The tall fingerlike pillar of Mt Jizō will soon come into view. ◄ Just before the crest of the ridge a path drops to the right: ignore this and stick to the main rock formations on your left. You will soon reach a junction marked 地蔵岳山頂 10分; take the right fork for the 10min descent to a saddle at the base of the obelisk.

There is a large signpost for **Mt Jizō-dake** 地蔵岳 (2764m) and most hikers take their summit photos here.

However, the true summit lies at the very tip of the obelisk and it requires a bit of rock-climbing skill and a lot of courage. If you're keen to scale the near-vertical rock, follow the scuff marks directly up the southern face to a final climb up the crack between the two highest boulders. Otherwise you can simply rest in its shadow. ▸

Hike to the top of the saddle above the summit signpost to see an impressive collection of stone **jizō statues**. Jizō is a bodhisattva (Buddha) believed to protect children, deceased infants, women and travellers. The statues were placed here by couples wishing to have children.

Retrace your steps south back up to the junction (地蔵岳山頂 10分) on the ridge and turn right at the weather-beaten sign for 白鳳峠 (Hakuhō-tōge). The path turns west towards Mt Kai-koma-ga-take (which is 7hr of tough hiking away). Continue traversing through the narrow sandy granite to reach a saddle below a lush green peak. This is the aptly named Takamine ('tall peak') and is a steep 45min climb through creeping pine. Arrive abruptly at a false summit and continue for another 10min to the narrow true summit of

Famed Englishman Walter Weston claimed the first ascent of Mt Jizō's obelisk back in 1904 in what is regarded as Japan's first recreational rock climb.

The broad ridge of coarse sand granite

Mt Takamine 高嶺 (2779m). This peak is not part of the Hō-ō range but the views are just as superb.

On the summit there is a signpost for 白鳳峠; follow this and quickly lose altitude on what is the steepest section so far, lowering yourself down tall boulders for 30min to reach the tree-covered **Hakuhō pass** at 2450m. There is a new signpost in English mislabeled as 'Hirokawara'; leave the ridge along this trail left.

Enter an immense field of rocks that stretches all the way to the horizon, with fantastic views of Kita-dake directly ahead. Take care hopping from wobbly rock to rock. After losing about 250m of elevation you'll reach a forest of silver fir. Follow markings, and after 20min veer left for a narrow traverse with ropes strewn across exposed drops to the right.

Climb down a series of six steel **ladders** at the edge of a rocky cliff. After the last ladder the trail drops through forest with fixed ropes at trickier sections. In about 10min you'll reach another rock formation adorned with a rotting wooden ladder; drop carefully down and cross a dilapidated log bridge that will hopefully be replaced soon. ◄

Continue traversing the tape-marked track down via log steps and fixed ropes. Bear left to the top of a spur and a series of long switchbacks, and proceed carefully to reach a paved road about 2hr after leaving the Hakuhō pass. Turn left on the road for an easy 15min walk to the visitor centre and bus stop at **Hirogawara** 広河原. If you have time before the next bus, cross the suspension bridge over the river to Hirogawara sansō hut for a curry lunch (served from 11am until 2pm).

Take care on the steel ladders on the descent from Hakuhō pass to Hirogawara.

SOUTH AREA – 南アルプス南部

The entire South Alps ridge (Trek 13) as seen from Mt Hō-ō (Trek 10)

The southern section of the South Alps requires a full day of train and bus travel just to reach the base camp of Sawarajima, where several options await. The Arakawa-Akaishi traverse (Trek 11) is a tough three-day trek that provides outstanding views of Mt Fuji while scaling Japan's sixth and seventh highest peaks. Mt Hijiri (Trek 12) is Japan's southernmost 3000m peak and involves a long approach crossing suspension bridges to the remote Hijiridaira plateau.

Hut bookings are generally not required in this area, with the exception of Akaishi-dake hinan-goya (Treks 11 and 13) and Hijiridaira-goya (Treks 12 and 13), but aim to arrive at the huts by 3pm as dinner is generally served early.

Shizuoka静岡 is the best gateway to the southern section of the South Alps. There's not much to see near the station apart from the ruins of Sunpu Castle, and the lack of budget accommodation is surprising for such a large city. Since the bus to Hatanagi Dai-ichi Dam (for the connecting shuttle bus to Sawarajima) leaves at 9:50am (see below), it may be easier to base yourself in Kyoto or Tokyo and board an early-morning Hikari Shinkansen train instead of staying overnight in Shizuoka.

Sawarajima 椹島 is the start for hikes to Mt Hijiri, Mt Akaishi, and Mt Arakawa (Mt Warusawa). The grass campground here is spectacular and underutilised as most visitors stay at Sawarajima Lodge to qualify for the return shuttle bus back to Hatanagi Dai-ichi Dam. In addition to the campground there is a rest house that serves lunch and sells basic supplies (including rubber trekking pole tip protectors) but there are no ATMs.

Seasonal buses run from Shizuoka to Hatanagi Dai-ichi Dam (3hr, one bus daily from mid July to late August; www.justline.co.jp (English-language option)). The bus leaves at 9:50am from bus stop no.8 at the North Exit of Shizuoka Station. Advanced booking is required one day prior to departure (tel 054-252-0505 or visit the bus ticket office バス案内所 next to bus stop no. 8). Get off at the Rinji-chūshajo bus stop (follow the other hikers) and change to the shuttle bus for Sawarajima (1hr, three buses daily from late April to early November, five buses daily from mid July to late August; www.t-forest.com/alpsinfo/bus (Japanese link)). The shuttle bus fee includes a voucher that can be used for your accommodation at Sawarajima Lodge (or other mountain huts owned by the Tokushu Tokai Paper Company). Be aware that you must stay in one of the mountain huts owned by this company if you want to board the return shuttle bus from Sawarajima back to Hatanagi Dai-ichi Dam (for the connecting bus to Shizuoka). The cheapest accommodation to qualify for the shuttle bus is the Tozan Goya at Sawarajima (no meals). Campers will be refused a ride on the shuttle bus and must walk on the narrow gravel forest road for 18km to reach the bus stop for the Shizuoka bus at Hatanagi Dai-ichi Dam. Private cars are only allowed as far as the Rinji-chūshajo parking lot.

Alternatively you could try to hitch a ride from the Rinji-chūshajo car park back to Shizuoka, or another option is to walk down the road for 45min to Akaishi Onsen Shirakaba-sō (Trek 13). This hot-spring facility is served by local bus to Ikawa Station 井川駅, for infrequent trains to Shizuoka (4hr, multiple transfers involved).

MAPS

Treks 11 and 12 are covered at 1:50,000 by the Yama-to-Kogen (No. 43) Shiomi, Akaishi and Hijiri-dake 塩見・赤石・聖岳 sheet. Trek 13 requires both this sheet and (No. 42) Kita-dake and Kai-koma 北岳・甲斐駒.

TREK 11

Mt Arakawa-Higashidake (Mt Warusawa-dake) and Mt Akaishi-dake 荒川東岳（悪沢岳）～赤石岳

Start/finish	Sawarajima 椹島
Distance	27.5km (17 miles)
Total ascent/descent	3235m (10,620ft)
Grade	3 *
Time	3–4 days (+1 extra day for transport to Sawarajima)
Terrain	Rugged forest paths then a rocky ridge with plenty of elevation gain and loss between two +3100m peaks. Switchbacks and a narrow traverse on wooden stairs down to the tree line, followed by more forest paths.
Access	See South Area chapter introduction
Accommodation	Huts and camping along the way. Take your own sleeping bag for a discount if staying at the mountain huts (no prior booking required, except at Akaishi-dake hinan-goya), and take extra 100 yen coins for tipping at the toilets.
Facilities	Huts sell food, drinks and some mountain goods. Hot coffee is available at Akaishi-dake hinan-goya hut near the summit of Mt Akaishi.
When to go	Aim to go between mid July and late August when the bus is running from Shizuoka. Sawarajima Lodge is open from late April to early November, so those with their own transport can go earlier/later in the season by driving as far as Hatanagi Dai-ichi Dam and taking a shuttle bus to Sawarajima.

This loop is one of the most strenuous routes in the South Alps, but the views of Mt Fuji make the effort worthwhile, especially on Mt Senmai-dake, the closest alpine peak to Mt Fuji (50km away). Access by public transport is long and requires an entire day just to reach the Sawarajima trailhead, thus only the most dedicated hikers are attracted. The route here heads up to the three peaks of Mt Arakawa (3141m, also known as Mt Warusawa), Japan's sixth highest mountain, then drops and regains 500m of vertical elevation to reach Mt Akaishi (3120m), a peak famous for its sedimentary deposits of red chert. The 'mountain' day (Stage 2) is particularly long

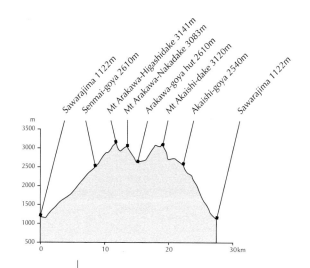

Mt Arakawa-Nakadake (right) and Mt Akaishi (left) (Stage 2)

and demanding and a very early start is required in order to avoid being caught in thunderstorms, although the stage can be broken up by staying at Arakawa-goya. The trek ends with

268

a long descent back down to the tree line and Sawarajima for the long bus ride to Shizuoka.

When boarding the bus from Shizuoka you will receive a paper to register your hiking plans (*tozantodoke* in Japanese). Fill it out and give it to the bus staff. Submit another form (*gezantodoke* in Japanese) on your safe return if asked.

STAGE 1
Sawarajima to Senmai-goya 椹島~千枚小屋

Start	Sawarajima Lodge 椹島ロッジ
Finish	Senmai-goya hut 千枚小屋
Distance	9.5km (5¾ miles)
Total ascent	1620m (5310ft)
Total descent	135m (450ft)
Time	6hr 30min
Terrain	A long steady climb through deciduous woodland then planted forests of pine and fir above 2000m
Accommodation	Huts and camping at Sawarajima and Senmai-goya hut

The day starts at Sawarajima (elevation 1122m) and it is a long, steady climb to Senmai-goya (elevation 2610m) at the edge of the tree line. The route is well marked with red paint and waymarks at roughly every 200 vertical metres. Daily thunderstorms usually roll in around 3pm, so start early to avoid being caught in the rain. It is a steady hike through verdant forest and past a picturesque pond before reaching a field of wildflowers just before the hut.

Walk on the gravel road through **Sawarajima**, keeping the rest house and campground on your right. Note a metal sign that reads 赤石岳・千枚岳 (Akaishi-dake, Senmai-dake) in white, and continue straight to enter the forest through a shrine gate on your right.

Follow switchbacks up to a gravel road and in a few minutes turn right towards a green metal bridge spanning the river. At the bridge, look left to see a sign for 千枚岳登山口 (Senmai-dake Tozanguchi), and turn left onto the track

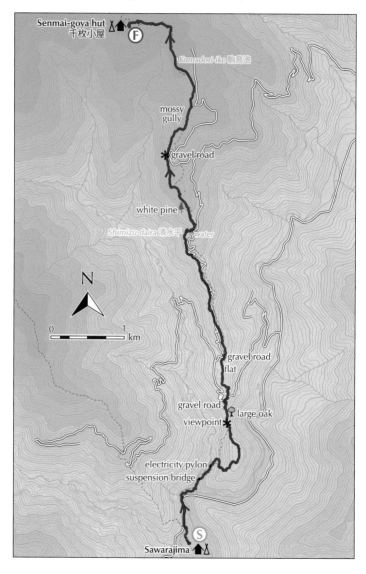

Senmai-goya hut
千枚小屋 **F**

Komadori-ike 駒鳥池

mossy gully

* gravel road

white pine

Shimizu-daira 清水平 water

N

0   1
km

gravel road
flat

gravel road
* large oak
viewpoint *

electricity pylon
suspension bridge

S

Sawarajima

to cross metal bridges on a narrow traverse to a **suspension bridge**. Cross and drift left, following red paint marks through a rocky forest of birch, beech and rhododendrons, to reach an electricity pylon after roughly 1hr – a good place to rest.

Beyond the pylon follow the sign for 千枚小屋 (Senmai-goya) and navigate a thin spur of rock before reaching a drop on the right. The path straight along the ridge is blocked off, so skirt right down a fixed rope and back to the spur to a small **viewpoint** marked 岩頭 (Iwakashira). ▶

Continue along the track past a **large oak** tree (ミズナラ) to arrive at a **gravel road**. Turn right on the road and then left up a metal staircase signposted 千枚小屋 (Senmai-goya). The route is now clearly marked in sections from 1 to 7, with the final waymark just before Senmai-goya hut.

Enter the forest of beech trees, passing a sign marked '2/7 標高 1500m' (elevation 1500m), and proceed along a **flat** section to a large wooden post that indicates 4hr 30min to Senmai-goya (千枚小屋 4 時間 3 0 分). Continue straight for 10min before reaching a **gravel road**. Cross the road and re-enter forest of pine, hemlock and birch trees for a steady 1hr 30min climb to a rest spot with a water source at 1900m called **Shimizu-daira** 清水平.

Follow red paint marks through a broad strand of **white pine** trees. ▶ After passing through a flattened area called 蕨段 (Warabidan) dotted with large birch and rowan trees, you will reach the halfway point, signposted as 千枚小屋 3 時間 (3hr to Senmai-goya). From here it is a short climb to an unmarked junction with a trail to the right; take this side

Through a gap in the trees you can see to the northwest the ridge that you will traverse the next day.

The path is usually blanketed in pine needles, making for a pleasant, soft ascent.

Mossy forests of white pine and fir

Sections of white pine and silver fir trees on the approach were planted for pulp cultivation.

The hut has been completely destroyed by fire on two occasions. It was rebuilt in 2012 and is one of the nicer huts in the South Alps.

trail and climb to the gravel road for a **viewpoint** of both Mt Akaishi and Mt Arakawa/Warusawa. ◄

Return to the main track and continue into pine and fir forest and then ascend a **mossy gully**. Paint marks lead the way to a flat area with a side-path branching right; drop your rucksack at the signpost and descend this path for 1min to reach **Komadori-ike** 駒鳥池 – a small, pretty pond surrounded by moss.

From the pond, retrace your steps and turn right up the main path over loose rocks and tree roots. Ignore a side-trail to 管理道路 (Kanri-doro – leading to a gravel access road for hut workers) and keep straight to cross a field of yellow ragwort and purple Japanese monkshood wildflowers. Continue for 30min to reach the relatively new **Senmai-goya** hut 千枚小屋. ◄

STAGE 2
Senmai-goya to Akaishi-goya 千枚小屋~赤石小屋

Start	Senmai-goya hut 千枚小屋
Finish	Akaishi-goya hut 赤石小屋
Distance	13.5km (8¼ miles)
Total ascent	1565m (5140ft)
Total descent	1625m (5330ft)
Time	11hr 30min
Terrain	Rocky alpine terrain, passing wildflowers and creeping pine. The path is mostly above the tree line with exposed sections and wooden bridges.
Accommodation	Huts and camping at Senmai-goya, Arakawa-goya and Akaishi-goya huts

This is one of the toughest sections of the South Alps and involves an ascent of two 3100m high peaks, with a 500m vertical drop and climb sandwiched between. However, your hard work will be rewarded with unobstructed views of Mt Fuji for the entire day in breathtaking alpine scenery that feels very remote. Those who prefer to take their time could consider breaking this long stage in half by staying at Arakawa-goya.

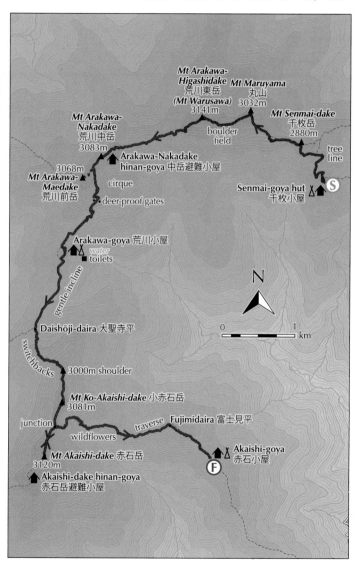

Mt Arakawa-Higashidake
荒川東岳
(Mt Warusawa)
3141m

Mt Maruyama
丸山
3032m

Mt Arakawa-Nakadake
荒川中岳
3083m

Mt Senmai-dake
千枚岳
2880m

boulder field

tree line

3068m

Arakawa-Nakadake hinan-goya 中岳避難小屋

Mt Arakawa-Maedake
荒川前岳

cirque

Senmai-goya hut
千枚小屋

S

deer-proof gates

Arakawa-goya 荒川小屋

water
toilets

N

0   1
km

Daishōji-daira 大聖寺平

gentle incline

switchbacks

3000m shoulder

Mt Ko-Akaishi-dake 小赤石岳
3081m

junction

traverse

Fujimidaira 富士見平

wildflowers

Akaishi-goya
赤石小屋

F

Mt Akaishi-dake 赤石岳
3120m

Akaishi-dake hinan-goya
赤石岳避難小屋

The view of Mt Fuji from Mt Senmai-dake

Aim to leave by 4am in order to avoid being caught out in afternoon thunderstorms.

◀ Exit **Senmai-goya hut** 千枚小屋 and turn left at a signpost for Arakawa-Nakadake Shelter, then follow switchbacks for 30min up to a junction at the edge of the tree line. Follow the track left, signed for 千枚岳 (Senmai-dake), and pass through a birch grove dotted with starwort and creeping sibbaldia flowers, with views left across the valley to Mt Fuji. After reaching creeping pine, turn and ascend for 20min via rocky zigzags to the top of **Mt Senmai-dake** 千枚岳 (2880m) for panoramic alpine vistas.

Ignore the track to your right for 二軒小屋 and stay left for 荒川三山 (Arakawa-sanzan) along a rocky ridge trail, passing colourful wildflowers. The path skirts just below the main ridge before dropping steeply to a saddle. Follow the paint marks through a short, exposed section to a **col** and then navigate rocky switchbacks for 45min to arrive at the summit of **Mt Maruyama** 丸山 (3032m).

Views out towards Mt Akaishi dominate to the left, with the red roof of Arakawa-goya hut visible in a col below.

Continue west, heading gently down to a saddle, and navigate a boulder field painted with red circles and arrows. ◀ Scramble over large boulders and past red chert for 20min to **Mt Arakawa-Higashidake** 荒川東岳 (3141m), the first and highest of Arakawa's three peaks. This summit is also known as Mt Warusawa-dake 悪沢岳, and has splendid panoramic views.

Continue west for a steep 200m zigzagging descent to a **saddle**, and then a steady 40min climb to **Arakawa-Nakadake hinan-goya** 中岳避難小屋, a basic hut offering accommodation without meals or water. The trail continues to the right of the hut, past roped-off sections to protect the wildflowers. You will soon reach **Mt Arakawa-Nakadake** 荒川中岳 (3083m), from where the route drops to a three-way junction. You can leave your rucksack here (but take valuables with you) for the optional 20min return climb to **Mt Arakawa-Maedake** 荒川前岳 (3068m), or to omit the climb just head left at the weathered signpost for 荒川小屋・赤石岳.

The onward path skirts past a glacial **cirque** dotted with wildflowers. Pass through two **deer-proof gates** and follow steep switchbacks through meadows, then continue descending towards the mountain hut that should now come into view. It is a long and sometimes steep path, passing an unreliable water source and dropping over 400m to reach **Arakawa-goya** hut 荒川小屋 in 1hr 30min.

Here you should make a decision about whether to carry on, based on your fitness and time. If it's before 9am then you're in good time to reach Akaishi-goya before the weather turns. If not, consider staying at the hut and breaking the stage in two. Lunch is served from 9am and there is a toilet (tip required) and a water source.

A deer-proof gate protects the wildflowers

To continue, walk towards the toilets and turn right at the painted sign for 赤石岳 (Akaishi-dake). Climb a short distance through birch then follow a **gentle incline** for 40min to the 大聖寺平 (**Daishōji-daira**) saddle. Here turn left, taking care not to follow the trail that drops west off the ridge. The path soon reaches a large stone cairn, steepening through an area of loose rock. Follow the **switchbacks** for 30min to reach the **summit shoulder** at 3000m, flanked by a mound of red chert boulders and lots of creeping pine.

Turn south along the ridge for 15min, passing sprinkles of white bistort and purple dwarf bellflowers to reach **Mt Ko-Akaishi-dake** 小赤石岳 (3081m). ◀ From the summit, drop to a trail branching left for 赤石小屋 (Akaishi-goya). You can leave your rucksack here (but take your valuables) as you'll need to return to this junction after climbing the main summit.

In good weather you can see the summit of Akaishi directly in front of you across a small saddle.

Continue along the summit ridge, following orange paint marks on the rocks and keeping an eye out for birds such as the alpine accentor, ptarmigan and spotted nutcracker. You will reach the top of **Mt Akaishi-dake** 赤石岳 (3120m) in about 20min; it is marked by a large signpost and affords excellent views of Mt Hijiri to the south. There is a small refuge hut (**Akaishi-dake hinan-goya**) just below the summit offering accommodation (advanced booking required) and the highest fresh-drip coffee in the Japan Alps.

Return to the junction and head right (east) off the summit and down along a series of steep switchbacks, following a stream towards a gully. The route is lined with colourful **wildflowers**, and it loses around 400m of elevation to reach the bottom of a col.

Cross a pair of small streams and ascend the fixed rope for a narrow **traverse** on wooden bridges and ladders rising above a ravine. Some 40min from the col, reach the **Fujimidaira** 富士見平 plateau for views of Mt Fuji and Mt Akaishi. ◀ Head southeast beyond the far side of the viewpoint through a maze of creeping pine for a steep descent through a forest of hemlock, beech and silver fir to reach **Akaishi-goya** hut 赤石小屋 in 30min. The hut's helipad affords views of Mt Akaishi, Mt Arakawa/Warusawa and Mt Hijiri. (Double-check the shuttle bus schedule at Akaishi-goya hut before setting out on Stage 3 as the bus service is infrequent.)

This viewpoint is often misty in the afternoon, so if you have the energy consider returning here for sunrise.

STAGE 3
Akaishi-goya to Sawarajima 赤石小屋~椹島

Start	Akaishi-goya hut 赤石小屋
Finish	Sawarajima Lodge 椹島
Distance	4.5km (3 miles)
Total ascent	50m (165ft)
Total descent	1475m (4840ft)
Time	2hr 30min
Terrain	Steep path through forests of beech, hemlock, fir, oak and cypress
Accommodation	Huts and camping at Sawarajima

This final day involves a short but steep descent back to Sawarajima to complete the loop. If you are keen on a hot spring bath, then start very early and aim to arrive at Sawarajima in time for the first shuttle bus to Rinji-chūshajo, then walk south along the road for 45min to Akaishi Onsen Shirakabasō. The bath house opens at 10am and also serves lunch, making it a great place to relax as the bus to Shizuoka (booking required) also stops here.

Head southeast from **Akaishi-goya hut** 赤石小屋 through a **mossy forest** of beech, hemlock, and fir with views out to Mt Akaishi and Mt Hijiri through gaps in the trees. Follow the pink tape and clamber over tree roots and large rocks to a painted '30' sign (indicating 30min to Akaishi-goya). Descend along the rocky trail, passing a field of baneberry flowers and bearded lichen hanging from trees to the left.

The gradient steepens to reach a flat area 歩荷返し (**Hokkakaeshi**) before once again dropping along a series of switchbacks. Continue for about 1hr to reach a **flat** area and signpost for 椹島ロッジ (Sawarajima Lodge, 90 minutes). This is a good resting point at about 2000m, but there is still almost 1000m of descent remaining. ▶

Zigzag past a sign warning of **hornets** (ハチ注意) and down to a flat area called **kanbadan** 樺段, then continue straight among large birch trees and along a couple of metal walkways to reach a **dirt road**. Cross it and follow the pink

Japanese hornets (*suzumebachi*) found here can be aggressive and are attracted to the colour black. Avoid aggravating them as stings can require medical attention.

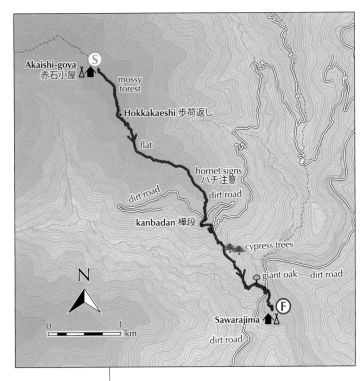

tape to wind through a forest of Sawara **cypress trees**, from which Sawarajima derives its name.

Soon pass by a **giant oak** tree (ミズナラ) and turn onto a long steel staircase to arrive at the gravel forest road you started on two days ago. Turn left and then quickly right for the **Sawarajima** rest house, from where the shuttle bus departs. You will need to show your hut accommodation receipt to the staff in order to receive a numbered ticket that allows boarding for the shuttle bus to Hatanagi Dai-ichi Dam.

Mt Kamikōchi-dake and Mt Hijiri-dake
上河内岳〜聖岳

Start/finish	Hijiri-dake tozanguchi 聖岳登山口
Distance	30km (18½ miles) including Mt Kamikōchi or 21km (13 miles)
Total ascent/descent	2970m (9745ft) including Mt Kamikōchi or 2390m (7840ft)
Grade	3
Time	2 or 3 days (+ 1 extra day for transport to Sawarajima)
Terrain	Forested path followed by a long climb with fixed ropes, steel suspension bridges and wooden log planks in places. Rocky trail through creeping pine and wildflower meadows above the tree line.
Access	See South Area chapter introduction: Hijiri-dake tozanguchi is on the shuttle bus route between Hatanagi Dai-ichi Dam and Sawarajima. At the end of the trek there are shuttle buses (advanced booking only) to Hatanagi Dai-ichi Dam (and the hot spring at Shirakaba-sō). Register for the shuttle bus when you make a phone booking for Hijiridaira-goya hut. Campers will be refused boarding. Those without a shuttle bus booking could walk back to Sawarajima and board their shuttle bus (only for those who stayed at Sawarajima Lodge before starting the hike). Another option is to walk south along the gravel road for 5hr (18km) to Akaishi Onsen Shirakaba-sō which has a hot spring and is served by local bus to Ikawa Station 井川駅, for infrequent trains to Shizuoka.
Accommodation	Hut and camping at Hijiridaira-goya (advanced booking required) and Sawarajima. Take your own sleeping bag for a discount to stay in Hijiridaira-goya hut.
Facilities	Huts sell food, drinks and some mountain goods.
When to go	Aim to go between mid July and late August when the bus is running from Shizuoka. Sawarajima Lodge is open from late April to early November, so those with their own transport can go earlier/later in the season by driving as far as Hatanagi Dai-ichi Dam and taking a shuttle bus to Sawarajima. Hijiridaira-goya hut is only open from mid July to mid September.

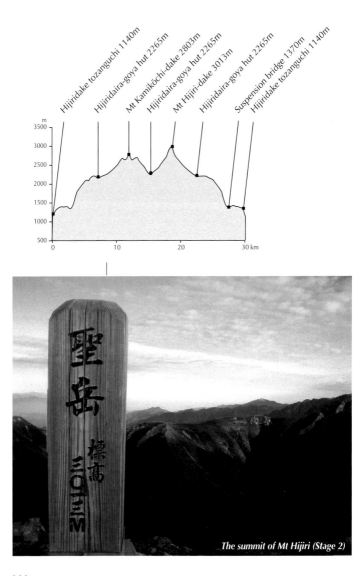

The summit of Mt Hijiri (Stage 2)

Mt Hijiri (3013m) is the southernmost 3000m peak in Japan and one of the most remote, attracting only a fraction of the hikers found in other parts of the South Alps. The route described here is a variation of sorts, with a warm-up climb to the summit of Mt Kamikōchi (2803m, not to be confused with Kamikōchi in the North Alps) before the big climb to Mt Hijiri and the long walk back to the trailhead. The trek can easily be extended to three days by staying two nights at Hijiridaira-goya hut, a lovely spot on a broad saddle between the two mountains.

When boarding the bus from Shizuoka you will receive a paper to register your hiking plans (*tozantodoke* in Japanese). Submit it to bus staff. At the trailhead at the end of Stage 2 you will receive another form proving that you have safely descended (*gezantodoke* in Japanese). Shizuoka Prefecture is pretty strict about this, so follow the guidelines and ask other hikers for assistance with the Japanese form if necessary.

STAGE 1

Hijiridake tozanguchi to Hijiridaira-goya via
Mt Kamikōchi-dake 聖岳登山口~上河内岳~聖平小屋

Start	Hijiridake tozanguchi 聖岳登山口
Finish	Hijiridaira-goya hut 聖平小屋
Distance	14.5km (9 miles) including Mt Kamikōchi or 5.5km (3½ miles)
Total ascent	1990m (6530ft) including Mt Kamikōchi or 1410m (4625ft)
Total descent	1005m (3295ft) including Mt Kamikōchi or 425m (1395ft)
Time	9hr including Mt Kamikōchi or 5hr
Terrain	A path through planted spruce and cedar forests and natural woodland, followed by an exposed traverse on suspension bridges, fixed ropes and log planks, ending with a short riverside walk. Steep rocky alpine terrain above the tree line.
Accommodation	Huts and camping at Hijiridaira-goya

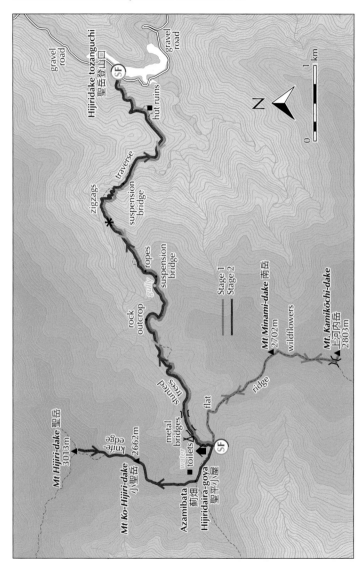

This is a strenuous day involving a long approach above a river gorge to reach the alpine plateau of Hijiridaira. The route features log planks, fixed ropes and suspension bridges along a well-marked trail. A very early start will allow time for the optional ascent of Mt Kamikōchi, one of the quietest and most isolated peaks in the Japan Alps. Stay at Sawarajima Lodge the previous night and aim to catch the 6.15am shuttle bus from there to the trailhead, or walk south along the road for 40min (2.5km) if you would like an earlier start.

From the shuttle bus stop at **Hijiridake tozanguchi** 聖岳登山口, take the track that runs perpendicular to the gravel road, marked for 聖岳 (Hijiridake), and zigzag steeply through cedar forest to reach a spur. Continue west with occasional views of the Hatanagi lake on your left, following red and yellow markings to reach forestry **hut ruins** after 30min, with a sign indicating 290 minutes to Hijiridaira hut.

Follow the sign and soon reach a metal bridge across a small stream; you can fill up on water here before crossing the bridge and climbing a gentle incline through spruce trees planted in the 1960s for pulp production. The path soon swings abruptly right (southwest) and drops through a cedar grove giving way to beech, hemlock and fir trees. Begin a

A suspension bridge spanning the river

long and narrow **traverse** along metal planks, fixed ropes and construction scaffolding, then cross a swaying **suspension bridge** after 45min.

Veer right and ascend **zigzags** to gain altitude quickly in a mossy forest of beech, oak and hemlock. Follow the markings around an exposed cliff face to reach the top of the spur and a nice flat area with a sign in English indicating 160 minutes to Hijiridaira hut.

Continue along a flatter section marked with red tape, passing through a grove of rhododendrons and walking up to a small **viewpoint**. You will need to negotiate an old log walkway and skirt past a landslide as the trail turns left, then zigzag further up the spur with occasional views to Mt Hijiri across a steep gorge to the right. At a recently washed-out section of trail, turn sharply left, clambering over tree roots aided by **ropes** to reach another **suspension bridge** (elevation 2000m) 50min after leaving the viewpoint. ◄

Cross the bridge and navigate loose scree on the eroding path, with fixed ropes and metal bridges at tricky sections. Drop to a rocky **gully** (fill up on water if necessary), cross the stream and turn left, then follow paint marks through an area of abundant Stellaria, Japanese meadowsweet and summer ragwort wildflowers.

After passing through another gully, climb fixed ropes and pass over tree roots to reach a viewpoint in 20min, overlooking a large waterfall on the right. From here continue along an old section of track with rotting log bridges to another waypoint. Beyond this, find a **rock outcrop** with views straight down into the Hijirisawa gorge. ◄

Continue straight along a rocky path past more wildflowers, cross a small stream and climb up and over a short spur before dropping quickly on fixed ropes to reach the river seen from the viewpoint above. Cross the metal bridge and turn left upstream, following the right river bank, and go straight through a forest of **stunted trees** to reach another bridge. Cross the bridge and turn right to navigate across a large landslide to a gentler path on red chert.

> Red chert is predominant throughout the southern part of the South Alps which gives the mountains their red appearance. The range is also called the Akaishi Sanmyaku (**red rock mountains**).

The suspension bridges on the route sway heavily, so take care and cross one at a time.

A stone plaque commemorates a mountaineer who perished here back in 1970.

Cross another metal bridge and pass a few tent spots. A final bridge soon leads to **Hijiridaira-goya** hut 聖平小屋 at 2264m. Enjoy the complementary fruit punch at check-in. Lunch is served from 10am to 2pm, so you can take a rest before the optional afternoon climb to Mt Kamikōchi.

Optional climb to Mt Kamikōchi-dake 上河内岳

This is a highly recommended return hike to Mt Kamikōchi, a quiet peak offering refreshing solitude and outstanding views of Mt Fuji and Mt Hijiri, along with a chance to acclimatise before the long climb to 3000m the following morning. You'll need to allow 4–5hr for the return journey, so make sure you depart the hut by 1pm to return before dark.

Turn right out of the hut and into the forest to reach a pleasant path on wooden planks. ▶ Continue to the end of the boardwalks and turn left on the heavily eroded zigzags, ascending to the top of a spur which flattens out after 30min. Steadily climb southeast through dwarf pine and birch, passing above the tree line to the ridge. The route now veers left and follows switchbacks, reaching the top of **Mt Minami-dake** 南岳 (2702m) for panoramic views after another 40mins.

Descend steeply to a col and follow the undulating ridge, which is dotted with **wildflowers**. Enter a broad gully

Fog usually settles here quite early each day but you will likely rise above the cloud at the 2600m tree line.

Mt Kamikōchi

and ascend steadily to a saddle (上河内岳肩 – Kamikōchi-dake kata) where you can drop your rucksack and turn left for a short climb to the top of **Mt Kamikōchi-dake** 上河内岳 (2803m) and more panoramic vistas. Return the same way to **Hijiridaira-goya**.

STAGE 2

Hijiridaira-goya hut to Hijiridake tozanguchi
聖平小屋~聖岳登山口

Start	Hijiridaira-goya hut 聖平小屋
Finish	Hijiridake tozanguchi 聖岳登山口
Distance	15.5km (9½ miles)
Total ascent	980m (3215ft)
Total descent	1965m (6445ft)
Time	9hr
Terrain	Sub-alpine forests, a short knife-edge ridge and long switchbacks to the summit. A long descent on wooden/metal planks, fixed ropes, and suspension bridges through forest.
Accommodation	Huts and camping at Hijiridaira-goya hut

An up-and-back ascent of Japan's southernmost 3000m peak, then retracing the route described in Stage 1. Make sure to start early in order to make the 1pm shuttle bus (advanced booking required) to Hatanagi Dai-ichi Dam. If you're fast then you can make the earlier 10am shuttle bus from the trailhead to Shirakaba-sō hot spring and the connecting bus to Ikawa/Shizuoka, although a more comfortable option might be to stay an additional night at Hijiridaira-goya hut after summiting Mt Hijiri-dake and then leave early the following morning for the 5–6hr return hike to Hijiridake tozanguchi.

For map, see Stage 1.

You can leave most of your things in the annex next to the main building at **Hijiridaira-goya hut** 聖平小屋 to lighten your load. Then turn right out of the hut and follow the path across the wooden boardwalks to a junction. Turn right on the path marked for 'Mt Hijiri-dake (160 minutes)' and pass through fields of white bistort and purple bellflowers lined

Wooden boardwalks lead the way from Hijiridaira-goya hut

with deer-proof fences, to reach a junction in 20min (薊畑 – **Azamibata**).

Turn right and climb steeply through more wildflower fields, then through birch forest along a muddy track. Ascend fixed rope and switchbacks on a rocky path to a ridge and the first sight of the summit, then veer right and zigzag across scree to **Mt Ko-Hijiri-dake** 小聖岳 (2662m), reached in 1hr from the junction and marked by a weather-beaten signpost.

Descend to a small saddle for the start of a **knife-edge traverse**, and then pick your way carefully along the undulating trail, avoiding the near-vertical drops to the left. Beyond here, zigzag up the southern face of the mountain for about 50min to reach the summit of **Mt Hijiri-dake** 聖岳 (3013m). ▶

Retrace your steps back to **Hijiridaira-goya** hut and pick up your rucksack. The return to the trailhead follows the same route as Stage 1 and should take 5–6hr. Consider staying an extra night in the hut if you don't have enough time to catch the 1pm shuttle bus.

The view from the top is spectacular, as it looks directly across a deep valley to Mt Akaishi and further afield to the Central and North Alps and Mt Fuji.

TREK 13
South Alps traverse 南アルプス縦走

Start	Hirogawara 広河原
Finish	Akaishi Onsen Shirakaba-sō hot spring 赤石温泉白樺荘
Distance	97km (60½ miles) or 77.5km (48½ miles) omitting Stage 7
Total ascent	9775m (32,070ft) or 7835m (25,705ft) omitting Stage 7
Total descent	10,490m (35,070ft) or 8550m (28,705ft) omitting Stage 7
Grade	3+ *
Time	7 or 8 days
Terrain	Rugged well-travelled paths with lots of ups and downs. Rocky terrain of loose scree and chert, mostly staying above 2400m all the way until the final day. Some narrow and exposed sections but nothing overly technical or challenging, and some steeper parts are aided with fixed ropes or handrails. Sometimes muddy conditions.
Access	See South Area chapter introduction. From the end of the trek, there is a bus to Shizuoka (one bus daily, advanced booking required) or Ikawa (two buses daily, infrequent trains to Shizuoka via Senzu and Kanaya). Double-check the bus times before leaving the hut and consider staying at Shirakaba-sō to make the long journey back to Shizuoka easier. Hitchhiking from the road in front of Shirakaba-sō is also an option, as other hikers are usually willing to give fellow trekkers a lift.
Accommodation	Huts and camping at start and finish and at regular intervals along the route
Facilities	Water, other drinks and snacks available at most mountain huts
When to go	Mid July to late August is the best time to hike, as all of the huts are open and the buses are running. Expect daily afternoon thunderstorms and dense fog from mid morning.

This full-length traverse of the entire South Alps is Japan's toughest yet most rewarding multi-day hike. After climbing into the alpine zone you will enjoy an entire week of near-constant views of Mt Fuji's perfect cone floating above a sea of clouds just across the valley, abundant wildflowers and the range's distinctive red chert rock. The route stretches for nearly 100km, climbing up and over six different 3000m peaks with significant elevation losses between each one due to the steep drops back below the tree line. Many huts along the route require advanced booking, making prior planning crucial for those relying on huts. Campers have more flexibility as bookings are not needed for tents.

This trek should only be attempted by those with hiking experience and excellent fitness, as the days are long and the terrain is steep. There is an escape route at roughly the halfway point of the traverse if necessary. It rains nearly every day in the summer, so early starts are essential in order to avoid being caught out in the mid-afternoon deluges.

The trek starts at Hirogawara and heads south up Kita-dake and Ai-no-dake (Japan's second and fourth tallest peaks) and follows the ridge over Mt Shiomi to Sanpuku-tōge, the dividing line of the north and south areas of the South Alps. From here it is a long climb over a tough stretch between Mt Arakawa and Mt Hijiri before reaching Mt Chausu. An optional stage leads to Mt Tekari – the southernmost point in the world for creeping pine and ptarmigan – and then the

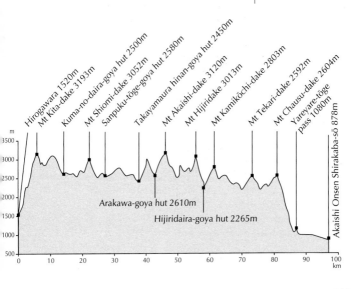

289

Red chert and greenstone are found throughout the South Alps (Stage 6)

route descends back to the valley and finishes at a hot spring where you can enjoy a well-deserved bath!

Yama-to-Kōgen's 'Japan Alps Overview' map (1:150,000 Nihon Arupusu sōzu 日本アルプス総図 – No. 34) covers the entire route (and every hike in this book apart from the Mt Fuji area walks), although it is large scale and so the individual area maps are recommended.

STAGE 1
Hirogawara to Kitadake Kata-no-goya
広河原~北岳肩ノ小屋

Start	Hirogawara 広河原
Finish	Kitadake Kata-no-goya hut 北岳肩ノ小屋
Distance	5.5km (3½ miles)
Total ascent	1650m (5410ft)
Total descent	290m (950ft)
Time	6hr
Terrain	A steady climb through forest, then steeply up to a rough rocky ridge below summit
Accommodation	Huts (advanced booking required) and camping near the trailhead and at Shirane-oike and Kitadake Kata-no-goya hut

This stage follows the same route as the start of the Mt Kita-dake trek (Trek 10), with almost 1500m of elevation gain, climbing through three different forest zones to rise above the tree line and ascending to Kata-no-goya hut at 3000m. Sunsets and views of Mt Fuji here are some of the best in the Alps. Note that bookings at Kata-no-goya hut are essential on weekends if you plan on staying in the hut. Tent spaces soon fill up so an early start is recommended. Pick up a free copy of the English-language *Road to the Minami-Alps* pamphlet from the information centre at Hirogawara before setting off; it includes a handy pocket map of Stage 1.

From the bus stop at **Hirogawara** 広河原 head northwest on the paved road between the river and information centre, then turn left at the fork in the road and pass a log building and a gate across the road. Just past the gate, drop down left to a suspension bridge, cross it and turn right to reach **Hirogawara sansō** 広河原山荘.

From the hut take the trail marked for Ōkanbasawa 大樺沢. You'll soon see an English sign for Shirane-oike 白根御池, followed by another sign at a junction for Mt Kita-dake. The well-marked path meanders for 15min through a forest of beech, fir, oak and hemlock to reach a junction. Take the right branch marked for 白根御池 (Shirane-oike)

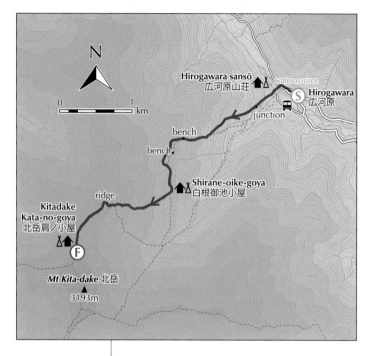

and follow the very steep spur over exposed tree roots and through green ferns. There are wooden ladders and steps on the steeper parts.

After about 1hr of relentless climbing you'll reach a wooden bench. Pass a second wooden bench 30min later as the angle finally starts to ease at roughly 2000m, then veer left for a relatively flat traverse, passing a wooden signpost indicating that Shirane-oike-goya is 20min away (白根御池小屋まであと 2 0 分です). Follow the path across wooden bridges to **Shirane-oike-goya** 白根御池小屋. Water and lunch are available at the hut and Shirane-oike pond nearby has reflections of Kita-dake.

The trail passes through fields of wild plants and purple flowers with views to the pond and Mt Hō-ō directly behind.

At a junction just past the hut, take the right fork marked Kata-no-goya 肩の小屋・北岳山頂. ◀ After 1hr 30min, pass through an open area of rocks at the edge of the tree line, then veer right to a vast field of wildflowers lined with deer-proof fencing. Just above this clearing, turn right at the junction and climb for 20min to the ridgeline for the first of many views of Mt Fuji to the southeast.

Turn left on the **ridge** and follow the well-trodden path towards the summit massif, skirting over a small pinnacle aided by fixed rope and painted red arrows before reaching **Kitadake Kata-no-goya** 北岳肩ノ小屋 in 20min. Here you can select a tent spot or check in at the hut.

STAGE 2

Kitadake Kata-no-goya to Kuma-no-daira-goya
北岳肩ノ小屋~熊ノ平小屋

Start	Kitadake Kata-no-goya hut 北岳肩ノ小屋
Finish	Kuma-no-daira-goya hut 熊ノ平小屋
Distance	8km (5 miles)
Total ascent	850m (2790ft)
Total descent	1020m (3350ft)
Time	6hr
Terrain	Steep, rocky alpine terrain dotted with fields of wildflowers
Accommodation	Camping and accommodation at Kitadake sansō and Kuma-no-daira huts
Note	Carry plenty of water, wear sunscreen, and be wary of afternoon thunderstorms and mist

This stage is spent mostly above the tree line, with unobstructed views of Mt Fuji across the Kofū Basin on your left, and of the Central Alps across Ina Valley on your right. The day begins with an ascent of Kita-dake, Japan's second tallest peak, and continues along a rocky alpine ridge to the top of Ai-no-dake, just 3m lower and Japan's fourth highest mountain. The route then veers west over the summit of Mt Mibu and drops back to the tree line at the idyllic Kuma-no-daira hut and campgound.

Take the path left of **Kitadake Kata-no-goya hut** 北岳肩ノ小屋 and follow the ridge of dwarf pine and loose stones towards the summit plateau, using handrails and fixed rope on steeper sections. At the top of the first major pinnacle turn

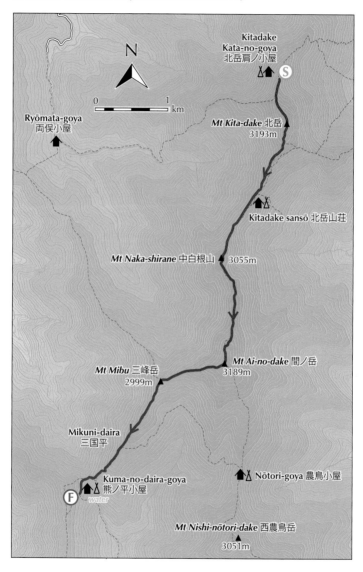

N

0 ____ 1 km

Kitadake
Kata-no-goya
北岳肩ノ小屋   **S**

Ryōmata-goya
両俣小屋

Mt Kita-dake 北岳
3193m

Kitadake sansō 北岳山荘

Mt Naka-shirane 中白根山   3055m

Mt Mibu 三峰岳
2999m

Mt Ai-no-dake 間ノ岳
3189m

Mikuni-daira
三国平

Kuma-no-daira-goya
熊ノ平小屋
F   water

Nōtori-goya 農鳥小屋

Mt Nishi-nōtori-dake 西農鳥岳
3051m

*Mt Ai-no-dake with
Mt Shiomi behind*

left at the signpost for Kitadake sanchō 北岳山頂, taking care
not to descend off the ridge on the trail for Ryōmata-goya 両
俣小屋 where many cairns are scattered west of the main
ridge. Scramble up through boulders for 20min to reach a
false summit, then drop down to a small saddle and climb a
few metres for panoramic views at the top of **Mt Kita-dake** 北
岳 (3193m), Japan's second tallest mountain.

From the summit, continue south along the ridge to a
long saddle from where you can trace the route to Mt Ai-no-
dake, with the rest of the South Alps spread out behind.
Follow the path just to the right of the true ridge, staying clear
of the long drops to the right. There is a short exposed section
with chain-link handrails, followed by a steep descent on
loose scree lined with wooden logs for erosion protection. At
a junction, ignore the trail left.

After a couple of short ups and downs you'll reach
another exposed area with chain-link handrails and a
wooden staircase. Descend the long drop to the saddle,
ignore another junction left and follow the sign for 北岳山
荘. The route flattens out and **Kitadake sansō** 北岳山荘 is left
down a short path just off the main trail. You can refill water
and rest at this hut, 45min beyond the summit.

Go back to the main ridge trail and turn left, passing a series of rock cairns to start the steady 40min climb to the summit of **Mt Naka-shirane** 中白根山 (3055m). From here drop to a small saddle and climb left on a narrow trail marked by yellow arrows. After traversing past two unmarked peaks you will reach a large cairn pierced with a rusty metal pipe.

Continue south just below the main ridge for another rock scramble and a series of ups and downs to reach another large cairn on the main ridge. Stay on the ridge and climb over two false summits before reaching **Mt Ai-no-dake** 間ノ岳 (3189m), Japan's fourth highest mountain, 90min from Kitadake sansō hut.

Take the right fork on the summit, heading west (away from Mt Fuji) for Mt Mibu. Descend gradually and follow an elongated ridge for 20min to a saddle, then a short rock scramble to the bulbous top of **Mt Mibu** 三峰岳 (2999m), which sits on the border of Nagano, Yamanashi, and Shizuoka prefectures.

At the summit, turn left (southwest) at an English sign for 'Kumanodaira Hut' and pass a big cairn to descend over large boulders marked by yellow arrows. The track soon widens through broad swathes of dwarf pine interspersed with yellow buttercups and pink dainthus wildflowers.

After about 45min you'll reach a plateau and the **Mikuni-daira** 三国平 junction. Ignore the left track and head straight at the signpost reading 塩見岳・熊の平小屋 (Shiomi-dake, Kumanodaira-goya). Ahead you can see the mountain hut tucked in a forest below the ridge. Drop down switchbacks to a saddle at the tree line for a short, undulating ridge walk and wooden boardwalks to reach **Kuma-no-daira-goya** hut at 2500m. ◂

There are great views back to Mt Ai-no-dake from the deck of the hut.

STAGE 3
Kuma-no-daira-goya to Sanpuku-tōge-goya
熊ノ平小屋~三伏峠小屋

Start	Kuma-no-daira-goya hut 熊ノ平小屋
Finish	Sanpuku-tōge-goya hut 三伏峠小屋
Distance	15.5km (9½ miles)
Total ascent	1420m (4660ft)
Total descent	1380m (4530ft)
Time	10hr 30min
Terrain	Rough rocky alpine trail, exposed in places
Access	It is possible to leave the trek at Sanpuku-tōge-goya, taking a trail to the Torikura trailhead 鳥倉登山口, where two buses daily (mid July to late August only) go to Ina-Oshima Station, for trains to either Okaya or Toyohashi (connections to Tokyo and Nagoya).
Accommodation	Camping and accommodation at Sanpuku-tōge-goya. Lodging at Shiomi-goya, but no camping.
Note	Carry enough water for the entire day, as water sources are a long side-trip off the ridge and the water at Shiomi-goya hut is expensive.

This is a long day, half of which is spent high up and exposed to the wind. The descent from the summit of Mt Shiomi is steep and exposed, with risk of rockfall. The final part of the route from Shiomi-goya hut to Sanpuku-tōge-goya involves a lot of up-and-down over two separate peaks. The day can be broken in two by staying at Shiomi-goya hut (advanced booking required, no camping allowed).

Exit **Kuma-no-daira-goya hut** 熊ノ平小屋 and turn right, passing by a sign ('360 minutes to Shiomi Lodge'). Pass a field of yellow summer ragwort flowers and climb steadily through fir trees just below the main ridge, then continue straight to reach a faint junction in 20min with a sign pointing for Mt Abe-Arakura-dake 安部荒倉岳. Ignore this (as there are better views further on) and carry straight on through forest dotted with pink Japanese geraniums and blue gentians to reach

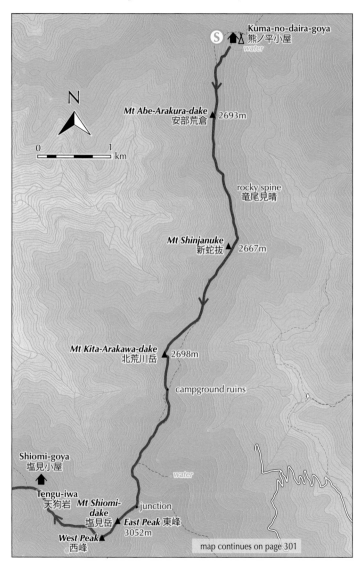

Kuma-no-daira-goya 熊ノ平小屋
water

Mt Abe-Arakura-dake 安部荒倉 2693m

rocky spine 竜尾見晴

Mt Shinjanuke 新蛇抜 2667m

Mt Kita-Arakawa-dake 北荒川岳 2698m

campground ruins

water

Shiomi-goya 塩見小屋

Tengu-iwa 天狗岩

Mt Shiomi-dake 塩見岳

East Peak 東峰 3052m

West Peak 西峰

map continues on page 301

a rocky spine marked on the map as 竜尾見晴 ('dragon-tail viewpoint'), where a sign indicates 1hr 20min to Kuma-no-daira hut. Pick your way across the dragon's tail with vistas of the undulating ridge of Mt Shiomi to the southeast.

After re-entering the forest, gradually ascend for 20min to find a faint trail leading to the ridge on the right for Mt Shinjanuke 新蛇抜山. Climb this trail for 5min to the **summit** (2667m) for another view with which you can gauge your progress. Now carry on straight, dipping below the tree line and then going up along a rocky path through birch and wildflowers. The angle steepens and the trail splits, with an easier path below the ridge to the left and a ridge trail leading right. Take the right fork and further on emerge from the trees, then climb a short way to the unmarked summit of **Mt Kita-Arakawa-dake** 北荒川岳 (2698m), where steep cliffs of sandy scree drop away dramatically. ▶

Drop left off the summit and negotiate a trail of loose scree before dropping off the ridge to a flat area with a dilapidated wooden hut. These are the **ruins of an old campground** and a signpost reads 幕営禁止 (no camping allowed). Veer right and climb gently through a wonderful grassy field with yellow summer ragwort flowers, easily the most scenic part of the stage.

Sub-alpine forest of Erman's birch is encountered frequently on the route

There is a fantastic view of the steep, crumbly ridge leading to the summit of Mt Shiomi directly in front of you.

Keep to the east of the heavily eroded main ridge before rejoining it a bit further, passing through dwarf pine above a col dotted with dirt clearings, the remnants of a campground (雪投沢). An unmarked side-trail leads down to a water source on the plateau (20min return). Climb the steep, rocky ridge for 50min, topping out at a **junction** on the edge of Mt Shiomi's summit plateau. The ridge splits here, so be careful not to drop off left (east) to Mt Kōmori-dake 蝙蝠岳 (2865m) in times of poor visibility. Instead, follow the old signpost right (southwest) for 塩見岳 and a gentle 40min climb to the **East Peak** of Mt Shiomi-dake 塩見岳東峰 (3052m), the higher of Shiomi's twin peaks and a good place to rest.

To continue, walk west along the ridge for 3min to the **West Peak** of Mt Shiomi-dake (3047m) before descending the northwest face of the mountain. It is a steep and somewhat exposed drop on red chert with yellow paint and signs warning of rockfall (落石注意) before the path flattens at a narrow saddle and skirts around to the left of **Tengu-iwa** 天狗岩, a pointy peak that juts abruptly out of the ridge. Traverse a narrow path dotted with pink thyme flowers for a steep drop to a saddle, then a gentle up-and-down leads to the red-roofed **Shiomi-goya** hut 塩見小屋 – a great place to rest (lunch served from 10am to 2pm). ◀

Shiomi-goya used to be a poorly run hut but has been completely rebuilt under new ownership. However, there is no camping and staying usually requires prior booking.

mont·bell

The crowded campground at Sanpuku-tōge

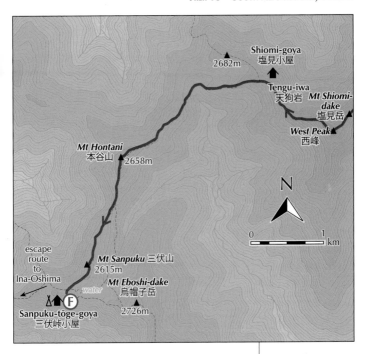

Continue west from the hut, drop below the tree line to a junction and turn left at the signpost marked for 三伏峠 (Sanpuku-tōge). Descend a rocky trail to a **col** before turning west to traverse well below the ridge through a stunning mossy fir forest. After descending gently to a broad saddle, swing south for a long, steady 1hr climb to the summit of **Mt Hontani** 本谷山 (2658m) just above the tree line. A sign on the summit indicates 1hr 20min to Sanpuku-toge hut.

Now drop back into birch trees and yellow ragwort and pass an unmarked side-trail to a lookout on the right. Descend to a saddle and roped-off track on your left with a sign prohibiting camping (幕営禁止). This trail leads to the old Sanpuku-tōge hut ruins; ignore it and keep going for 30min to the top of **Mt Sanpuku** 三伏山 (2615m), which has excellent panoramic views. Continue south from here, dipping below the tree line to reach a junction where you turn right for the short stroll to **Sanpuku-tōge-goya** hut 三伏峠小屋.

Escape route to Ina-Oshima Station

There is a well-used trail marked in 10 stages, taking about 3hr, that leads out of the mountains to Torikura trailhead 鳥倉登山口, where two buses daily (mid July to late August only) go to Ina-Oshima Station for trains to either Okaya or Toyohashi (connections to Tokyo and Nagoya). The trail passes Sanpuku-tōge-goya hut and zigzags down to a junction. A trail right is roped off, so continue straight on a long traverse along wooden log bridges for 1hr before the final steep drop to the bus stop. If you miss the bus, turn right on the tarmac road and walk 40min to reach a parking lot, where hitching with a fellow hiker may be an option.

STAGE 4

Sanpuku-tōge-goya to Arakawa-goya
三伏峠小屋~荒川小屋

Start	Sanpuku-tōge hut 三伏峠小屋
Finish	Arakawa-goya hut 荒川小屋
Distance	14.5km (9¼ miles)
Total ascent	1260m (4130ft)
Total descent	1680m (5510ft)
Time	11hr
Terrain	Rugged mountain path frequently rising and falling below the tree line. Steep alpine terrain with plenty of switchbacks.
Accommodation	Camping and accommodation at Arakawa-goya hut. Camping available at Takayamaura hinan-goya hut.

This is another long yet rewarding day, with beautiful sections of wildflowers and Erman's birch, and very few other hikers. Once you have passed Takayamaura hinan-goya hut (a possible stopover for those wishing to break the stage in two) the real climb back above 3000m begins, with the stage finishing at the idyllic Arakawa-goya hut that sits in a deep valley with views of Mt Fuji.

From **Sanpuku-tōge hut** 三伏峠小屋 go back past the camp-ground to a junction and turn right at the signpost for 荒川岳 (Mt Arakawa-dake) and Kogōchi-goya 小河内小屋, and enter a large grassy field of wildflowers lined with deer-proof fences and ropes. ▶ A trail leads left to a water source (水場) but ignore this and go right, climbing log stairs to the top of the ridge. Turn left to re-enter a birch forest and follow the undulating ridge for 40min to reach **Mt Eboshi-dake** 烏帽子

There are a wide variety of flowers here including purple pincushions, white apiaceae and yellow hypericaceae.

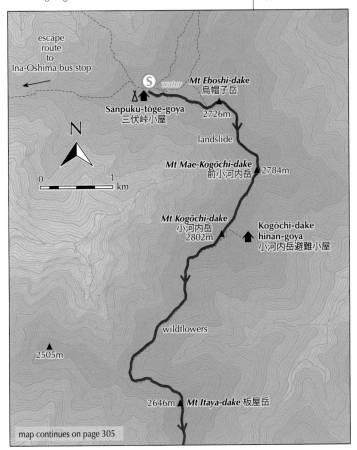

escape route to Ina-Oshima bus stop

S water

Mt Eboshi-dake 烏帽子岳
2726m

Sanpuku-tōge-goya 三伏峠小屋

landslide

N

0   1
└─────┴─────┘ km

Mt Mae-Kogōchi-dake 前小河内岳 ─ 2784m

Mt Kogōchi-dake 小河内岳 2802m

Kogōchi-dake hinan-goya 小河内岳避難小屋

wildflowers

▲ 2505m

2646m ▲ *Mt Itaya-dake* 板屋岳

map continues on page 305

岳 (2726m), from where there is an impressive view of Mt Shiomi across a narrow gorge to the northeast and Mt Fuji to the east.

From the summit, drop east off the broad ridge and skirt past a landslide before a steady 45min climb to the unmarked summit of **Mt Mae-Kogōchi-dake** 前小河内岳 (2784m). A hut is clearly visible on the saddle of the peak ahead, with Mt Arakawa dominating the horizon behind. Follow the undulating contours of the ridge for 45min to reach a junction just below the summit of Mt Kogōchi. A side-trail to the left leads in 3min to Kogōchi-dake hinan-goya 小河内岳避難小屋, a hut selling drinks only. ◄ Unless you're thirsty, ignore this track and arrive at the summit of **Mt Kogōchi-dake** 小河内岳 (2802m) for unobstructed 360-degree views.

Kogōchi hut is a staffed shelter offering accommodation without meals. There are no basic amenities and camping is not permitted.

Descend gradually southwest on a broad ridge, passing another landslide to drop below the tree line for a series of gentle ups and downs through grasslands. Walk through fir and birch forest interspersed with **wildflowers**. After 1hr in the forest, turn east and traverse below the ridge to reach the forested summit of **Mt Itaya-dake** 板屋岳 (2646m).

Continue south, skirting by a series of **landslides** and a beautiful field of summer ragwort flowers near **Takayamaura hinan-goya** 高山裏避難小屋 at 2450m. This barebones hut

The undulating ridge to Mt Kogōchi-dake

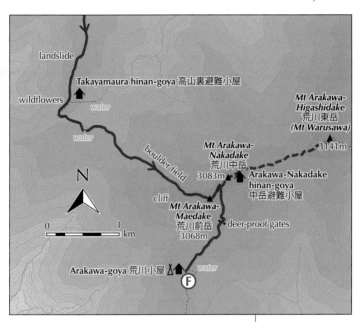

is similar to Kogōchi hut except that camping is allowed; if you're tired you may want to break the stage in two by staying here. The water source is a 20min return hike down a gully. ▶

From the hut, follow the sign for 荒川 (Arakawa) to a saddle and turn southeast below the main ridge, passing a water source after about 20min. Continue on the narrow trail through forest and up a short fixed chain to reach the edge of a scree field; from here it is a 500m vertical ascent straight up through a rocky col. Climb gently to the tree line and enter a **boulder field** sandwiched between two ridges, then follow paint marks up through dwarf pine, rowan trees and yellow avens. Despite the steepness, it is a nice climb and the final one of the day.

After reaching the summit ridge, traverse the edge of a crumbly **cliff**, skirting around a sharp pinnacle to arrive at the summit of **Mt Arakawa-Maedake** 荒川前岳 (3068m) – the first of Arakawa's trio of summits – around 3hr after leaving Takayamaura hinan-goya.

There's a more convenient water source on the trail ahead, although it can be reduced to a trickle in mid summer.

305

Misty forests in the late afternoon

Mountains in Japan are often grouped together in threes, called **Sanzan** in Japanese. The Arakawa Sanzan are no exception, with the Mae (Front), Naka (Middle) and Higashi (East) peaks all above 3000m in height.

Turn left off the peak and drop to a junction on a broad saddle.

Optional ascent of Mt Arakawa-Higashidake (Mt Warusawa)
If you are interested in climbing Japan's sixth tallest mountain, then drop your rucksack here for the 3hr return trip to Mt Arakawa-Higashidake, also known as Mt Warusawa (3141m). The route climbs over Nakadake 中岳 (where there is a refuge hut) before dropping to a col, then follows a steep 200m ascent to the top. Return the same way or continue on to Senmai-goya hut (Trek 11) for an escape route to Sawarajima.

To continue south on the main route, turn right at the weathered waymark for 荒川小屋・赤石岳 (Arakawa-goya・Akaishidake) then skirt below the main ridge and past a glacial cirque dotted with wildflowers. Pass through two **deer-proof gates** and follow steep switchbacks through meadows.

Continue descending towards the mountain hut that should now come into view. It is a long and sometimes steep path, passing an unreliable water source and dropping over 400m back below the tree line to reach **Arakawa-goya** hut 荒川小屋 in 1hr 30min from Mt Arakawa-Maedake.

STAGE 5
Arakawa-goya to Hijiridaira-goya 荒川小屋~聖平小屋

Start	Arakawa-goya hut 荒川小屋
Finish	Hijiridaira-goya hut 聖平小屋
Distance	15.5km (9½ miles)
Total ascent	1820m (5970ft)
Total descent	1950m (6400ft)
Time	11hr 30min
Terrain	Rough, rocky alpine trail with large losses of altitude between peaks
Access	It is possible to leave the trek at Hijiridaira-goya, picking up a long trail to Sawarajima, where a shuttle bus (only for staying guests at the lodge) runs to Hatanagi Dai-ichi Dam and a connecting bus (advanced booking only) to Shizuoka.
Accommodation	Huts on the way and camping and accommodation at Hijiridaira-goya

Views, wildflowers and alpine terrain dominate this strenuous section. The morning starts off with an ascent of Mt Akaishi, then drops to a narrow col before climbing over Mt Nakamori-Maruyama and Mt Usagi to the summit of 3000m Mt Hijiri and back down to the tree line. Most of the day is spent in the alpine zone exposed to the elements, so beware of changes in the weather.

From **Arakawa-goya hut** 荒川小屋, walk towards the toilets, turn right at the sign for 赤石岳 (Akaishi-dake) and climb a short distance through birch trees then along a gentle 40min incline towards a saddle (大聖寺平 **Daishōji-daira**). Here turn left, taking care not to take the trail that drops west off the ridge. The path climbs before flattening out at a large

307

stone cairn, then steepens in an area of loose rock. Follow switchbacks for 30min to reach the summit shoulder, flanked by a mound of red chert boulders and lots of creeping pine.

Turn south along the ridge for 15min, passing patches of white bistort and purple dwarf bellflowers to reach **Mt Ko-Akaishi-dake** 小赤石岳 (3081m), and drop down to a trail branching left for 赤石小屋 (Akaishi-goya). Ignore this and continue straight for 20min to reach **Mt Akaishi-dake** 赤石岳 (3120m), the main peak marked by a large signpost and excellent views of Mt Hijiri to the south.

Having enjoyed the views, drop to the small hut (**Akaishi-dake hinan-goya**) in a saddle directly below the summit. ◀ Turn right just before reaching the hut at a weathered sign reading 百間洞山の家 (Hyakkenborayama-no-ie), then follow switchbacks and red paint marks before turning west for a 1hr rocky **traverse** to a small col. From here a short

Stop in at the hut for a cup of fresh coffee if time permits.

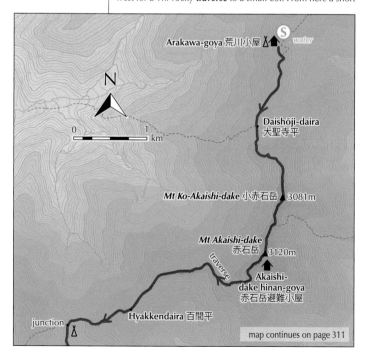

Arakawa-goya 荒川小屋

Daishōji-daira 大聖寺平

Mt Ko-Akaishi-dake 小赤石岳 ▲ 3081m

Mt Akaishi-dake 赤石岳 ▲ 3120m

Akaishi-dake hinan-goya 赤石岳避難小屋

traverse

junction

Hyakkendaira 百間平

map continues on page 311

Turn right at this weathered signpost in front of Akaishi-dake hinan-goya hut

climb leads to a gentle series of rolling green hills; enjoy their easy gradient before the tough climbing ahead.

Descend a narrow rope-lined path to the broad plateau of 百間平 (**Hyakkendaira**), where camping is prohibited. ▸ Follow the route for 45min as it continues west along the plateau to a series of switchbacks and a **junction** at the tree line. The route splits here; continue straight on a faint path for the steep climb to Mt Ōsawa 大沢岳 (2819m), or turn left for the well-used path through a campground and wildflowers to **Hyakkenborayama-no-ie** 百間洞山の家, a hut at 2470m. Both trails meet up on the ridge later, but at the hut you can fill up on water and rest for lunch.

Follow the sign for 聖岳 (Hijiri-dake) and go west past the hut for a steady 1hr traverse through birch back up to the ridgeline. Turn left at the **junction** (the track over Mt Ōsawa converges here) with an orange signpost for 兎岳 (Usagi-dake) and zigzag through creeping pine to the rotund summit of **Mt Nakamori-Maruyama** 中盛丸山 (2807m), offering fantastic panoramic views. This round pointy peak has been visible ever since leaving Mt Akaishi and is about 1hr 30min from the last hut.

Orange paint marks lead down the peak's south face through prime ptarmigan habitat, then along a narrow ridge

Mt Hijiri's flat top dominates the view south, then to the right are Mt Usagi, Mt Nakamori-Maruyama and Mt Ōsawa.

to a col at the edge of the tree line. Ascend through creeping pine to the rocky top of **Mt Ko-Usagi-dake** 子兎岳 (2738m). From here descend to a saddle with a water source 5min off the ridge to the left (marked by a painted red arrow on a rock), then climb a small peak and drop to another col before a zigzagging ascent through creeping pine for 45min to the summit of **Mt Usagi-dake** 兎岳 (2818m). You might want to rest and enjoy the impressive views here before the toughest section of the day.

Ignoring a faint path to your right that heads to the triangulation point, veer east through dense creeping pine to reach a stone emergency hut, **Usagi-dake hinan-goya** 兎岳非難小屋. ◄ Scuff marks lead to a **knife-edge** ridge with exposed drops to the right; continue carefully on the path, which loses nearly 200m of altitude to arrive at the bottom of a small col.

Veer left away from the ridge along a narrow trail through birch to another col below the final summit climb. From here it is a steep 1hr **scramble** on loose red chert rocks to the flat, broad summit of **Mt Hijiri-dake** 聖岳 (3013m), Japan's southernmost 3000m peak. Turn around for vistas of the rugged ridgeline you just crossed.

This aging structure was renovated in 2009 and offers a place to escape from the wind but little else in terms of comfort or amenities.

Looking back towards Mt Akaishi from the top of Mt Hijiri

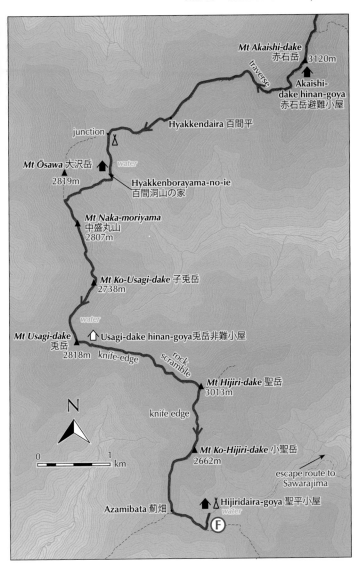

Mt Akaishi-dake
赤石岳 3120m

traverse

Akaishi-dake hinan-goya
赤石岳避難小屋

junction

Hyakkendaira 百間平

Mt Ōsawa 大沢岳
2819m

water

Hyakkenborayama-no-ie
百間洞山の家

Mt Naka-moriyama
中盛丸山
2807m

Mt Ko-Usagi-dake 子兎岳
2738m

water

Mt Usagi-dake
兎岳
2818m

knife-edge

Usagi-dake hinan-goya 兎岳非難小屋

rock scramble

Mt Hijiri-dake 聖岳
3013m

knife edge

Mt Ko-Hijiri-dake 小聖岳
2662m

escape route to Sawarajima

Azamibata 薊畑

Hijiridaira-goya 聖平小屋

water

F

N

0   1
km

Drop south off the summit down switchbacks to reach another **knife-edge** section, then mind the near-vertical drops to the right on a series of small ups and downs to reach **Mt Ko-Hijiri-dake** 小聖岳 (2662m), marked by a weather-beaten signpost. The terrain now becomes gentler, descending a short way to the tree line.

Drop down a fixed rope and follow the often muddy track through fields of wildflowers (mostly yellow ragwort and pink lousewort) to reach a junction, 薊畑 (**Azamibata**). Go left, passing fenced-off patches of wildflowers, then turn left at a col and follow wooden boardwalks to **Hijiridaira-goya** 聖平小屋, a hut with a campground and complimentary fruit punch.

Escape route to Sawarajima 椹島

A long trail leads from Hijiridaira-goya to Sawarajima in 5–6hr. A detailed description is covered in Trek 12, but it involves following the Hijirisawa stream via a series of metal bridges, then a long walk paralleling the river valley, followed by a steep descent to a suspension bridge. Continue above the river for a final drop to a gravel forest road. Turn left on the road for a 45min walk to the lodge and camping facilities at Sawarajima, where a shuttle bus (only for staying guests at the lodge) runs to Hatanagi Dai-ichi Dam and a connecting bus (advanced booking only) to Shizuoka.

STAGE 6
Hijiridaira-goya to Chausu-goya 聖平小屋~茶臼小屋

Start	Hijiridaira-goya hut 聖平小屋
Finish	Chausu-goya hut 茶臼小屋
Distance	7km (4¼ miles)
Total ascent	730m (2400ft)
Total descent	610m (2000ft)
Time	5hr
Terrain	Rough rocky alpine trail turning into a broad gentle ridge dotted with wildflowers
Accommodation	Camping and accommodation at Chausu-goya hut

An easier day after the last five days of tough hiking, so take your time and enjoy the steady climb to Mt Kamikōchi and the gentle descent to Chausu-goya hut.

Exit **Hijiridaira-goya hut** 聖平小屋 and turn right to return to the main ridge, then turn left and zigzag along the heavily eroded trail to reach the top of a spur that flattens out after 30min. Continue southeast for a steady climb through

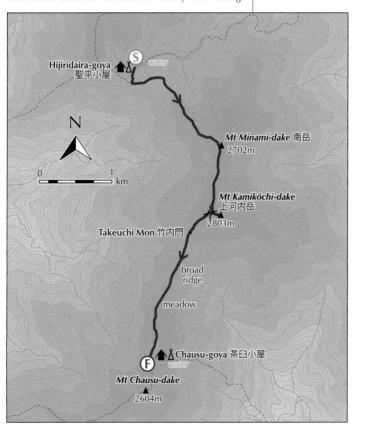

The rough ridge just below Mt Minami-dake

Panoramic views include many mountains from the last few days (Mt Hijiri, Mt Akaishi, Mt Arakawa) to the north, Mt Fuji to the east, and Mt Kamikōchi due south.

creeping pine and Erman's birch, then at the ridge turn left and follow switchbacks to the summit of **Mt Minami-dake** 南岳 (2702m). ◀

Now descend steeply to a saddle and follow the undulating ridge, which is dotted with wildflowers. At a col, ascend steadily to a junction 上河内岳肩 (Kamikōchi-dake kata). You can drop your rucksack here and turn left for a steep 15min climb and panoramic vistas from the top of **Mt Kamikōchi-dake** 上河内岳 (2803m).

Backtrack to the junction and descend left for 20min to a small collection of jagged head-high boulders referred to as 竹内門 (**Takeuchi Mon**, or Takeuchi's Gate). The gradient eases; gently descend a **broad ridge** to the tree line. Walk through birch, heading just west of the main ridge, then through a broad grassy **meadow** bustling with wildflowers and fir trees. This is the remnant of an ancient glacial cirque and it affords fantastic views back to Mt Kamikōchi's impressive pyramidal form.

The meadow is home to a geological phenomenon called '**patterned ground**'. Typically found in periglacial climates, hexagonal patterns are formed by repeated freezing/thawing of the soil.

Continue south to rejoin the broad ridgeline of loose scree at a well-marked junction, and turn left to soon reach **Chausu-goya** hut 茶臼小屋. If you want to leave the mountains today, continue past the hut to reach Hatanagi Dam in 5hr (see Stage 8).

STAGE 7
Optional Mt Tekari-dake side trip 光岳

Start/finish	Chausu-goya hut 茶臼小屋
Distance	19.5km (12 miles)
Total ascent/descent	1940m (6365ft)
Time	9hr
Terrain	Rugged mountain path with many ups and downs, alternating between creeping pine and sub-alpine forests
Accommodation	Chausu-goya hut and Tekari-dake-goya hut

This is an optional return trip to the summit of Mt Tekari, the southernmost point in the world for creeping pine and ptarmigan. It is an all-day hike with plenty of up-and-down that can be broken in two by staying at Tekari-dake-goya hut (reservations required). The warden at Chausu-goya hut can make a booking for you.

From **Chausu-goya hut** 茶臼小屋, return to the ridge you left yesterday and turn left to follow the rock cairns for a steady 30min ascent of **Mt Chausu-dake** 茶臼岳 (2604m). ▶ Take a sharp right here, descending west to reach the tree line and a series of wooden boardwalks through a grove of birch. After passing a small **pond** framed with yellow ragwort, continue back above the tree line through thick creeping pine to reach 希望峰 (**Kibohō**) junction in another 30min.

A side-path leads south (30min return) to the summit of Mt Nitta-dake 仁田岳 (2524m); ignore this and descend west to a saddle and then a steady traverse with occasional views of Mt Tekari to the south. After passing through a wildflower **meadow**, pick your way for 1hr through a maze of fallen trees and a thick grove of beech and fir to reach a junction on the tree-covered summit of **Mt Irō-dake** 易老岳 (2354m).

The rocky spire is a great place to catch the sunrise and enjoy vistas of Mt Hijiri and Mt Kamikōchi.

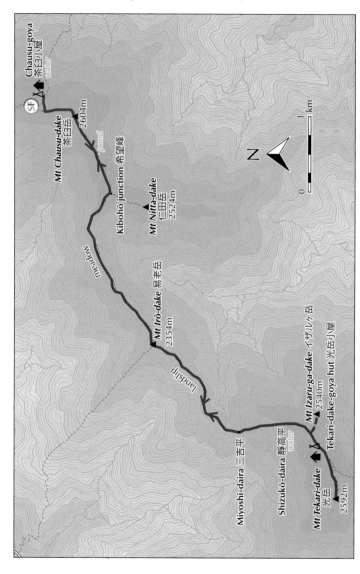

Do not head northwest on the well-defined path to 易老渡, but veer left at the sign reading '160 min. to Tekari Lodge'. Make a steady descent through ferns amid toppled trees, then through grasslands, to reach a clearing with a **landslip** off the ridge to the right. (Mobile phone reception is good in this area, so you may see a hiker or two using their phones.) Walk for 40min through a wet section of forest to a saddle indicated by a small sign 三吉平 (**Miyoshi-daira**) and then start a very long and rocky climb.

Scramble up to a grassy gully lined with birch, rowan and cherry trees, climbing west of the main ridge, then ascend steadily for 45min to an unreliable water source at 静高平 (**Shizukō-daira**). Wildflowers dominate as the path flattens out and enters creeping pine along the tree line.

A further 30min on, a path to the left leads to a short optional return climb up Mt Izaru-ga-dake イザルケ岳 (2540m). ▶ Otherwise keep heading west along wooden boardwalks on a wonderful plateau. The roof of **Tekari-dake-goya** hut 光岳小屋 soon comes into view and is reached in 10min. Continue past the hut for another 10min (ignore the junction on your left) to the summit of **Mt Tekari-dake** 光岳 (2592m). The top is covered with trees, so head west for 10 metres to reach a viewpoint. Your can then stay or camp at the hut, or retrace your steps all the way back to **Chausu-goya** hut.

This peak offers panoramic views of Mt Fuji from a broad clearing in the creeping pine.

STAGE 8
Chausu-goya to Shirakaba-sō 茶臼小屋~白樺荘

Start	Chausu-goya hut 茶臼小屋
Finish	Akaishi Onsen Shirakaba-sō hot spring 赤石温泉白樺荘
Distance	11.5km (7 miles)
Total ascent	105m (340ft)
Total descent	1620m (5320ft)
Time	6hr 30min
Terrain	Well-maintained trail through mostly deciduous forests, followed by an exposed traverse through a narrow gorge. Gravel and tarmac road to the hot spring.
Accommodation	Accommodation at Yokokubozawa-goya hut and Akaishi Onsen Shirakaba-sō (advanced booking required)

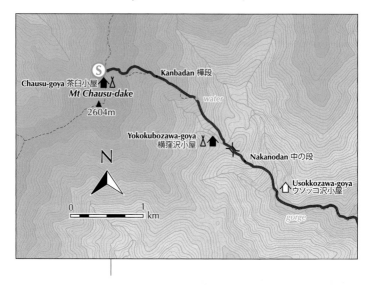

After a week above the tree line, say farewell to views of Mt Fuji and return to green valleys 1500m below. Plenty of suspension bridges, including one of Japan's longest, provide safe passage through a narrow gorge and across Hatanagi Lake, then an easy walk on a gravel forest road and a final section of tarmac lead to a well-deserved bath at a hot spring.

From **Chausu-goya hut** 茶臼小屋 follow the painted sign 畑ナギ下山 down wooden steps to cross flower meadows and reach the tree line. Pink tape marks lead through a grove of silver fir, and you'll pass a white elevation mark (2200m) before reaching a flat area with an old sign for 樺段 (**Kanbadan**) in 30min. Veer left at a painted sign for 横窪沢 (Yokokubosawa).

The track steepens, with wooden log bridges in places and a water source marked 水呑場 (Mizunomiba). Continue down switchbacks, with rest spots and vistas of Mt Daimugen through gaps in the foliage. Descend for another 30min to reach **Yokokubozawa-goya** 横窪沢小屋, a hut situated along the banks of a stream. This is a good place to rest and refill water if necessary.

From the hut, cross the metal bridge and climb a short distance to a mountain **pass**, Yokokubo-tōge 横窪峠. From here, drop a couple of hundred vertical metres through

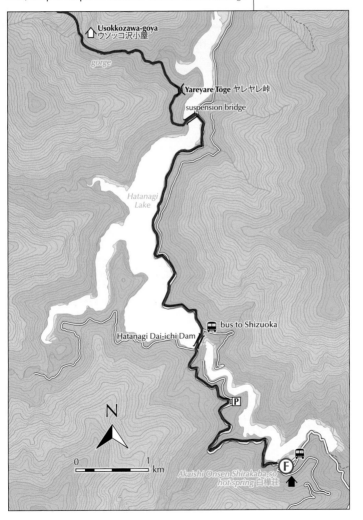

Usokkozawa-goya ウソッコ沢小屋

gorge

Yareyare Tōge ヤレヤレ峠

suspension bridge

Hatanagi Lake

bus to Shizuoka

Hatanagi Dai-ichi Dam

P

N

0   1 km

Akaishi Onsen Shirakaba-sō hot spring 白樺荘

F

mixed forests of beech and hemlock on a rough trail for 30min, going past a spot called 中の段 (**Nakanodan**) and through a washed-out section affixed with ropes and metal waymarks. Descend roughly for another 40min on a rocky trail then down metal staircases, ending at a green suspension bridge spanning a waterfall. Just past this, arrive at **Usokkozawa-goya** ウソッコ沢小屋, an unmanned emergency hut. ◄

From here it is just 1hr 20min to the end of the trek.

From the hut it is a thrilling 40min traverse through a narrow **gorge**, zigzagging down a rocky trail to the first of four suspension bridges spanning the river. Cross the first one and negotiate a narrow section of metal staircases down to the second bridge. Cross this and turn left on mossy rocks near the river bank before crossing again and reaching an elevation marker (1000m) just before a metal staircase leading to the final bridge. After this crossing head left, close to the river's edge, to pass a painted sign for 畑薙大吊橋 (Hatanagi Ōtsuribashi). Take care if the river is swollen and be on the lookout for mountain leeches that can sometimes be found in this area. ◄

Yamahiru, or mountain leeches, are relatively harmless but their painless bites bleed for a long time. If a leech attaches to you, pull it off gently using your fingernail.

Leave the river bank for the final short climb to the pass called ヤレヤレ峠 (**Yareyare Tōge** – *yareyare* is Japanese for 'thank God'), then turn south and descend using fixed ropes over an eroded section of trail to reach a long **suspension bridge** spanning Hatanagi Lake. This is the 182m Hatanagi Long Rope Bridge 畑薙大吊橋, one of the longest in Japan.

On the other side of the bridge, turn right on the gravel road and walk for 40min, going through the guarded checkpoint to reach **Hatanagi Dai-ichi Dam**. Turn right and walk across the top of the dam, turning left on the other side past the summer parking lot and going down the tarmac road for another 40min to reach the hot spring baths at **Akaishi Onsen Shirakaba-sō** 赤石温泉白樺荘.

MT FUJI – 富士山

Mt Fuji and Lake Kawaguchiko

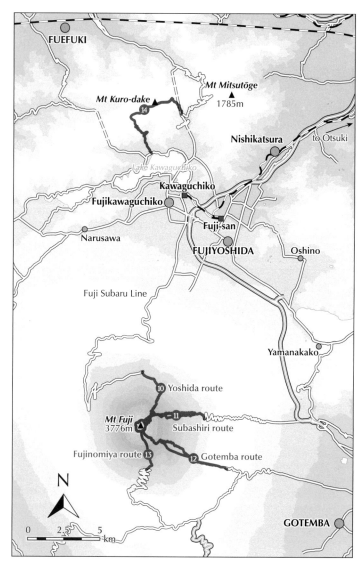

FUEFUKI

Mt Mitsutōge
▲
1785m

Mt Kuro-dake ▲
14

Lake Kawaguchiko

Nishikatsura

to Otsuki

Kawaguchiko

Fujikawaguchiko

Fuji-san

Narusawa

FUJIYOSHIDA

Oshino

Fuji Subaru Line

Yamanakako

10 Yoshida route

Mt Fuji
3776m ▲

11

Subashiri route

Fujinomiya route 13

12 Gotemba route

N

0   2.5   5
        km

GOTEMBA

Mt Fuji, or Fuji-san as it is known in Japanese, is a striking and almost symmetrical conical-shaped volcano roughly 100km southwest of Tokyo. At 3776m it is the tallest peak in the country and one of Japan's most iconic symbols, revered since ancient times and a frequent subject of art and literature. It is listed as one of Japan's 'Three Holy Mountains', along with Haku-san and Tateyama. Snowcapped for half of the year, a climb to the top of the mountain is a hugely popular pursuit for locals and visitors alike during the summer climbing season, when it is estimated that up to 300,000 people each year make the slow and laborious ascent up the rocky and barren black slopes, many staying in huts and climbing in the dark with the intention of watching the sunrise from the summit.

The level of development on the mountain can be quite startling (and is one of the reasons why it was made a cultural, rather than a natural world heritage site in 2013), with vending machines and even a post office at the summit. But that doesn't mean it is a mountain that should be taken lightly, as inclement weather along with the effects of altitude can provide a challenge, and due to its impressive height and prominence a successful ascent of Mt Fuji does feel like an accomplishment – even if you have to fight for space with hundreds of other people. In fact, it is the sense of camaraderie, the wide range of nationalities and the friendliness of most Japanese hikers that makes climbing Mt Fuji a truly unique experience.

Despite its serene and stately appearance, Mt Fuji has quite an explosive history. The first eruptions occurred about 700,000 years ago,

with subsequent episodes of volcanic activity moulding the mountain into its current shape by about 5000 years ago. The most recent eruption was in 1707–8 when a secondary crater, Mt Hōei, was formed on the southeastern flank of the mountain, with the fallout covering Tokyo in ash. Mt Fuji is classed as an active volcano but is under constant surveillance and is currently considered to be at low risk of erupting.

The official climbing season is quite short, starting at the beginning of July and ending in the second week of September. During this time thousands of people clamber up the mountain every day, huts and facilities are open for business and buses take people to and from the trailheads. There are four main routes to the summit; running clockwise from the north they are the Yoshida trail, the Subashiri trail, the Gotemba trail and the Fujinomiya trail.

Like many volcanoes in Japan, the trails on Mt Fuji are split into 10 stages or stations, called *gō-me* (合目) in Japanese – used by hikers for measuring progress. Buses run as far as the fifth stations, so most people start their climbs from there (although for purists it is perfectly possible to start at the first station at the foot of the mountain). The stations are all at different elevations on each route, but they give you a rough idea of how far there is to go and are the places where most of the huts are located.

The summit of Mt Fuji is dominated by a huge 100m-deep crater which often holds patches of snow until late in the year. There are eight minor peaks around the crater rim, including the true high-point, Mt Ken-ga-mine. This peak is home to a weather station which was

OVERVIEW	
Location:	On the border of Shizuoka and Yamanashi prefectures, 100km southwest of Tokyo. Part of the Fuji-Hakone-Izu National Park.
When to go:	Official climbing season is from the beginning of July until early September. Outside of this time climbing is discouraged, with facilities and transport options greatly reduced.
Access:	Frequent buses to and from the four main trails' fifth stations during climbing season; see www.japan-guide.com/bus/fuji_season.html for full schedules. Parking for private vehicles available at all the fifth stations but only out of season; during the climbing season shuttle buses run from parking areas lower down the mountain.
Information:	See the official website for Mt Fuji – www.fujisan-climb.jp/en

manned year-round for 72 years until it was replaced with an automatic system in 2004. There are a few huts, shops and shrines along the summit ridge and the path around the crater has a bit of up-and-down, a loop of which takes about 1hr to complete.

BASES

Kawaguchiko 河口湖 is the largest and most developed of the Fuji Five Lakes and is a popular base from which to climb the mountain. It is a major tourist destination in its own right, with easy access from Tokyo and year-round buses to the Yoshida trail's fifth station. The best views of Mt Fuji are from the northern shore of the lake, while the eastern shore has the highest concentration of hotels, shops, hostels and hot spring resorts. Just outside Kawaguchiko's train station is a large tourist information centre where you can pick up free maps and detailed bus schedules.

If coming from Tokyo, take a train from Shinjuku on the JR Chuo Main Line to Otsuki and then change to the Fujikyu Railway Line (note the JR Pass is not valid on this line). There is also the JR Fuji Excursion (Fuji Kaiyū), a direct limited express train between Shinjuku and Kawaguchiko. The bus terminal just in front of the station serves highway buses from Tokyo, Kyoto/Osaka and other cities (www.willerexpress.com/en), while local buses provide transportation around the Fuji Five Lakes area (http://bus-en.fujikyu.co.jp). This is also the place to catch the bus for the Fuji Subaru Line 5th Station (Yoshida trail).

Fujiyoshida 富士吉田市 is the city just before Kawaguchiko on the Fujikyu Railway Line, and it has a decent number of hotels and amenities. It is also home to Fuji-Q Highland (one of Japan's best theme parks), an annual fire festival at the end of August, the historic Fuji Sengen Shrine and Chureito Pagoda with its famous view of Mt Fuji. The main train station is called Fujisan, which is the starting point for buses to the Yoshida trail, and highway buses stop here too.

The summit crater

Gotemba 御殿場市 is a rather small city on the eastern side of Mt Fuji from where buses service the Gotemba and Subashiri routes. There are a handful of shops and places to stay, but most people tend to pass through here as there are regular buses onwards to Kawaguchiko, and the station is only 1hr 20min from Tokyo on the JR Gotemba Line (requires a change to the Tokaido Main Line at Kozu). Another option is the Odakyu Limited Express Romance Car, a reservation-only direct train between Shinjuku and Gotemba, which can be booked online.

Numazu 沼津市 is a seaside town 30min south of Gotemba by train. It has more in the way of facilities and accommodation options, especially around the station, which is on the Tokaido Main Line to Tokyo. Just 5min east of Numazu by train is Mishima 三島市, the gateway to the Izu Peninsular. It too has

numerous accommodation options, and is a stop for Hikari and Kodama *shinkansen* (bullet trains). Both Mishima and Numazu have highway bus connections and are good bases for the Gotemba, Subashiri and Fujinomiya routes on Mt Fuji.

Fuji 富士市 is a fairly large industrial city looking over Suruga Bay, around 25km due south of Mt Fuji. The city enjoys clear views of the famous peak, and is the place where *shinkansen* passengers can sometimes get a glimpse of the mountain as they whizz by (Hikari and Kodama trains do stop here, however). Fuji is not a particularly touristy city and most accommodation options are located around Fuji Station or in the slightly less convenient Fujiwara district just to the northeast.

Fujinomiya 富士宮市 is an old market town with a few basic hotels and guesthouses, and is the starting point for the Fuji Skyline road which winds half-way up Mt Fuji. Highway express buses stop at both Fuji and Fujinomiya, where there are plenty of buses to and from the Fujinomiya fifth station, so these are by far the closest and most convenient bases for the Fujinomiya trail.

MAPS

Mt Fuji is covered at 1:50,000 by Yama-to-Kogen (No. 32) Fuji-san 富士山. There are also free maps available at tourist information centres and bus stations. Mt Kuro-dake (Walk 14) is also on the Fuji-san map (No. 32).

GETTING THERE

In the climbing season all four trails are easily accessible by public transport. Outside of the climbing season transport options are considerably reduced.

To save a bit of money there is a special 'climbers bus pass' which is valid for three days and allows you to ride a bus to one of the fifth-station trailheads and then take a return bus from any trail after climbing the mountain. This flexibility is good for those who plan to ascend and descend by different trails. The ticket costs about 3000 yen and is available from most of the main bus/train stations in the Mt Fuji area.

Yoshida trail fifth station

For the Yoshida trail, buses operated by Fujikyu run to the fifth station (Fuji-Subaru Line 5th Station) from Kawaguchiko and Fujisan train stations all year round. The journey takes 1hr and costs about 1500 yen (one-way). During the climbing season there are buses

roughly every 30min from about 6.30am until 8pm, and in the other direction from 8am until around 8.30pm. During the rest of the year there are hourly buses between 8.30am and 4.30pm. Direct express buses from Shinjuku Bus Terminal (Tokyo) to the fifth station run from late April to early November.

There are parking spaces at various points along the Subaru Line (the scenic toll road to the fifth station) and at the fifth station itself, but there are restrictions for private vehicles during climbing season, when shuttle buses run from the Fujihokuroku parking area 富士北麓駐車場.

Subashiri trail fifth station

For the Subashiri trail, during the climbing season Fujikyu operates six to 10 daily buses between JR Gotemba station and Subashiri 5th Station, with the first bus leaving Gotemba at 7.35am, the last one at 5.25pm (6.25pm on weekends and holidays). For the reverse journey, buses depart the fifth station at 8.45am until 6.45pm (7.45pm on weekends and holidays). Outside of climbing season there is a limited service of three buses a day on weekends and holidays from mid May until early July. Another service operates from mid July to early September between Odakyu Line Shin-Matsuda Station and the fifth station, stopping at Subashiri Sengen shrine on the way. It runs five times a day on weekends and holidays, and just twice a day on weekdays.

Private vehicles can drive to the Subashiri fifth station, although there are restrictions during climbing season, with shuttle buses running from the car parks at the bottom of the Fuji Azami Line.

Gotemba trail fifth station

The Gotemba trail is the least developed of the four routes, but there are six or seven buses a day from JR Gotemba station to the fifth station (Gotemba New 5th Station), with the first bus departing at 7.35am and the last one at 4.45pm. From there the first bus back to civilisation is at 9.25am and the last one leaves at 6.45pm. Outside of climbing season there are only three buses a day on weekends and holidays from mid May until early July.

It is possible to drive all the way to the fifth station, with no restrictions even during climbing season, and there is plenty of parking space available.

Fujinomiya trail fifth station

For the Fujinomiya trail, during climbing season Fujikyu runs regular buses from JR Shin-Fuji Station to Fujinomiya 5th Station, stopping at Fuji and Fujinomiya train stations on the way. These run every day from about 8.25am to 5.55pm. There are earlier buses from Fujinomiya Station only, departing at 6.30am and 7.30am. Buses in the other direction run from 8.30am to 7pm. There are also buses roughly every two hours from Mishima and one a day from Shizuoka. Outside of climbing season there is a much-reduced schedule with three buses a day from Shin-Fuji Station on weekends and holidays only, operating from the end of April until the end of October.

There is ample parking at the fifth station, but the Fujisan Skyline road is closed to private vehicles during climbing season, when shuttle buses operate from car parks lower down. The road is completely closed for winter from late November until late April.

Futons stacked up ready for evening at 9.5 station on the Fujinomiya trail (Walk 13)

MOUNTAIN HUTS

Mountain huts, offering food and accommodation, can be found along all four of the main routes on Mt Fuji, from the trailheads at the fifth stations and at regular intervals right up to the summit. Many have toilets (for a small fee) and a few run medical centres during the peak season. Still, it's best to take as many snacks and drinks as you feel comfortable carrying, as the prices increase with altitude.

Accommodation is usually mixed dorm-style, with everyone sleeping in very close quarters. Take ear plugs and an eye mask if you don't want to be disturbed by people shuffling around at night. Dinner is served from about 5pm, and lights out is usually at around 9pm, with wake-up calls from about 1.30am onwards (depending on how far up the mountain the hut is). If the weather is bad or you just need a break, huts usually let you take shelter for a while if you buy some food.

Unlike refuges in the Japan Alps, on Mt Fuji it is essential to book if you plan on staying at a hut, and many of them sell out weeks in advance for weekends and holidays. A few of the huts have online booking on their websites or via email, but for most you must call to make a reservation. Some huts have English-speaking staff, but if not, try to speak slowly and clearly or get a Japanese speaker to call. Hotel staff will often happily help to make a reservation if you ask politely and provide details of your stay.

See Appendix C for mountain hut details, including phone numbers.

As the goal for many people is to see the sunrise from the summit, it is common practice to climb part of the way up, stay at a hut for a few restless hours' sleep, and set off in the dark to arrive at the summit just in time for sunrise. Most of the huts can accommodate between 100 and 200 people, but on busy weekends and holidays they can be completely full and you may find yourself sharing a futon with two other people! It can be quite difficult to get even a couple of hours' good sleep with hikers coming and going at all hours plus the cramped sleeping conditions, so another option is to start from the fifth station late at night and climb without staying at a hut, to arrive on the summit just before sunrise.

Camping on Mt Fuji is strictly prohibited. There is, however, a small campground near the Yoshida route trailhead at Satōgoya hut.

WHEN TO GO

The official climbing season is generally from the beginning of July until around the second week in September, although dates vary every year so it's best to check online (www.fujisan-climb.jp/en). During this season the huts are open for business, there are plenty of buses to trailheads and the mountain is crowded with people. Weekends and public holidays (especially the week-long Obon holiday in mid August) are particularly busy and mountain huts may be fully booked, so it's best to avoid these times if possible.

Mt Fuji is often shrouded in cloud during the summer, and afternoon thunderstorms are a risk, but due to its great elevation the summit is often clear even if it's misty at the trailhead. Temperatures are generally pleasant, but the summit can be cold and close to freezing (particularly at night and early in the morning), even when it's hot and humid at sea level. If a typhoon is forecast, it's best to change your climbing plans as the trails on Mt Fuji are unforgiving in the driving wind and rain.

There is an argument that a good time to climb Fuji-san is just before or after the climbing season, as a few of the huts are open for a couple of weeks either side of the main season and some buses are scheduled to run. The trails are much less crowded during these times, making for a much more pleasant climbing experience. The earlier or later you go then the colder and tougher the conditions be, with the upper parts of the mountain usually covered in snow

from around mid November until early June. Winter climbs are very serious undertakings beyond the scope of this book, with numerous fatalities reported every year and so are discouraged (but permitted) by the authorities, to whom climbing plans must be submitted.

WHAT TO TAKE

While it's not uncommon to see people (usually foreigners) reach the top of Mt Fuji in nothing more than shorts, t-shirt and a pair of trainers, it is advisable to come a little better prepared. See 'What to take' in the introduction to this guide for recommendations. Crampons are not necessary during a summer ascent, but cheap surgical masks (popular in Japan and available in convenience stores)

Expect big crowds at the summit for sunrise

help to prevent breathing in dust which is often a problem on Mt Fuji's rocky and sandy trails, particularly after a few days of dry weather.

CLIMBING NOTES

The classic way to climb Mt Fuji is to set off during the day, arrive at a hut by late afternoon, have an early dinner and try to get a few hours' sleep before waking very early to continue hiking in the dark so as to arrive on the summit just in time for sunrise. This being the 'land of the rising sun', viewing the sunrise from a high mountain even has its own word, *goraikō*. If this is your plan, be prepared to approach the summit at a snail's pace, as hundreds of other people will have the same idea, and the steep, narrow paths below the summit

become clogged with hikers. It's a hiking experience quite unlike anywhere else, and however you view it, the sight of hundreds of headlamps snaking up the mountain in the dark is a memorable one. During the hiking season sunrise is at around 4.30am, but it's best not to arrive at the summit too early as it can be bitterly cold if you have to wait around for long.

If the prospect of spending the night squeezed into a hut with hundreds of other hikers doesn't appeal, then it is perfectly feasible to start the walk later and climb through the night to arrive at the summit in time for sunrise. The last buses of the day arrive at the Yoshida and Fujinomiya fifth station trailheads at about 8pm during climbing season, so if you start climbing at around 10pm you

Capturing Mt Fuji's shadow

will have ample time to reach the summit before it gets light.

Alternatively, if you're not interested in seeing the sunrise then it is possible to climb to the top of Mt Fuji and descend in one day. It's a fairly long and tiring day however, so you'll need decent fitness and should catch one of the early buses to the trailhead.

A huge number of people ascend and descend by the same trail, but it is perfectly possible, and sometimes preferable, to combine different routes. The Yoshida and Fujinomiya trials are the shortest routes to the top, and so make for logical ascent trails. In contrast, the 'sand runs' of the Subashiri and Gotemba trails are arguably more fun in descent. So a good combination would be an ascent of the popular Yoshida trail followed by a return down the Subashiri trail (buses from this trailhead go to JR Gotemba Station, from where there are convenient transport links back to Kawaguchiko and Tokyo). The Fujinomiya trail is the shortest ascent route and it can easily be combined with a descent of the Gotemba trail (which even has a detour leading back to the Fujinomiya trailhead if you'd rather finish there) for a satisfying and varied outing. But any combination of routes is possible, and as there are good transport links at all the trailheads during the climbing season, you can choose the best combination to suit your ability and itinerary.

When climbing Mt Fuji it is important to stay on the trails, keep off the bulldozer tracks and pay attention to signs and notices (there are plenty in English). Also be careful to only go up the ascent trails and down the descent ones, all of which are clearly marked. At all of the trailheads there will be someone asking for a modest donation which goes towards the upkeep of the mountain, and this should be paid by each climber (although is not mandatory).

The top of Mt Fuji is in the zone where altitude sickness, or acute mountain sickness (AMS) can start to occur due to the lower levels of oxygen in the air. The effects can kick in from 2500m, and anyone can be afflicted regardless of age, fitness or experience, with an increased risk if you ascend quickly. At these altitudes the effects are generally on the mild side but can include headaches, dizziness, breathlessness and nausea, and so if someone displays these symptoms it's important to take a break, and if necessary, head back down the mountain. Bottled oxygen is sold at the trailheads and at many huts, and it may slightly alleviate the effects of altitude sickness or give a boost to people not accustomed to such strenuous activity.

People of all ages and abilities scale the mountain during the climbing season, with some clearly better equipped than others, but if caught out by poor conditions and lack of planning it can be a very miserable and potentially dangerous experience, even in the summer. Some people would argue that Mt Fuji is a mountain best observed from a distance, and there can be little arguing that it is a fairly monotonous and tiring hike, compounded by crowds of people all trying to get to the same place at the same time. But for many, a climb to the roof of Japan and to the summit of one of the world's most famous mountains is a major bucket-list item, and an experience never to be forgotten.

WALK 10
Mt Fuji – Yoshida route 吉田ルート

Start/finish	Fuji Subaru Line 5th Station
Distance	Ascent 7.5km (4½ miles); descent 7.5km (4½ miles)
Total ascent/descent	1470m (4830ft)
Grade	1+
Time	Ascent 6hr; descent 3hr
Terrain	A gentle start along a track, getting steeper from the sixth station onwards. Well-marked paths consisting of volcanic rock and gravel.
Access	See Mt Fuji part introduction
Accommodation	Huts at every station (reservation required)
Facilities	Huts sell food, drinks, souvenirs, some have free wi-fi. Coin lockers at trailhead. Toilets at regular intervals, requiring small donation. First-aid centres at fifth, seventh and eighth stations.

The Yoshida trail is the most popular route up Mt Fuji, with crowds of people starting the climb from the Fuji Subaru Line 5th Station (also sometimes referred to as Yoshidaguchi or Kawaguchiko 5th Station). Located at 2305m elevation, the station almost feels like a small village as it is open all year round and is very developed, with huts, shops, restaurants, coin lockers, a shrine and other facilities.

This trail is the second shortest route to the summit, and due to the abundance of huts all along the way and easy access from Tokyo, it is by far the busiest of the four. The route historically begins at the famous Fujiyoshida Sengen Shrine way down at the foot of the mountain, which is the traditional starting point for climbs to the summit (it also adds 5hr to the hike so few people attempt it nowadays). During the climbing season the trail can get very congested, especially above the eighth station, but there are still views of the sunrise even if you don't make it to the top in time.

Ascent
The trail starts at **Fuji Subaru Line 5th Station** beyond the shops, huts and information centre at the eastern end of the road terminus, and is marked by a large sign. A small path heads down to the left, but instead follow the crowds along

the wide and flat black gravel track to the right. Despite Mt Fuji's arid image, there is quite a lot of greenery lining the path in the early stages. After 1km of easy walking, turn right where the trail dips a little at the **Izumi-ga-daki Falls** 泉ケ滝.

Climb gradually for 20min, and pass through a concrete tunnel (which protects against rockfall) to reach the **sixth station** where you can find toilets and the Mt Fuji Safety Guidance Centre. Shortly after this the trail splits into ascending and descending paths, so continue up the right

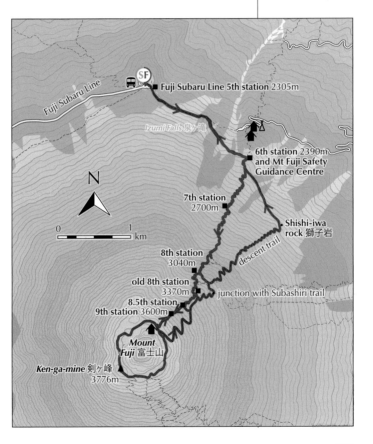

Torii gate (sacred entrance) at the top of the Yoshida route

There are patches of grass and knotweed around the trail and the view up the mountain is impressive if the weather is clear.

branch which soon steepens into a long series of wide zig-zags and ugly walls to prevent erosion. ◄

The **seventh station** is reached in less than 1hr and there are many huts and a first-aid centre here. Continue upwards past more huts, climbing over rugged rock and up occasional stone stairs. In about another 1hr arrive at the **eighth station** at an elevation of 3040m, where there are more huts and a medical facility.

Carry on upwards, past many more huts, and ignore any trails leading off to the left (they connect to the descent

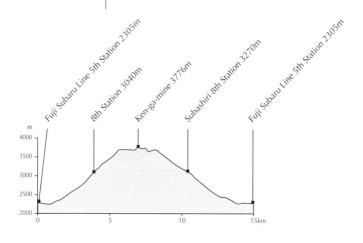

path). The eighth stage seems to go on for a long time, but in 1hr 20min you'll arrive at the **'old' eighth station** at 3370m. There are plenty of huts here and it is a major junction, as it is the place where the Yoshida and Subashiri trails merge.

Follow the crowds and continue climbing for 15min to reach the **8.5 station**, where the gentle-looking descent path is visible to the left. Ascend the well-marked but barren and rocky slope and pass under a wooden *torii* gate to arrive at the **ninth station** after a further 45min.

Continue upwards for another 30min to pass between two stone *komainu* (guardian lion-dog) statues and another *torii* gate, and finally emerge onto the summit rim. There are huts, shops and toilets here, and the true summit of **Ken-ga-mine** 剣ケ峰 (3776m) is on the opposite side of the crater, a 30–40min undulating walk in either direction.

Descent

The Yoshida trail takes about 3hr to descend, with the descent branch (which also serves as the Subashiri descent trail) located just south of the huts at the top end of the ascent trail. You can also go down the ascent trail for a short way,

Huts, shops and even vending machines at the top of Mt Fuji

as far as the **8.5 station** and then take the designated descent
route from there. The descent trail is an initially reddish and
dusty gravel track (shared also by the bulldozers servicing the
summit huts) which winds gently downwards via some large
zigzags, and is much less rough underfoot than the ascent
path.

Eventually reach the **'old' eighth station**, and descend
on a trail running parallel to the Subashiri trail for 15min.
Once at the (Subashiri) **eighth station**, be careful to follow
the descent trail for the Yoshida 吉田 route, as many people
go wrong here and end up descending the Subashiri trail all
the way! The two trails split at the Shita-edoya hut 下江戸屋,
so pay attention to the signs and it should be clear enough.

The Yoshida descent trail zigzags incessantly down the
mountain, and swings left at the **'Shishi-iwa' rock** 獅子岩
about 1hr after leaving the eighth station. There is only one
emergency hut and one toilet until the sixth station, where
the ascent and descent trails meet again, and then it's an
easy 35min walk back to the bus stop at **Fuji Subaru Line
5th Station**.

WALK 11
Mt Fuji – Subashiri route 須走ルート

Start/finish	Subashiri 5th Station
Distance	Ascent 8km (5 miles); descent 6km (3¾ miles)
Total ascent/descent	1805m (5930ft)
Grade	1+
Time	Ascent 6hr 30min; descent 3hr
Terrain	Forest trail at first; open sandy, rocky slopes later
Access	See Mt Fuji part introduction
Accommodation	Huts at regular intervals (reservation required)
Facilities	Huts sell food, drinks, souvenirs, some have free wi-fi. Toilets (small donation required) at huts.

Starting at 1970m, the Subashiri trail is the most varied of the four routes up Mt Fuji. Attractive alpine flowers bloom in the rich forests at the lower elevations, there is a moon-like 'sand run' section on the way down, and higher up the mountain there are plenty of huts (and crowds) after the path merges with the Yoshida trail. The Subashiri trail is a relatively popular route, but quieter and much less developed than the Yoshida trail, and the sunabashiri 'sand run' makes for an enjoyable descent from the seventh station down to the trailhead.

Ascent

From the bus stop at **Subashiri 5th Station**, walk down the paved track which is lined with huts, shops and benches. Beyond this is the donation collecting booth, and a map and information boards. Walk up the concrete steps which lead into the forest and pass a small shrine. A path to the right goes to a panoramic viewpoint called Mt Kofuji 小富士 in 20min, but instead follow the well-marked route which climbs gently up through the woods, where pink bellflowers and other alpine plants grow in abundance. The trail is mostly fine black gravel and rocky in places, with occasional clear views up the mountain.

Take the 'up' branch when the path splits and then climb steadily for 1hr to reach the **'new' sixth station**, where there is a small hut selling snacks and drinks. Continue up the

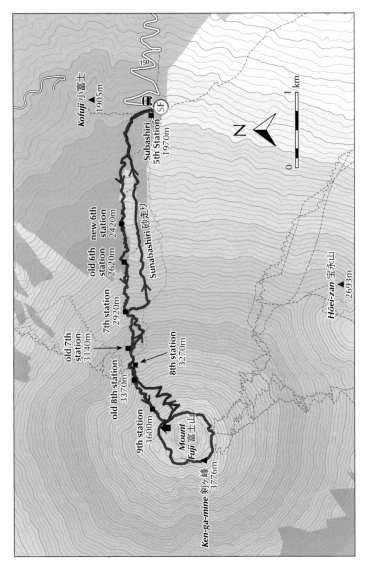

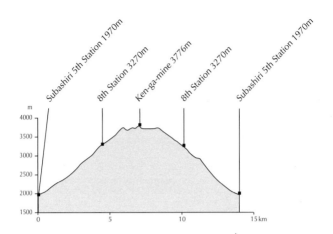

steepening forest trail, which is fringed with flowers such as orange lilies and wild mushrooms. The forest thins out before the hut at the **'old' sixth station** is reached in 50min. Climb through thickets of alpine brush as the twisting trail gets

Mt Fuji isn't all black scoria – there are occasional tinges of red too

rougher and rockier, and after 1hr 30min arrive at the Taiyō-kan hut 大陽館 at the **seventh station**.

Climb for another 50min along a zigzagging path up the black sandy slopes, the barren landscape livened up with tufts of knotweed. There is another hut at the **'old' seventh station**, and then it is a 30min slog up to the **eighth station** and the Shita-edoya hut 下江戸屋, where the Yoshida and Subashiri trails converge and the crowds begin to increase. Follow the winding ascent path for 25min to arrive at the **'old' eighth station**. There are lots of huts here as this is on the main Yoshida ascent trail which the Subashiri trail now joins. ◄

The summit is now less than 1hr 30min away.

Follow the crowds and continue climbing for 15min to reach the 8.5 station, where the gentle-looking descent path is visible to the left. Ascend the well-marked but barren and rocky slope and pass under a wooden *torii* gate to arrive at the **ninth station** after 45min.

Unkai 雲海 *is the Japanese word for 'sea of clouds'*

Continue upwards for another 30min to pass between two stone *komainu* (guardian lion-dog) statues and another *torii* gate, and finally emerge on the summit rim. There are huts, shops and toilets here, and the true summit of

Ken-ga-mine 剣ケ峰 (3776m) is on the opposite side of the crater, a 30–40min undulating walk in either direction.

Descent

The Subashiri and Yoshida descent trails follow the same path initially, which starts just south of the huts at the top end of the ascent trail. The descent trail is an initially reddish and dusty gravel track (also shared by the bulldozers servicing the summit huts) which winds gently downwards via some large zigzags, and is much less rough underfoot than the ascent path.

Eventually reach the **'old' eighth station**, and descend on a trail running parallel to the Subashiri ascent trail for 15min as far as the Shita-edoya hut 下江戸屋 at the **eighth station**. Be careful to follow the signs for the Subashiri trail and take the right descent path (if you reach the zigzags at the top of the Yoshida descent trail then you've gone too far!).

Leave most of the crowds behind and descend the trail, which soon merges with the ascent path, and in less than 20min arrive at the **'old' seventh station**. The 'up' and 'down' paths split again, so take the right-hand branch and crunch down a sandier path to reach the **seventh station** in 25min.

After the hut, follow the right-hand trail for the *sunaba-shiri* 砂走り, or 'sand run' – a long and steady descent on loose volcanic scoria which tends to get in your shoes (and sometimes the dust in your eyes). Walk or run downhill for about 1hr to rejoin the ascent path, and then it's a 20min stroll through the forest to reach the bus stop at **Subashiri 5th Station**.

WALK 12
Mt Fuji – Gotemba route 御殿場ルート

Start/finish	Gotemba New 5th Station
Distance	Ascent 11km (6¾ miles); descent 8.5km (5¼ miles)
Total ascent/descent	2335m (7660ft)
Grade	Ascent 2/descent 1+
Time	Ascent 7hr 30min; descent 3hr
Terrain	Very loose volcanic sand and gravel paths between fifth and seventh stations; steep and rockier near summit
Access	See Mt Fuji part introduction
Accommodation	A few huts along the way (reservation required)
Facilities	Huts sell food, drinks, souvenirs, some have free wi-fi. Toilets at huts (small donation required).

A wonderful descent trail, the Gotemba route is the longest of the four trails on Mt Fuji, and the fifth station is by far the lowest of all the fifth stations, at an elevation of just 1440m. This makes it a long and tough route in ascent, only compounded by the black sandy ground which makes climbing a bit of a slog. In descent, however, it can actually be one of the quickest routes, as the loose volcanic soil means you can take large sliding strides down the mountain, especially along the *osunabashiri*, or 'great sand run', which starts just below the seventh station. There are few huts along the way and it is generally the least popular route, with none of the big crowds seen on other parts of the mountain. There is also the option of a short detour to the summit of Mt Hōei on the way down.

Ascent

At the **Gotemba New 5th Station** there is parking, a bus stop, toilets, a small shop and a man in a shack asking for donations, but not a lot else. Take the black sandy trail to the left of the building, and climb gently for 15min to reach the **Ōishi-chaya** hut 大石茶屋, the last place to buy supplies for a while. A path leads off to nearby Mt Futago 双子山, two very minor peaks on Fuji-san's lower slopes, but instead follow the signs for the Gotemba trail. The trail splits into ascending and descending branches; follow the left-hand ascent branch

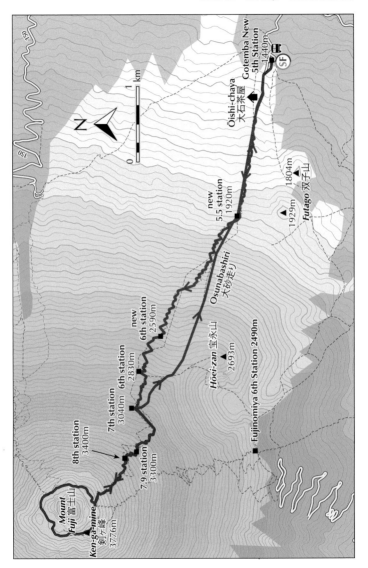

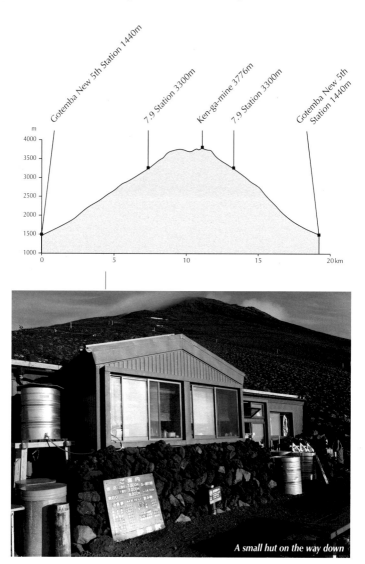

Gotemba New 5th Station 1440m

7.9 Station 3300m

Ken-ga-mine 3776m

7.9 Station 3300m

Gotemba New 5th Station 1440m

A small hut on the way down

for about 1hr, along a lengthy and gradual incline of loose black scoria.

At the **'new' 5.5 station**, formerly known as Jirōbō 次郎坊, the ascent and descent paths cross. Continue up the sandy trail, and try not to be disheartened by the sight of hikers descending with apparent ease over to the left. After 30min the path crosses the main bulldozer track, and then crosses it again at an old station marker after another 40min of climbing. Ascend the trail as it zigzags upwards for 1hr to arrive at the **'new' sixth station** where there is a hut which is currently not in service.

Continue the meandering climb and arrive at a junction and meteorological agency shelter after another 1hr. From here carry on for 50min up a steep path of many switch-backs to reach the **seventh station**, where there are finally a few huts open for business and good views up and down the mountain.

Follow the path around and climb steadily for 50min to reach the awkwardly named **7.9 station** and the Akaiwahachigō-kan hut 赤岩八合館. The terrain has a distinct reddish tinge and it is only a 20min climb to the **eighth**

The trail leading to Mt Hōei (straight on) or left for the Osunabashiri ('great sand run')

station along a twisting and stony gravel trail. There is nothing here apart from the remnants of an old hut.

The last 1hr is fairly steep, the path zigzagging between and sometimes over large grey boulders which litter the red slopes. Scramble over rocks and finally pass through a wooden *torii* gate to arrive on the **summit rim**. Take the path left for the true summit, Ken-ga-mine 剣ケ峰 (3776m).

Descent

The descent uses the same trail as the ascent as far as the seventh station. It begins in a saddle along the crater rim where there are some stone markers, a *torii* gate and a boarded-up old hut. Follow the trail down the stone steps and descend steeply down a winding and rocky path. The long stony zigzag section down to the **eighth station** should only take about 30min. ◄ It is then another 30min to reach the huts at the **seventh station** and the point where the trail splits.

There are splendid views of Mt Hōei on the way down.

Follow the path to the right which is marked as 'Osunabashiri' 大砂走り, meaning 'the great sand run'. The gently winding path is marked by ropes, and is a loose mix of black volcanic sand and small rocks underfoot, making it great fun to slip, slide or run down. After about 600 metres another path comes in from the left and the trail splits. The path to the right is known as the 'Prince Route' プリンスルート after the Crown Prince of Japan went this way in 2008. It snakes over to the summit of Mt Hōei (2693m) in 15min and then carries on around the mountain for 40min to the Fujinomiya sixth station, and so is a good route to take if you want to head to the Fujinomiya trailhead.

Take time to remove all the black dust and scoria from your boots!

Otherwise follow the left path down the black sandy slopes, and descend steadily for 2.3km to the **'new' 5.5 station** where the 'up' and 'down' paths cross. It is then a 30min descent, sometimes following the bulldozer track, to reach the **Ōishi-chaya** hut 大石茶屋, beyond which lies the **fifth station** bus stop, a 10min walk away. ◄

WALK 13
Mt Fuji – Fujinomiya route 富士宮ルート

Start/finish	Fujinomiya 5th Station
Distance	Ascent 5km (3 miles); descent 5km (3 miles)
Total ascent/descent	1395m (4580ft)
Grade	1+
Time	Ascent 5hr; descent 3hr 30min
Terrain	Fairly steep, rocky and loose gravel paths, with some simple short scrambles over rough rocks
Access	See Mt Fuji part introduction
Accommodation	Huts at every station (reservation required)
Facilities	Huts sell food, drinks, souvenirs, some have free wi-fi. Toilets at huts (small donation required). Small medical centre at the eighth station.

The Fujinomiya trail is the second most popular route, with the fifth station at 2380m the highest starting point on the mountain. It is the shortest trail to the top and is also the route that arrives closest to the true summit of Mt Ken-ga-mine, so its popularity is easy to understand. There are plenty of huts but it's an unrelenting climb, and there are no separate ascending and descending branches, so expect to meet a lot of people on the way, with congestion on the final steep section just below the summit (especially before sunrise).

Ascent
Fujinomiya 5th Station is well developed, with shops, a restaurant and information centre and the trail starts just beyond the buildings, right at the edge of the tree line. The black sandy path is stony in places and starts climbing immediately, but very gently, and soon arrives at the **sixth station**. Walk past the huts and turn left to continue climbing.

Another path follows the contours of the mountain and leads to **Mt Hōei** 宝永山 (2693m), the most recently formed secondary crater and peak. It makes for an interesting short hike if you don't have

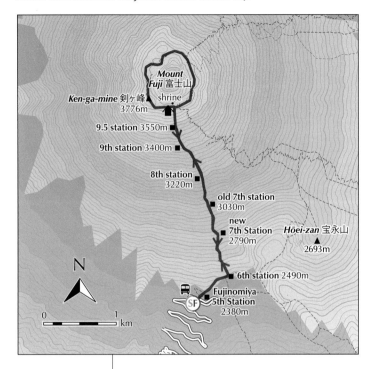

time to scale Mt Fuji itself. Allow at least 1hr 30min there and back.

Continue up the suddenly steeper, rougher and zigzagging path, the surrounding black slopes littered with boulders and tufts of vegetation. In less than 1hr you'll reach the **'new' seventh station** 新七合目, where there is a large hut and still just under 1000m of height to gain before the summit. Follow the loose gravel and boulder-strewn path upwards for 50min to arrive at the **'old' seventh station** where there is a nice and somewhat rustic-looking hut nestled on the hillside.

Carry on climbing for another 50min, the terrain becoming rockier and steeper in places, and pass through a narrow rocky section to arrive at the **eighth station**, where there is a hut, toilet and temporary medical centre. Just past this station

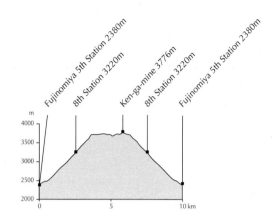

there is a large *torii* gate to the left of the trail. Continue up the rocky, scree-covered slope for 40min and reach the sturdy looking **ninth station** hut, which offers great views down the mountain and out to Suruga Bay. Pass through a

The Fujinomiya route becomes rockier near the top

349

The summit hut at the top of the Fujinomiya route

The large gully below and to the right holds snow until late in the season.

wooden *torii* gate and zigzag upwards towards the **9.5 station** which should be reached in around 30min. ◄

The final section is along a fairly narrow path which is quite steep and rocky, and can become very slow and congested in the pre-dawn 'rush', but usually takes about 40min. Pass another wooden *torii* gate to reach the crater rim where you'll find the Chōjō Fujikan summit hut 頂上富士館 on the left, a post office and the Sengen-taisha Okumiya **shrine**. Head left to climb to the true summit of **Mt Ken-ga-mine** 剣ヶ峰 (3776m) in 20min.

Descent
As there is no separate path down, just follow the same route in reverse. The knee-knocking descent takes about 3hr 30min.

WALK 14
Mt Kuro-dake 黒岳

Start	Mitsutōge-iriguchi bus stop 三ツ峠入口
Alternative start	Tenkachaya 天下茶屋
Finish	Kawaguchiko Healthy Living Centre 河口湖自然生活館
Alternative finish	Itchiku Kubota Art Museum bus stop 久保田一竹美術館
Distance	11.5km (7 miles); alternative start adds 0.7km (½ mile). Alternative finish is 3.5km (2¼ mile) shorter.
Total ascent	855m (2810ft); alternative start is 180m less
Total descent	1025m (3370ft)
Grade	1+
Time	6hr
Terrain	A steady climb on a leafy forest path, followed by a gentle ridge walk (with one or two very easy scrambles) and then a steep descent on a narrow and little-used path. Finish on paved road.
Access	See below
Accommodation	Hotels, hostels and campgrounds around Kawaguchiko
Facilities	Shops and hot springs in Kawaguchiko
When to go	All year, but snow and winter conditions are likely from mid December to March. The descent from Shindō-tōge is not recommended in snow as the route is steep and poorly marked.
Note	Winter is the best time to have a chance of viewing Mt Fuji, especially early mornings. However, great care should be taken if snow is on the ground, and crampons are recommended. If in doubt, retrace steps rather than attempting either of the descents described here.

Climbing Mt Fuji may be the ultimate goal for many people interested in walking in Japan, but it is usually said that the famous peak is best appreciated – and certainly at its most beautiful – when viewed from afar. The Fuji Five Lakes region boasts countless great viewpoints of the famous peak, including from the tops of the many smaller mountains that encircle Mt Fuji to the west, north and east.

Mt Kuro-dake (1793m) is a modest peak that sits almost directly north of Fuji-san, with its wooded slopes looming over the northern shores of Lake Kawaguchiko.

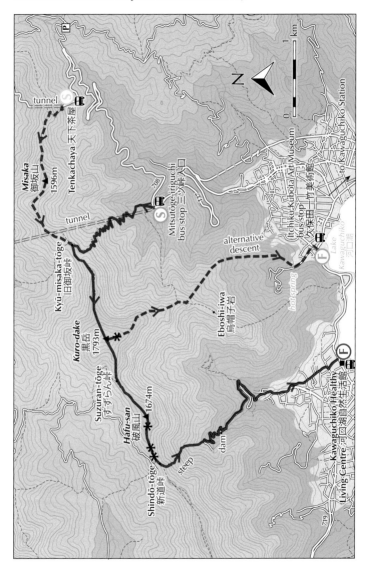

It is one of many small promontories on the mostly forested Mt Misaka ridgeline, and where there are occasional breaks in the trees the magnificent panoramic views of Mt Fuji, Lake Kawaguchiko and the lakeside town of the same name are jaw-droppingly good (when the weather is clear at least). Kuro-dake is far quieter and less developed than the nearby Mt Mitsutōge, a popular mountain to the northeast of Kawaguchiko that is somewhat tarnished by a number of ugly antennas near its summit, crowds of people and arguably inferior views.

ACCESS

The 'hiking bus' bound for Tenkachaya leaves from Kawaguchiko Station around 9am every day (times differ on weekends). See http://bus-en.fujikyu.co.jp; under 'Route bus' at the bottom of the page, select the Kofu Station option for a timetable in English. Get off at the Mitsutōge-iriguchi bus stop 三ツ峠入口 (also called Mitsutōge Entrance in English). If attempting the alternative start, ride the bus all the way to Tenkachaya 天下茶屋. Most hikers walk down the mountain so there are no return buses from there in the afternoon.

Alternatively, there are much more frequent (and early-morning) buses from Kawaguchiko Station bound for Kofu 甲府, stopping at Mitsutōge-iriguchi; see previous link. If ending the walk at Mitsutōge-iriguchi bus stop, there are buses heading for Kawaguchiko and Fuji stations almost every hour until around 9pm.

At the other end of the walk, the Kawaguchiko sightseeing bus (red line) runs between Kawaguchiko Healthy Living Centre and Kawaguchiko Station. Check the 'Retro Bus/Omnibus' tab at http://bus-en.fujikyu.co.jp/heritage-tour for the timetable. There are also infrequent local buses.

Bus schedules for the whole region are available in English from Kawaguchiko's tourist information centre.

For drivers there is plenty of parking around Kawaguchiko. There is also parking high up the mountain before reaching Tenkachaya, up the track from the Mitsutōge-tozanguchi bus stop 三ツ峠登山口.

From the **Mitsutōge-iriguchi** bus stop 三ツ峠入口, cross the road and walk north towards the tunnel. Turn right at the road just before the tunnel, walk a few metres and take the path heading left signposted 'Misaka tōge' 御坂峠. You will soon reach a large board map of the area where a path branches left, but continue straight on and follow the path into the woods, passing large boulders and a series of small

Admiring Mt Fuji from the viewpoint at the summit of Mt Kuro-dake

There are many kinds of sasa in Japan, and it is ubiquitous at higher altitudes and latitudes.

concrete dams. Continue climbing on the clear and moderately steep, leafy path up through the forest of cedar trees. There are countless switchbacks all the way up the mountain, and also occasional tantalising views of Mt Fuji through the gaps in the trees.

Near the top of the ridge the trees thin out a little and *sasa* grass (broadleaf bamboo) grows on the ground. ◄ Just over to the east, Mt Mitsutōge 三ツ峠山 sometimes pops into view. After around 1hr 30min of steady climbing you'll reach a grassy spot called **Kyū-misaka-tōge** 旧御坂峠, a major junction for various trails. It is marked by signposts and an abandoned old corrugated-iron hut.

Alternative start

The 'hiking bus' runs further up the mountain all the way to **Tenkachaya** 天下茶屋. Starting from here is slightly easier as it cuts around 200m of ascent, although the walking time is roughly the same (about 1hr 30min to the abandoned hut at Kyū-misaka-tōge).

Walk past the large and attractive old wooden Tenkachaya teahouse 天下茶屋, then climb the stairs just before the road tunnel and walk up through forest to reach a trail junction on the ridgeline in about 15min. Turn left and walk along the ridge for about 1km to gently ascend to the wooded summit of **Mt Misaka** 御坂山 (1596m), and from here carry on along the slightly undulating ridge for 30min to arrive at **Kyū-misaka-tōge** 旧御坂峠, a large trail junction marked by a decrepit hut.

Take the path heading left past the hut, labelled for 'Kurodake' 黒岳. Pass a wooden shed-like shrine and some old breezeblock toilets. The walk along the undulating ridge path is reasonably gentle, with a few short, steady climbs and occasional views of Mt Fuji or the mountains to the north. There are a couple of simple scrambles up over rocks before arriving at the top of the flat and forested peak of **Mt Kuro-dake** 黒岳. Ignore the path to the right and soon reach the summit sign (1793m).

To continue, look for a sign marked as 'Observatory' and follow it left. After 200 metres you'll reach a gap in the trees which serves as a spectacular **viewpoint** high up on the mountainside. ▸ A small path leads down to the left for an alternative return to Kawaguchiko, ending at a hot spring (see alternative finish). In winter, if there is any snow and ice it is safer to retrace your steps back to the Mitsutōge-iriguchi bus

If the weather is clear, the views of Mt Fuji and Lake Kawaguchi below are staggering. The South Japan Alps are also visible to the west.

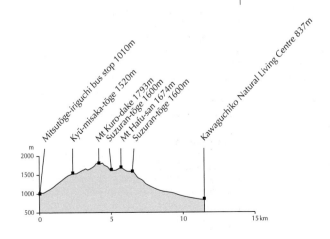

The narrow and indistinct path on the descent

stop, rather than attempting either the full route described here or the alternative finish, both of which are steep and difficult in winter conditions.

For the 'main' descent route, go back to the trail junction near the summit, turn left, and follow the path which immediately twists and turns steeply downhill. In 15min there is another great view of Mt Fuji near a trail junction marked as **Suzuran-tōge** すずらん峠. Ignore the path branching right and carry on along the ridge, following the sign for Ōishi 大石.

The route rises very gently through nice woodland to arrive at an unassuming minor peak called **Hafū-san** 破風山 (1674m) in about 20min. From here stroll downwards again to soon reach another great Mt Fuji **viewpoint** at a clearing on the left, then continue down the trail a little further to soon reach another wonderful **viewpoint**. This one has some large bare rocks to sit on and admire the views.

Carry on down the path for a few minutes to reach yet another **viewpoint** just off the trail to the left, and shortly afterwards reach a trail junction known as **Shindō-tōge** 新道峠. There are more good Fuji-san views from here and a number of paths branching off. The path heading right leads to a small car park at the end of a rough forest road, while the trail straight on continues along the ridge for many more kilometres towards Mt Settō-ga-take 節刀ヶ岳. The way back to Kawaguchiko is down a very narrow, indistinct grassy forest path which branches leftwards and is easy to miss. This route doesn't look that frequently used, and due to the steep terrain and minimal markings should be avoided if there is a covering of snow in the winter.

Follow the path between the trees and soon begin to descend very steeply, down countless zigzagging switchbacks. The lack of signs or trail markings is unusual for Japan, but partway down you should pass a signpost for 'Ōishi and Lake Kawaguchiko'. Continue descending down into cedar forest; eventually the steep gradient lessens and the forest floor becomes stonier. About 40min after leaving the ridge you will reach a rough gravel track. A large hiking course map indicates 120 minutes to the lake, but it is possible in half that time.

Head left and follow the winding track down through the forest, passing multiple small waterfalls. Skirt by a huge

Wandering down through the village

357

concrete **dam** on the right with Mt Fuji looming in the distance. The track turns into a paved road and passes many curious holiday homes, some of which precariously overhang the steep mountainside with the support of stilts. Follow the road as it winds down through the village, the constant presence of Mt Fuji in the background providing plenty of interesting photo opportunities.

Cross a bridge, and at a road junction with two mirrors turn right and then left to head towards the lake. You will soon reach the main road. Here you can either turn right for Akebonosō-mae bus stop あけぼの荘前 (local buses back to Kawaguchiko Station are fairly infrequent, but it's worth checking the timetable on the sign) or for buses on the 'red line' walk across the road to the **Kawaguchiko Natural Living Centre** 河口湖自然生活館 near the lake. This touristy place sells mostly blueberry-related goods, and if you still have the will or energy for taking photos then there are great lakeside views of Mt Fuji from nearby Ōishi Park 大石公園.

Alternative finish

This way offers a shorter and slightly quicker route off the mountain, but lacks the various Mt Fuji viewpoints encountered along the main route. As a bonus, however, this descent ends near a nice hot spring if you want a bath after the walk. Unrelentingly steep in places, the path may also be difficult to follow if there is snow on the ground, so caution is advised.

At the **viewpoint** near the summit of Mt Kuro-dake, follow the unmarked path that heads off to the left (southeast) of the rocks. After a short distance pass a sign for Eboshi-iwa 烏帽子岩, and then descend steeply. There are fixed ropes on some of the steeper sections for you to grab onto, but it is relatively straightforward in good conditions. Occasional green signs read 至広瀬 (for Hirose) and indicate that you are on the right path. After around 40min you'll reach a trail junction. The path left is for 'Misaka tunnel' 御坂トンネル, and leads back to the Mitsutōge-iriguchi bus stop 三ツ峠入口 at the start of the walk in about 1hr. If you are not enjoying the steep descent then this is a slightly gentler escape route.

For the hot spring, head right and continue following the green signs. Soon another path branches to the right and heads down to Eboshi-iwa 烏帽子岩, but ignore this. The ground remains steep, with a few rocky sections to

scramble down. There are ropes to aid the descent in places too. After about 1hr, turn right to cross a small stream and reach a paved road. Walk left down the road and the first building on the right is Notenburo Tensui hot spring 野天風呂天水 – a splendid outdoor *onsen* (10am–10pm). Continue down the road for a few minutes to pass **Itchiku Kubota Art Museum** on the right and after 1min turn right and then left onto 'Route 21' to reach the bus stop 久保田一竹美術館 for local and 'red line' buses back to Kawaguchiko Station.

Mt Kuro-dake from the southeast side of Lake Kawaguchiko

APPENDIX A
Route summary table – walks

Route	Start/Finish	Distance	Total ascent/descent	Time	Page
North (Kita) Alps					
Hakuba Area					
Walk 1 Mt Shirouma-dake	Sarukura or Tsugaike Ropeway	14km (8½ miles) or 18km (11 miles)	1700m (5580ft) or 1080m (3550ft)	9hr 30min or 12hr	56
Tateyama Area					
Walk 2 Mt Tateyama	Murodō	9.5km (6 miles)	900m (2950ft)	6hr 30min	83
Walk 3 Mt Oku-dainichi	Murodō	10km (6¼ miles)	580m (1900ft)	6hr	89
Hotaka Area					
Walk 4 Mt Yake-dake	Kamikōchi	10.5km (6½ miles)	920m (3020ft)	6–7hr	140
Walk 5 Mt Nishiho-Doppyō	Shin-Hotaka Ropeway	7.5km (4¾ miles)	545m (1790ft)	4hr 30min	146
Norikura Area					
Walk 6 Mt Norikura-dake	Norikura bus terminal	6.5km (3¾ miles)	330m (1080ft)	2hr 30min	205

Route	Start/Finish	Distance	Total ascent/descent	Time	Page
Central (Chūō) Alps					
Walk 7 Mt Kiso-koma-ga-take	Senjōjiki Ropeway	4km (2½ miles)	380m (1250ft)	3hr	213
South (Minami) Alps					
North Area					
Walk 8 Mt Kai-koma-ga-take	Kitazawa-tōge or Chikuu-komagatake Jinja	8.5km (5¼ miles) or 16km (10 miles)	935m (3070ft) or 2200m (7220ft)	7hr 30min or 15hr	235
Walk 9 Mt Senjō-ga-take	Kitazawa-tōge	9km (5¾ miles)	1175m (3850ft)	6hr 30min	241
Mt Fuji Area					
Walk 10 Mt Fuji – Yoshida route	Fuji Subaru Line 5th Station	7.5km (4½ miles) ascent; 7.5km (4½ miles) descent	1470m (4830ft)	6hr ascent; 3hr descent	332
Walk 11 Mt Fuji – Subashiri route	Subashiri 5th Station	8km (5 miles) ascent; 6km (3¾ miles) descent	1805m (5930ft) ascent	6hr 30min ascent; 3hr descent	337
Walk 12 Mt Fuji – Gotemba route	Gotemba New 5th Station	11km (6¾ miles) ascent; 8.5km (5¼ miles) descent	2335m (7660ft)	7hr 30min ascent; 3hr descent	342
Walk 13 Mt Fuji – Fujinomiya route	Fujinomiya 5th Station	5km (3 miles) ascent; 5km (3 miles) descent	1395m (4580ft)	5hr ascent; 3hr 30min descent	347
Walk 14 Mt Kuro-dake	Mitsutōge-iriguchi bus stop/Kawaguchiko Healthy Living Centre	11.5km (7 miles)	855m (2810ft/ 1025m (3370ft)	6hr	351

APPENDIX B
Route summary table – treks

Route	Start/Finish	Distance	Total ascent/descent	Time	Page
North (Kita) Alps					
Hakuba Area					
Trek 1 Mt Shirouma-dake and Yari Onsen	Sarukura	20.5km (12½ miles)	2100m (6890ft)	2 or 3 days	66
Stage 1	*Sarukura/Hakuba sansō hut*	*7.5km (4½ miles)*	*1700m (5580ft)/ negligible*	*6hr*	67
Stage 2	*Hakuba sansō hut/Hakuba-Yari Onsen-goya hut*	*6.5km (4 miles)*	*310m (1010ft)/ 750m (2460ft)*	*5hr*	72
Stage 3	*Hakuba-Yari Onsen goya hut/Sarukura*	*6.5km (4 miles)*	*90m (300ft)/ 1350m (4430ft)*	*3hr 30min*	76
Tateyama Area					
Trek 2 Mt Tsurugi-dake	Murodō or Bambajima-sō	14km (8¾ miles) or 16.5km (10 miles)	1590m (5220ft) or 2250m (7410ft)	2 or 3 days	94
Stage 1	*Murodō/Kenzan-sō hut*	*5km (3 miles)*	*490m (1610ft)/ 425m (1400ft)*	*4–5hr*	97
Stage 2	*Kenzan-sō hut/Murodō*	*9km (5¾ miles)*	*1100m (3610ft)/ 1165m (3820ft)*	*7–8hr*	101
Trek 3 North Alps traverse	Murodō/Kamikōchi	63km (39 miles)	4365m (14,320ft)/ 5295m (17,370ft)	5–7 days	108
Stage 1	*Murodō/Goshiki-ga-hara sansō hut*	*7km (4¼ miles)*	*700m (2290ft)/ 680m (2230ft)*	*5–6hr*	111
Stage 2	*Goshiki-ga-hara sansō hut/*	*12km (7½ miles)*	*1335m (4390ft)*	*10–11hr*	115

Route	Start/Finish	Distance	Total ascent/descent	Time	Page
Stage 3	*Yakushi-dake sansō hut/ Kurobegorō-goya hut*	*14km (8¾ miles)*	*865m (2840ft)/ 1230m (4040ft)*	*7hr*	120
Stage 4	*Kurobegorō-goya hut/Yari-ga-take sansō hut*	*12km (7½ miles)*	*1365m (4470ft)/ 625m (2040ft)*	*9hr*	126
Stage 5	*Yari-ga-take sansō hut/ Kamikōchi*	*18km (11 miles)*	*100m (330ft)/ 1675m (5490ft)*	*7hr*	131
Hotaka Area					
Trek 4	Mt Oku-Hotaka-dake and Karasawa Cirque	Kamikōchi	25km (15½ miles)	1685m (5530ft)	2 or 3 days	151
Stage 1	*Kamikōchi/Hotaka-dake sansō hut*	*8km (5 miles)*	*1685m (5530ft)/ 210m (690ft)*	*8–9hr*	154
Stage 2	*Hotaka-dake sansō hut/ Kamikōchi*	*17km (10½ miles)*	*negligible/1475m (4840ft)*	*6–7hr*	160
Trek 5	Mt Yari-ga-take	Kamikōchi/Shin-Hotaka Onsen	34km (21 miles)	1675m (5500ft)/ 2090m (6860ft)	2 or 3 days	167
Stage 1	*Kamikōchi/Yari-ga-take sansō hut*	*20km (12½ miles)*	*1575m (5170ft)/ negligible*	*8hr*	169
Stage 2	*Yari-ga-take sansō hut/Shin-Hotaka Ropeway*	*14km (8½ miles)*	*100m (330ft)/ 2090m (6860ft)*	*7hr*	175
Trek 6	Mt Chō-ga-take and Mt Jōnen-dake	Kamikōchi	34km (21 miles)	1970m (6460ft)	2 or 3 days	182
Stage 1	*Kamikōchi/Chō-ga-take Hut*	*12km (7½ miles)*	*1170m (3840ft)/ negligible*	*7hr*	183
Stage 2	*Chō-ga-take Hut/Kamikōchi*	*22km (13½ miles)*	*800m (2630ft)/ 1970m (6460ft)*	*11hr*	187

Route		Start/Finish	Distance	Total ascent/descent	Time	Page
Trek 7	Mt Kasa-ga-take	Shin-Hotaka Onsen	18km (11 miles)	2010m (6600ft)/ 1910m (6260ft)	2 days	193
Stage 1		Nakao-kōgen-guchi bus stop/Kasa-ga-take sansō hut	8km (5 miles)	1910m (6270ft)/ 100m (330ft)	8–9hr	195
Stage 2		Kasa-ga-take sansō hut/Shin-Hotaka Ropeway	10km (6 miles)	100m (330ft)/ 1810m (5930ft)	5–6hr	199
Central (Chūō) Alps						
Trek 8	Central Alps traverse	Senjōjiki ropeway station/ Komagane Kōgen	17km (10½ miles)	755m (2480ft)/ 2520m (8270ft)	2 or 3 days	217
Stage 1		Senjōjiki ropeway station/ Kisodono sansō hut	7km (4¼ miles)	390m (1280ft)/ 520m (1710ft)	5–8hr	219
Stage 2		Kisodono sansō hut/ Komagane Kōgen	10km (6¼ miles)	365m (1200ft)/ 2000m (6560ft)	7hr 30min	224
South (Minami) Alps						
North Area						
Trek 9	Mt Kita-dake	Hirogawara	13.5km (8½ miles)	1705m (5490ft)	2 or 3 days	245
Stage 1		Hirogawara/Shirane-oike-goya hut	4km (2½ miles)	715m (2350ft)/ negligible	3hr	247
Stage 2		Shirane-oike-goya hut	6.5km (4 miles)	990m (3250ft)	7hr 30min	250
Stage 3		Shirane-oike-goya hut/ Hirogawara	3km (2 miles)	negligible/ 715m (2350ft)	3hr	253

Route		Start/Finish	Distance	Total ascent/descent	Time	Page
Trek 10	Mt Hō-ō	Yashajin-tōge/Hirogawara	17km (10½ km)	1450m (4760ft)/ 1320m (4330ft)	2 days	255
Stage 1		Yashajin-tōge/Minami-omuro-goya hut	7.5km (4¾ miles)	1050m (3445ft)/ negligible	5hr 30min	256
Stage 2		Minami-omuro-goya hut/ Hirogawara	9.5km (5¾ miles)	400m (1310ft)/ 1320m (4330ft)	8hr	260
South Area						
Trek 11	Mt Arakawa-Higashidake (Mt Warusawa-dake) and Mt Akaishi-dake	Sawarajima	27.5km (17 miles)	3235m (10,620ft)	3 or 4 days	267
Stage 1		Sawarajima/Senmai-goya hut	9.5km (5¾ miles)	1620m (5310ft)/ 135m (450ft)	6hr 30min	269
Stage 2		Senmai-goya hut/Akaishi-goya hut	13.5km (8¼ miles)	1565m (5140ft)/ 1625m (5330ft)	11hr 30min	272
Stage 3		Akaishi-goya hut/Sawarajima	4.5km (3 miles)	50m (165ft)/ 1475m (4840ft)	2hr 30min	277
Trek 12	Mt Kamikōchi-dake and Mt Hijiri-dake	Hijiri-dake tozanguchi	30km (18½ miles) or 21km (13 miles)	2970m (9745ft) or 2390m (7840ft)	2 or 3 days	279
Stage 1		Hijiridake tozanguchi/ Hijiridaira-goya hut	14.5km (9 miles) or 5.5km (3½ miles)	1990m (6530ft)/ 1005m (3295ft) or 1410m (4625ft)/ 425m (1395ft)	9hr or 5hr	281
Stage 2		Hijiridaira-goya hut/ Hijiridake tozanguchi	15.5km (9½ miles)	980m (3215ft)/ 1965m (6445ft)	9hr	286

Route		Start/Finish	Distance	Total ascent/descent	Time	Page
Trek 13	South Alps traverse	Hirogawara/Akaishi Onsen Shirakaba-sō hot spring	97km (60½ miles) or 77.5km (48½ miles)	9775m (32,070ft)/10,490m (34,420ft) or 7835m (25,705ft)/8550m (28,705ft)	7 or 8 days	288
Stage 1		Hirogawara/Kitadake Kata-no-goya hut	5.5km (3½ miles)	1650m (5410ft)/290m (950ft)	6hr	291
Stage 2		Kitadake Kata-no-goya hut/Kuma-no-daira-goya hut	8km (5 miles)	850m (2790ft)/1020m (3350ft)	6hr	293
Stage 3		Kuma-no-daira-goya hut/Sanpuku-tōge-goya hut	15.5km (9½ miles)	1420m (4660ft)/1380m (4530ft)	10hr 30min	297
Stage 4		Sanpuku-tōge hut/Arakawa-goya hut	14.5km (9¼ miles)	1260m (4130ft)/1680m (5510ft)	11hr	302
Stage 5		Arakawa-goya hut/Hijiridaira-goya hut	15.5km (9½ miles)	1820m (5970ft)/1950m (6400ft)	11hr 30min	307
Stage 6		Hijiridaira-goya hut/Chausu-goya hut	7km (4¼ miles)	730m (2400ft)/610m (2000ft)	5hr	312
Stage 7		Chausu-goya hut	19.5km (12 miles)	1940m (6365ft)	9hr	315
Stage 8		Chausu-goya hut/Akaishi Onsen Shirakaba-sō hot spring	11.5km (7 miles)	105m (340ft)/1620m (5320ft)	6hr 30min	317

APPENDIX C

Mountain huts

Most huts cost between 5000 and 10,000 yen per person per night. Prices at the higher end usually include dinner and breakfast; lower-end prices are *sudomari* (stay only, no meals). Huts only accept cash, and with a few exceptions reservations (especially for *sudomari*) are usually unnecessary – albeit recommended on national holidays in popular areas. A handful of huts open for the cluster of holidays known as Golden Week (late April to early May) but then close again until early summer, so check details carefully.

Note that most hut websites are in Japanese, but key information may be obtained with the help of an automatic translation tool such as Google Translate.

North (Kita) Alps

Hakuba area

Trek 1

Sarukura-sō
猿倉荘
Mt Shirouma
Golden Week (no meals) and mid June–early Oct
Stay, meals
tel 0261-72-4709 (0261-75-3788)
http://yamagoya.hakubakousha.com

Hakuba-jiri-goya
白馬尻小屋
Mt Shirouma
mid July–late Sep
Stay, meals, camping
tel 0261-72-2002
www.hakuba-sanso.co.jp

Hakuba-chōjō-shukusha
白馬頂上宿舎
Mt Shirouma
mid June–mid Oct
Stay, meals, camping
tel 0261-75-3788
http://yamagoya.hakubakousha.com

Hakuba sansō
白馬山荘
Mt Shirouma
Golden Week–mid Oct
Stay, restaurant, shop, medical centre
tel 0261-72-2002
www.hakuba-sanso.co.jp

Tsugaike hut
栂池ヒュッテ
Mt Shirouma
Golden Week and early June–mid Oct
Stay, meals, bath
tel 0261-83-3136 (090-4952-3122)
www.hakuba-sanso.co.jp

Tsugaike sansō
栂池山荘
Mt Shirouma
mid May–mid Oct
Stay, meals, bath
tel 0261-83-3113
www.tsugaikesansou.jp

Hakuba Ōike sansō
白馬大池山荘
Mt Shirouma
early July–mid Oct
Stay, meals, camping
tel 0261-72-2002
www.hakuba-sanso.co.jp

Hakuba-Yari Onsen-goya
白馬鑓温泉小屋
Mt Shirouma
late July–late Sep
Stay, meals, bath, camping
tel 0261-72-2002
www.hakuba-sanso.co.jp

Tengu sansō
天狗山荘
Mt Shirouma
late June–mid Sep
Stay, meals, camping
tel 0261-75-3788
http://yamagoya.hakubakousha.com

Tateyama area

Murodō

Hotel Tateyama
ホテル立山
mid April–late Nov
Stay, restaurant, shops, bath, Wi-Fi, coin lockers
tel 076-463-3345
https://h-tateyama.alpen-route.co.jp/en

Murodō sansō
室堂山荘
mid April–late Nov
Stay, meals, bath
tel 076-463-1228
www.murodou.co.jp

Trek 2

Mikuri-ga-ike Onsen
みくりが池温泉
mid April–late Nov
Stay, restaurant, café, shop, bath
tel 076-463-1441
www.mikuri.com

Raichō Onsen Raichōsō
らいちょう温泉 雷鳥荘
Murodō
mid April–late Nov

Stay, meals, bath
tel 076-463-1664 (076-463-1539)
www.raichoso.com

Raichōsawa Hut
雷鳥沢ヒュッテ
Murodō
mid April–late Oct
Stay, meals, bath
tel 076-463-1835
www.raichozawa.net/hyutte.html

Tsurugi-gozen-goya
劍御前小舎
Mt Tateyama
late April–mid Oct
Stay, meals
tel 080-8694-5076
www.tsurugigozengoya.net

Tsurugi-sawa-goya
劍澤小屋
Mt Tsurugi-dake
late April–mid Oct
Stay (from June), meals, shower
tel 076-482-1319 (080-1968-1620)
http://home.384.jp/tsuruqi1

Kenzan-sō
劍山荘
Mt Tsurugi-dake
early June–late Oct
Stay, meals, shower
tel 076-482-1564 (090-8967-9116)
www.net3-tv.net/~kenzansou

Tsurugi-dake Hayatsuki-goya
劍岳早月小屋
Mt Tsurugi-dake
mid July–mid Oct
Stay, meals, camping
tel 090-7740-9233 (076-482-1700)
www.net3-tv.net/~hayatsuki

Trek 3

Ichinokoshi sansō
一の越山荘
Mt Tateyama
late April–mid Oct
Stay, meals
tel 090-1632-4629 (076-421-1446)
http://tateyama-1nokoshi.in.coocan.jp

Goshikigahara sansō
五色ヶ原山荘
Mt Yakushi-dake
early July–early Oct
Stay, meals, camping
tel 090-2128-1857 (076-482-1940)
www.goshikigahara.com/f_sanso.htm

Sugo-no-koshi-goya
スゴ乗越小屋
Mt Yakushi-dake
mid July–mid Sep
Stay, meals, camping
tel 076-482-1917
http://sugohut.web.fc2.com/syoukai.html

Yakushi-dake sansō
薬師岳山荘
Mt Yakushi-dake
early July–early Oct
Stay, meals
tel 090-8263-2523 (076-451-9222)
www.yakushidake-sansou.com

Tarōdaira-goya
太郎平小屋
Mt Yakushi-dake
early June–late Oct
Stay, meals, camping
tel 076-482-1917 (080-1951-3030)
www.ltaro.com

Kurobegorō-goya
黒部五郎小舎
Mt Kurobegorō-dake
mid July–late Sep

Stay, meals, camping
tel 0577-34-6268
www.sugorokugoya.com

Mitsumata sansō
三俣山荘
Mt Washiba-dake
early July–mid Oct
Stay, meals, camping
tel 090-4672-8108
http://kumonodaira.net/mitsumata

Sugoroku-goya
双六小屋
Mt Sugoroku-dake
mid June–mid Oct
Stay, meals, camping
tel 090-3480-0434 (0577-34-6268)
www.sugorokugoya.com

Yari-ga-take sansō
槍ヶ岳山荘
Mt Yari-ga-take
late April–early Nov
Stay, meals, camping
tel 090-2641-1911
www.yarigatake.co.jp/english

Sesshō Hut
殺生ヒュッテ
Mt Yari-ga-take
mid June–mid Oct
Stay, meals
tel 0263-77-1488
www.nakabusa.com/lodge/lodge.html

Ōyari Hut
ヒュッテ大槍
Mt Yari-ga-take
early July–mid Oct
Stay, meals
tel 090-1402-1660 (0263-32-1535)
www.enzanso.co.jp/ooyari

Yarisawa Lodge
槍沢ロッジ
Mt Yari-ga-take
late April–early Nov
Stay, meals, bath, camping
tel 0263-95-2626 (090-3135-0003)
www.yarigatake.co.jp/yarisawa

Yoko-o sansō
横尾山荘
Kamikōchi
early May–early Nov
Stay, meals, bath, camping
tel 0263-95-2421
www.yokoo-sanso.co.jp/english

Tokusawa-en
徳澤園
Kamikōchi
early May–late Oct
Stay, meals, bath, camping
tel 0263-95-2508
www.tokusawaen.com/english.html

Tokusawa Lodge
徳澤ロッジ
Kamikōchi
early May–early Nov
Stay, meals, bath
tel 0263-95-2526
www.m-kamikouchi.jp/en

Myojinkan
明神館
Kamikōchi
late April–early Nov
Stay, meals, bath
tel 0263-95-2036
www.myojinkan.co.jp/index3.html

Kumo-no-daira variant

Yakushisawa-goya
薬師沢小屋
Mt Yakushi-dake
early July–early Oct

Stay, meals
tel 076-482-1917
www.ltaro.com

Kumonodaira sansō
雲ノ平山荘
Kumonodaira
early July–mid Oct
Stay, meals, camping
tel 070-3937-3980
https://kumonodaira.com/en

Kōtenbara sansō
高天原山荘
Kumonodaira
early July–late Sep
Stay, meals, outdoor bath
tel 076-482-1917
www.ltaro.com

Other

Lodge Tateyama-renpō
ロッジ立山連峰
Murodō
mid April–late Oct
Stay, meals, bath
tel 076-482-1617
www.raichozawa.net/lodge.html

Kuranosuke sansō
内蔵助山荘
Mt Tateyama
mid July–mid Oct
Stay, meals
tel 090-5686-1250

Kagamidaira sansō
鏡平山荘
Mt Kasa-ga-take
mid July–mid Oct
Stay, meals
tel 090-1566-7559
www.sugorokugoya.com

Hotaka area

Trek 4

Dakesawa-goya
岳沢小屋
Mt Hotaka
late April–early Nov
Stay, meals, camping
tel 090-2546-2100
www.yarigatake.co.jp/dakesawa

Hotaka-dake sansō
穂高岳山荘
Mt Hotaka
late April–early Nov
Stay, meals, camping
tel 090-7869-0045 (0578-82-2150)
www.hotakadakesanso.com

Karasawa-goya
涸沢小屋
Mt Hotaka
late April–early Nov
Stay, meals
tel 090-2204-1300
www.karasawagoya.com

Karasawa Hut
涸沢ヒュッテ
Mt Hotaka
late April–early Nov
Stay, meals, camping (tent/sleeping bag rental available mid July–early Oct, please call)
tel 090-9002-2534
www.karasawa-hyutte.com

Yoko-o sansō, Tokusawa-en and Myojinkan
横尾山荘, 徳澤園, 明神館
see Trek 3 above

Trek 5

Myojinkan, Tokusawa-en and Tokusawa Lodge
明神館, 徳澤園, 徳澤ロッジ
see Trek 3 above

Yoko-o sansō, Yarisawa Lodge, Sesshō Hut and Yari-ga-take sansō
横尾山荘, 槍沢ロッジ, 殺生ヒュッテ, 槍ヶ岳山荘
see Trek 3 above

Yaridaira-goya
槍平小屋
Mt Yari-ga-dake
early July–mid Oct
Stay, meals, camping
tel 090-8863-3021
www.yaridairagoya.sakura.ne.jp

Hotakadaira-goya
穂高平小屋
Mt Hotaka
early July–mid Oct (only weekends from Sept)
Stay, meals, bath
tel 0578-89-2842

Daikiretto and Hotaka ridgeline traverse

Yari-ga-take sansō
槍ヶ岳山荘
See Trek 3 above

Minami-dake-goya
南岳小屋
Mt Yari-ga-take
early July–mid Oct
Stay, meals, camping
tel 090-4524-9448
www.yarigatake.co.jp/minamidake

Kita-hotaka-goya
北穂高小屋
Mt Hotaka
late April–early Nov
Stay, meals, camping
tel 090-1422-8886
www.kitaho.co.jp

Karasawa-goya, Karasawa Hut and Hotaka-dake sansō
涸沢小屋, 涸沢ヒュッテ, 穂高岳山荘
see Trek 4 above

Trek 6

Myojinkan and Tokusawa-en
明神館, 徳澤園
see Trek 3 above

Chō-ga-take Hut
蝶ヶ岳ヒュッテ
Mt Chō-ga-take
late April–early Nov
Stay, meals, camping
tel 090-1056-3455
https://chougatake.com

Yoko-o sansō
横尾山荘
see Trek 3 above

Jōnen-goya
常念小屋
Mt Jōnen-dake
late April–early Nov
Stay, meals, camping
tel 090-1430-3328
www.mt-jonen.com

Trek 7

Kasa-ga-take sansō
笠ヶ岳山荘
Mt Kasa-ga-take
late June–mid Oct
Stay, meals, camping
tel 090-7020-5666
http://kasagatake.com/english.html

Wasabidaira-goya
わさび平小屋
Mt Kasa-ga-take
early July–mid Oct
Stay, meals, bath, camping
tel 0577-34-6268 (090-8074-7778)
www.sugorokugoya.com

Other

Suishō-goya
水晶小屋
Mt Suishō-dake

mid July–late Sep
Stay, meals
tel 090-4672-8108
http://kumonodaira.net/suisho

Yama-no-hidaya
山のひだや
Kamikōchi
late April–early Nov
Stay, meals, bath
tel 0263-95-2211
http://yamanohidaya.wixsite.com/hidaya

Kamonji-goya
嘉門次小屋
Kamikōchi
late April–mid Nov
Stay, meals, bath
tel 0263-95-2418 (0263-33-8434)
https://kamonjigoya.wordpress.com

Yake-dake-goya
焼岳小屋
Mt Yake-dake
mid June–late Oct
Stay, meals
tel 090-2753-2560
www.m-kamikouchi.jp/yakedake

Nishiho sansō
西穂山荘
Mt Hotaka
all year
Stay, meals, camping
tel 0263-36-7052
www.nishiho.com

Norikura area

Hakuunsō
白雲荘
Mt Norikura
mid June–mid Oct
Stay, meals, bath
tel 090-3480-3136
https://norikura-hakuunso.jimdo.com

Ginreisō
銀嶺荘
Mt Norikura
late July–late Oct
Stay, meals, bath
tel 0577-79-2026 (080-6926-3145)
http://norikura-ginreiso.com

Kata-no-koya
肩ノ小屋
Mt Norikura
late June–late Oct
Stay, meals
tel 0263-93-2002
www6.plala.or.jp/bell-suzuran

Norikura-chōjyō-goya
乗鞍岳頂上小屋
Mt Norikura
mid May–late Oct
Snacks, free wi-fi, no stay
tel 090-1561-6434
www.norikurahut.jp

Central (Chūō) Alps

Trek 8

Hotel Senjyōjiki
ホテル千畳敷
Mt Kiso-koma
all year
Stay, meals, bath
tel 0265-83-3844
www.chuo-alps.com/hotel

Kisodono sansō
木曽殿山荘
Mt Utsugi-dake
early July–early Oct
Stay, meals (reservation required)
tel 090-5638-8193 (0573-72-4380)

Komahō Hut
駒峰ヒュッテ
Mt Utsugi-dake
mid July–mid Oct

Stay only (futons available), snacks, no
meals
www.komaho.net/hutte/utsugi_hutte1.html

Other

Hōken-dake sansō
宝剣岳山荘
Mt Kiso-koma
late April–early Nov
Stay, meals
tel 090-7804-2185 (0265-95-1919)
http://miyadakankou.co.jp/houkensansou

Tengu-sō
天狗荘
Mt Kiso-koma
early July–early Oct
Stay, meals
tel 090-7804-2185 (0265-95-1919)
http://miyadakankou.co.jp/tengusou

Komagatake-chōjō sansō
駒ケ岳頂上山荘
Mt Kiso-koma
early July–early Oct
Stay, meals, camping
tel 090-7804-2185 (0265-95-1919)
http://miyadakankou.co.jp/chojosansou

Chōjō-Kiso-goya
頂上木曽小屋
Mt Kiso-koma
early June–early Nov
Stay, meals
tel 0264-52-3882

South (Minami) Alps

Most of the mountain huts in the South
Alps require advance booking if you plan
on having meals. Take your own sleeping
bag for a small discount at some of the
mountain huts.

North area

Trek 9

Hirogawara sansō
広河原山荘
Mt Kita-dake
mid June–early Nov
Stay, meals (reservation required), lunch,
camping
tel 090-2677-0828 (0552-83-2889)

Shirane-oike-goya
白根御池小屋
Mt Kita-dake
mid June–early Nov
Stay, meals (reservation required), lunch,
camping
tel 090-3201-7683 (0484-52-8663)
http://shiraneoike.com

Kitadake Kata-no-goya
北岳肩ノ小屋
Mt Kita-dake
mid June–early Nov
Stay, meals (reservation required), camping
tel 090-4606-0068 (0552-88-2421)
http://katanokoya.com

Kita-dake sansō
北岳山荘
Mt Kita-dake
mid June–early Nov
Stay, meals (reservation required for
groups of five or more), camping
tel 090-4529-4947 (0552-82-6294)
www.minamialps-net.jp

Daimonsawa-goya
大門沢小屋
Mt Nōtori-dake
early July–mid Oct
Stay, meals, camping, shower, lunch,
coffee
tel 090-7635-4244
www.daimonzawa.com

Trek 10

Yashajin Hütte
夜叉神ヒュッテ
Mt Hō-ō (Yashajin-tōge)
Late April–late Nov
Stay, meals (reservation required), lunch,
bath
tel 080-2182-2992
http://yashajin-hutte.com

Minami-omuro-goya
南御室小屋
Mt Hō-ō
New Year, Golden Week, May–June
(weekends only); July–Oct (daily)
Stay, meals (reservation required), camping
tel 090-3406-3404 (0551-22-6682)
www.houousan.com

Yakushi-dake-goya
薬師岳小屋
Mt Hō-ō
New Year, Golden Week, May–June
(weekends only); July–Oct (daily)
Stay, meals (reservation required)
tel 090-5561-1242 (0551-22-6682)
www.houousan.com

Yashajin-tōge-goya
夜叉神峠小屋
Mt Hō-ō
late April–mid Nov (weekends only); mid
July–late Aug (daily)
Stay, meals (reservation required), camping
tel 0552-88-2402
www.minamialps-net.jp

Hō-ō-goya
鳳凰小屋
Mt Hō-ō
New Year, late April–early Nov
Stay, meals (reservation required), camping
tel 0551-27-2018
http://houougoya.jp

Other

Shichijō-goya
七丈小屋
Mt Kai-koma (Kuroto-one route)
all year
Stay, meals (reservation required), camping
tel 090-3226-2967
www.kaikoma.info

Sensui-goya
仙水小屋
Mt Kai-koma
all year
Stay, meals (reservation required), camping
tel 080-5076-5494 (0551-28-8173)
www.minamialps-net.jp

Chōei-goya
長衛小屋
Kitazawa-tōge
New Year (no meals), Golden Week and
mid June–early Nov
Stay, meals (reservation required), camping
tel 090-2227-0360 (090-8485-2967)
www.minamialps-net.jp

Kitazawa-tōge Komorebi-sansō
北沢峠こもれび山荘
Kitazawa-tōge
New Year (no meals), late April–early Nov
Stay, meals (reservation required), lunch
tel 080-8760-4367 (0265-94-6001)
www.ina-city-kankou.co.jp/yamagoya

Ōdaira sansō
大平山荘
Kitazawa-tōge
early July–late Oct
Stay, meals (reservation required), coffee
tel 090-5810-2314 (0265-78-3761)
http://ohdaira.sakura.ne.jp

Senjō-goya
千丈小屋
Mt Senjō-ga-take
mid June–mid Oct

Stay, meals (reservation required)
tel 090-1883-3033 (0265-94-6001)
www.ina-city-kankou.co.jp/yamagoya

Umanose-hyutte
馬ノ背ヒュッテ
Mt Senjō-ga-take
mid July–mid Oct
Stay, meals (reservation required)
tel 090-2135-2500 (0265-98-2523)
www1.inacatv.ne.jp/umanose

Yabusawa-goya
藪沢小屋
Mt Senjō-ga-take
mid July–late Aug
Stay (no meals)
tel 0265-98-3130
www1.inacatv.ne.jp/umanose

Nōtori-goya
農鳥小屋
Mt Nōtori-dake
early July–mid Oct
Stay, meals (reservation required), camping
tel tel 0556-48-2533 (090-3342-5700)
www.minamialps-net.jp

South area

Trek 11

Sawarajima Lodge
椹島ロッヂ
Sawarajima
late April–early Nov
Stay, meals, camping, lunch, bath
tel 0547-46-4717
www.t-forest.com/alpsinfo/sawarajima-lodge

Senmai-goya
千枚小屋
Mt Arakawa-Higashidake (Mt Warusawa)
early July–mid Oct
Stay, meals (reservation required for
groups of 10 or more), camping
tel 0547-46-4717
www.t-forest.com/alpsinfo/climber/lodgeinfo

Arakawa-goya
荒川小屋
Mt Arakawa-Higashidake (Mt Warusawa)
early July–mid Oct
Stay, meals (reservation required for
groups of 10 or more), camping, lunch
tel 0547-46-4717
www.t-forest.com/alpsinfo/climber/
lodgeinfo

Arakawa-Nakadake hinan-goya
中岳避難小屋
Mt Arakawa-Higashidake (Mt Warusawa)
mid July–late Sept
Stay without meals (reservation required
for groups of 10 or more), bottled drinks,
instant noodles
tel 0547-46-4717
www.t-forest.com/alpsinfo/climber/
lodgeinfo

Nikengoya-lodge
二軒小屋ロッヂ
Mt Arakawa-Higashidake (Mt Warusawa)
late April–early Nov
Stay, meals (reservation required),
camping, bath
tel 0547-46-4717
www.t-forest.com/alpsinfo/
nikengoya-lodge

Akaishi-dake hinan-goya
赤石岳避難小屋
Mt Akaishi-dake
mid July–late Sept
Stay without meals (reservation required
for groups of 10 or more), bottled drinks,
instant noodles, fresh coffee
tel 0547-46-4717
www.t-forest.com/alpsinfo/climber/
lodgeinfo

Akaishi-goya
赤石小屋
Mt Akaishi-dake
early July–mid Oct
Stay, meals (reservation required for

groups of 10 or more), camping
tel 0547-46-4717
www.t-forest.com/alpsinfo/climber/
lodgeinfo

Trek 12

Hijiridaira-goya
聖平小屋
Mt Hijiri-dake
mid July–mid Sept
Stay, meals (reservation required),
camping, lunch
tel 080-1560-6309 (0542-60-2211)
https://hijiridairagoya.wixsite.com/hijiri

Trek 13

Hirogawara sansō, Shirane-oike-goya,
Kitadake Kata-no-goya and Kita-dake sansō
広河原山荘, 白根御池小屋, 北岳肩ノ小屋,
北岳山荘
see Trek 9 above

Kuma-no-daira-goya
熊ノ平小屋
Mt Mibu-dake
mid July–late Sept
Stay, meals (reservation required for
groups of five or more), camping, lunch
tel 0547-46-4717
www.t-forest.com/alpsinfo/climber/
lodgeinfo

Ryōmata-goya
両俣小屋
Mt Mibu-dake
early July–mid Oct
Stay, meals (reservation required for
groups of five or more), camping
tel 090-4529-4947 (0552-88-2146)
http://ryoumatagoya.com

Shiomi-goya
塩見小屋
Mt Shiomi-dake
early July–mid Oct

Stay, meals (reservation required), lunch
tel 070-4231-3164
www.ina-city-kankou.co.jp/yamagoya

Sanpuku-tōge-goya
三伏峠小屋
Sanpuku-tōge
early July–late Sept
Stay, meals (reservation required), camping
tel 0265-39-3110
http://sanpukutouge.com

Kogōchi-dake-hinan-goya
小河内岳避難小屋
Mt Kogōchi-dake
mid July–late Aug
Stay without meals (reservation required
for groups of 10 or more), bottled drinks
tel 0547-46-4717
www.t-forest.com/alpsinfo/climber/
lodgeinfo

Takayamaura-hinan-goya
高山裏避難小屋
Mt Arakawa-Higashidake (Mt Warusawa)
mid July–late Aug
Stay without meals (reservation required
for groups of 10 or more), camping,
bottled drinks, instant noodles
tel 0547-46-4717
www.t-forest.com/alps/lodge_takayama_
hinan.html

Arakawa-goya, Akaishi hinan-goya and
Akaishi-goya
荒川小屋, 赤石岳避難小屋, 赤石小屋
see Trek 11 above

Hyakkenborayama-no-ie
百間洞山の家
Hyakkendaira
mid July–mid Sept
Stay, meals (reservation required for
groups of 10 or more), camping
tel 0547-46-4717
www.t-forest.com/alpsinfo/climber/
lodgeinfo

Hijiridaira-goya
聖平小屋
see Trek 12 above

Sawarajima Lodge
椹島ロッヂ
see Trek 11 above

Chausu-goya
茶臼小屋
Mt Chausu-dake
mid July–mid Sept
Stay, meals (reservation required for groups
of five or more), bottled drinks, camping
tel 080-1560-6309 (0542-60-2211)
http://nanpusu.jp/yamagoya/report02.html

Tekari-dake-goya
光岳小屋
Mt Tekari-dake
mid July–mid Sept
Stay, meals (reservation required), bottled
drinks, camping
tel 090-6939-2356 (0466-27-7659)
http://alps2592.c.ooco.jp

Yokokubozawa-goya
横窪沢小屋
Mt Chausu-dake
mid July–late Aug
Stay, meals (reservation required), camping
tel 080-1560-6309 (0542-60-2211)
http://nanpusu.jp/yamagoya/report01.html

Akaishi Onsen Shirakaba-sō
赤石温泉白樺荘
Hatanagi Dai-ichi Dam
all year
Stay, meals (reservation required), hot
spring bath
tel 0542-60-2021
www.city.shizuoka.jp/000_007108.html

Mt Fuji
Mountain huts on Mt Fuji are operational
during the official climbing season (July
to early September; check www.fujisan-
climb.jp/en for exact dates), although some

huts are open a few weeks before and after this. Prices usually increase by 1000 or 2000 yen on Friday and Saturday nights. Reservations are strongly recommended.

Yoshida trail (Walk 10)

Fifth station

Satōgoya
佐藤小屋
2230m (7314ft)
all year
tel 090-3133-2230 (0555-22-1945)
www.fuji-satogoya.com

Okuniwasō
奥庭荘
2300m (7544ft)
mid April–late Nov
tel 0555-82-2910
www.digisco.com/okuniwa

Fujikyū Unjōkaku
富士急雲上閣
2305m (7560ft)
climbing season
tel 0555-72-1355
www.unjokaku.jp/en/

Fujisan Miharashi
富士山みはらし
2305m (7560ft)
late June–early Sept
tel 080-2681-3776 (0555-72-1266)
www.fujisan5.com

Sixth station

Satomidaira Seikansō
里見平星観荘
2325m (7872ft)
mid June–mid Oct
tel 0555-24-6524 (0555-24-6090)
www.seikanso.jp

Seventh station

Hanagoya
花小屋
2700m (8856ft)
climbing season
tel 090-7234-9955 (0555-22-2208)
www2.tbb.t-com.ne.jp/hanagoya

Hinodekan
日の出館
2720m (8921ft)
climbing season
tel 0555-24-6522 (0555-22-0396)
www10.plala.or.jp/hinodekan/hinodekan.
html

Nanagōme Tomoekan
七合目トモエ館
2740m (8987ft)
climbing season
tel 0555-24-6521
https://tomoekan.com/7tomoekan

Kamaiwakan
鎌岩館
2790m (9151ft)
climbing season
tel 080-1299-0223
www.kamaiwakan.jpn.org

Fuji-ichikan
富士一館
2800m (9184ft)
early July–early Sept
tel 080-1036-6691
www.mfi.or.jp/fujiichikan

Toriisō
鳥居荘
2900m (9512ft)
late June–early Sept
tel 080-2347-0514 (0555-84-2050)
http://toriiso.com

Tōyōkan
東洋館
3000m (9840ft)

late June–early Sept
tel 0555-22-1040
www.fuji-toyokan.jp

Eighth station

Taishikan
太子館
3100m (10,168ft)
late June–early Sept
tel 0555-24-6516 (0555-22-1947)
www.mfi.or.jp/taisikan

Hōraikan
蓬莱館
3150m (10,332ft)
climbing season
tel 0555-24-6515 (0555-22-3498)
www.horaikan.jp

Hakuunsō
白雲荘
3200m (10,496ft)
climbing season
tel 0555-24-6514 (0555-22-1322)
http://fujisan-hakuun.com/en

Gansōmuro
元祖室
3250m (10,660ft)
climbing season
tel 0555-24-6513 (090-4549-3250)
www.mfi.or.jp/fujisan/english

Honhachigōme Tomoekan
本八合目トモエ館
3400m (11,152ft)
climbing season
tel 0555-24-6511
https://tomoekan.com/8tomoekan

Fujisan Hotel
富士山ホテル
3400m (11,152ft)

late June–early Sept
tel 0555-24-6512 (0555-22-0237)
www.fujisanhotel.com

8.5 station

Goraikōkan
御来光館
3450m (11,316ft)
climbing season
tel 0555-73-8987 (0555-73-8815)
www.goraikoukan.jp/english

Subashiri trail (Walk 11)

Fifth station

Higashi-fuji sansō
東富士山荘
2000m (6560ft)
late April–early Nov
tel 090-3254-5057 (0550-75-2113)
www4.tokai.or.jp/yamagoya

Kikuya
菊屋
2000m (6560ft)
early May–early Nov
tel 090-8680-0686 (0550-75-5868)
http://fujisan-kikuya.jp

Yoshinoya
吉野屋
2300m (7545ft)
climbing season
tel 090-7854-7954 (0550-75-2119)
http://fujisan-sunaharaigogou.com

Sixth station

Osada sansō
長田山荘
2450m (8038ft)
late June–late Sept
tel 090-8324-6746 (0550-89-3058)
www4.tokai.or.jp/osadasanso

Setokan
瀬戸館
2700m (8856ft)
early July–late Aug
tel 090-3302-4466 (0550-89-0374)

Seventh station

Taiyōkan
太陽館
2920m (9708ft)
early June–late Sept
tel 090-3158-6624 (0550-75-4347)

7.5 station

Miharashi-kan
見晴館
3250m (10,660ft)
climbing season
tel 090-1622-1048
http://miharashi-kan.com

Eighth station

Edoya (Shimo-Edoya)
江戸屋 (下江戸屋)
3350m (10,988ft)
mid July–late Aug
tel 090-2770-3518 (0550-75-3600)
www.fujisan-edoya.com/edoya2

Munatsuki Edoya (Kami-Edoya)
胸突江戸屋 (上江戸屋)
3400m (11,155ft)
climbing season
tel 090-7031-3517 (0550-75-3600)
www.fujisan-edoya.com/edoya1

8.5 station

Goraikōkan
御来光館
3450m (11,316ft)
climbing season
tel 0555-73-8987 (0555-73-8815)
www.goraikoukan.jp/english

Tenth station (summit)

Yamaguchiya
山口屋
3740m (12,267ft)
mid July–mid Aug
tel 090-5858-3776 (0550-75-2012)
www.fujisan-yamaguchiya.com

Ōgiya
扇屋
3740m (12,267ft)
climbing season
tel 090-1563-3513 (0550-89-0069)

Gotemba trail (Walk 12)

Fifth station

Ōishijaya
大石茶屋
1500m (4920ft)
early July–late Aug
tel 090-8955-5076 (0550-89-2941)

7.4 station

Warajikan
わらじ館
3050m (10,007ft)
climbing season
tel 090-8678-3050 (0550-89-0911)
http://warazikan.main.jp

7.5 station

Sunabashirikan
砂走館
3090m (10,168ft)
early July–late Aug
tel 090-3155-5061 (0550-89-0703)
www.sunabashirikan.co.jp

7.9 station

Akaiwa-hachigōkan
赤岩八合館
3300m (10,824ft)

early July–early Sept
tel 090-3155-5061 (0550-89-0703)
www.sunabashirikan.co.jp/akaiwa

Fujinomiya trail (Walk 13)

Fifth station

Gogōme Resthouse
五合目レストハウス
2400m (7872ft)
early July–late Aug
tel 090-7618-2230 (0544-26-4655)

Sixth station

Unkaisō
雲海荘
2493m (8179ft)
early July–early Sept
tel 090-2618-2231 (0544-26-4533)
www.unkaiso.com

Hōei sansō
宝永山荘
2493m (8179ft)
late June–early Oct
tel 090-7607-2232 (0544-26-4887)
http://houeisansou.com

7th station

Goraikō sansō
御来光山荘
2780m (9118ft)
early July–early Sept
tel 090-4083-2233 (0544-26-3942)
www.goraikousansou.com

Yamaguchi sansō
山口山荘 (元祖七合目)
3010m (9872ft)
early July–early Sept
tel 090-7022-2234 (0544-23-3938)
http://fujisan-ganso.jp

Eighth station

Ikedakan
池田館 (富士山八合目)
3250m (10,660ft)
early July–early Sept
tel 090-2772-2235 (0544-26-0512)
www.fuji8.com

Ninth station

Mannenyuki sansō
万年雪山荘
3460m (11,348ft)
early July–early Sept
tel 090-7025-2236 (0544-27-2355)
http://mannnennyuki.wixsite.com/
mannennyuki

9.5 station

Munatsuki sansō
胸突山荘
3580m (11,775ft)
early July–early Sept
tel 090-5855-8759 (090-5855-8759)
www.munatsuki.com

Tenth station (summit)

Chōjō Fujikan
頂上富士館
3749m (12,267ft)
early July–early Sept
tel 0544-26-1519
http://fujisanchou.com

APPENDIX D
Glossary

Pronunciation

Luckily, Japanese pronunciation is relatively straightforward, as there are a rather limited number of sounds and none of the tonal systems as found throughout much of East Asia. The five main vowel sounds are:

- a, as in 'art'
- i, as in 'ski'
- u, as in 'flu'
- e, as in 'bed'
- o, as in 'old'.

In *rōmaji* (romanised versions of words as used in this book), vowels with a macron (small bar) over them are pronounced the same way as normal vowels, but the sound is held for twice as long. This can drastically change the meaning; for example, *kuki* refers to a plant's stem while *kūki* means 'air'.

Consonants sound almost the same as those in English apart from:

- g, as in 'give' at the start of words, or a slightly nasal 'sing' if it appears in the middle of a word
- f, as in the 'wh' of 'who', while pursing the lips and blowing gently
- r, is closer to an 'l' than an 'r'

Many trails, huts and signs have little in the way of English information, so it is useful to be able to recognise frequently occurring Japanese words, characters and place-name elements. Some of the most common ones are listed below.

Useful phrases

English	pronounced	Japanese
hello	konnichiwa	こんにちは
good morning	ohayō gozaimasu	おはようございます
good evening	konbanwa	こんばんは
goodbye	sayonara	さようなら
thank you	arigatō gozaimasu	ありがとうございます
sorry	gomen nasai	ごめんなさい
excuse me	sumimasen	すみません
yes	hai	はい
no	iie	いいえ

Signs

English	pronounced	Japanese
trailhead	tozan-guchi	登山口
path or trail	yama-michi/tozan-dō	山道 / 登山道
information	annai	案内
entrance	iriguchi	入口
exit	deguchi	出口
toilets	otearai/toire	お手洗い / トイレ
male/female	otoko/onna	男 / 女
water source/place	mizuba	水場
up/ascend	noboru	登る
down/descend	kudaru	下る
danger	kiken	危険
be careful/caution	chūi	注意
can't pass	tsūkōkinshi	通行禁止
closed/dead end	tsūkōdome	通行止
no entry	tachi-iri-kinshi	立入禁止
rockfall	rakuseki	落石
slippery	suberi-yasui	滑りやすい
bears	kuma	熊 / クマ

Mountain huts and camping

English	pronounced	Japanese
mountain hut	yamagoya	山小屋
hut (small)	koya	小屋
hut (large)	sansō	山荘
emergency hut/shelter	hinan-goya	非難小屋
campground	kyanpu-jyo	キャンプ所
reception desk	uketsuke	受付
dining area	shokudō	食堂
toilets	otearai/toire	お手洗い / トイレ
bath	ofuro	お風呂
shower	shawā	シャワー
one-night stay	ippaku	一泊

English	pronounced	Japanese
one-night stay (without meals)	sudomari	素泊まり

Food and drink

English	pronounced	Japanese
breakfast	chōshoku/asa-gohan	朝食 / 朝ご飯
lunch	chūshoku/hiru-gohan/ranchi	昼食 / 昼ご飯 / ランチ
dinner	yūshoku/ban-gohan	夕食 / 晩ご飯
set meal	teishoku	定食
water	mizu	水
hot water	oyu	お湯
tea	ocha	お茶
coffee	kōhī	コーヒー
beer	bīru	ビール
draft/can/bottle of beer	nama-bīru/kanbīru/bin-bīru	生ビール/缶ビール/ビンビール
Japanese sake	osake/nihon-shu	お酒 / 日本酒
curry and rice	karēraisu	カレーライス
miso soup	misoshiru	味噌汁
pork cutlet	tonkatsu	豚カツ
ramen noodles	rāmen	ラーメン
rice ball	onigiri	おにぎり
udon noodles	udon	うどん

Infrastructure

English	pronounced	Japanese
airport	kūkō	空港
bus stop	basu-tei	バス停
city	shi	市
convenience store	konbini	コンビニ
highway/motorway	kōsokudōro	高速道路
hot spring bath	onsen	温泉
hotel	hoteru	ホテル
hospital	byōin	病院

English	pronounced	Japanese
Japanese-style inn	ryokan	旅館
outdoor bath	rotenburo	露天風呂
pharmacy/drugstore	yakkyoku/doraggu-sutoa	薬局 / ドラッグストア
post office	yūbinkyoku	郵便局
road/track	michi	道
ropeway	rōpuwei	ロープウエイ
shop	mise	店
taxi stand	takushī-sutando	タクシースタンド
train station	eki	駅
village	mura	村

Physical features

English	pronounced	Japanese
avalanche	nadare	なだれ
bog/marsh/swamp	numa	沼
bridge	hashi	橋
cave	dōkutsu	洞窟
cirque/cwm/corrie	kāru	カール
cliff	zeppeki	絶壁
col/saddle	koru	コル
crag	gake	崖
crater	funkakō	噴火口
crevasse	kurebasu	クレバス
dam	damu	ダム
fixed chains	kusari	鎖 / クサリ
flat/level ground	taira	平
forest	mori	森
gorge	keikoku	渓谷
hill	oka	丘
hole	ana	穴
hot spring	onsen	温泉
island	shima	島
lake	mizuumi	湖

English	pronounced	Japanese
ladder	hashigo	ハシゴ
landslide	gake-kuzure	崖崩れ
lingering snow	zansetsu	残雪
marshland/wetland	numachi	沼地
moor	kōya	荒野
mountain	yama	山
pass	tōge	峠
peak/point	dake	岳
plain	heigen	平原
plateau	kōgen	高原
pond	ike	池
rapids	kyūryū	急流
rice paddy	tanbo	田んぼ
ridge/spur	one	尾根
ridgeline	ryōsen	稜線
river	kawa	川
rock	iwa	岩
scree	gare	ガレ
slope/incline	saka	坂
snowfield	setsugen	雪原
snow valley	sekkei	雪渓
steep	kyū/kitsui	急 / きつい
stream	ogawa	小川
summit	chōjō/sanchō	頂上 / 山頂
suspension bridge	tsuribashi	吊橋
valley	tani	谷
volcano	kazan	火山
waterfall	taki	滝

Weather

English	pronounced	Japanese
cloudy	kumori	曇り
frost	shimo	霜

English	pronounced	Japanese
ice	kōri	氷
rain	ame	雨
snow	yuki	雪
storm	arashi	嵐
sunny	hareru	晴れる
thunder	kaminari	雷
typhoon	taifū	台風
wind/windy	kaze/kyōfū	風 / 強風
weather forecast	tenki-yohō	天気予報

General

English	pronounced	Japanese
hiking	haikingu	ハイキング
mountain climbing	tozan	登山
mountain climber	tozansha	登山者
to climb/ascend	agaru/noboru	上がる / 登る
to descend	kudaru/oriru	下る / 降りる
today	kyō	今日
tomorrow	ashita	明日
yesterday	kinō	昨日
morning	asa	朝
noon	ohiru	お昼
afternoon	gogo	午後
evening	yūgata	夕方
night	yoru	夜
left	hidari	左
right	migi	右
north	kita	北
south	minami	南
east	higashi	東
west	nishi	西
tent	tento	テント
sleeping bag	shurafu	シュラフ

APPENDIX E
Useful contacts and further resources

General information

www.japan.travel/en
Official site of the Japan National Tourism Organization

www.seejapan.co.uk
Japan National Tourism Organization's UK-based website

www.japan-guide.com
Comprehensive travel information guide

www.japan-alps.com/en
Information hub for the main cities around the Japan Alps

Travel to Japan

Airlines

This is not an exhaustive list: check online and locally for further options.

Europe–Japan

Air France
www.airfrance.co.uk

ANA
www.ana.co.jp/en/eur

British Airways
www.britishairways.com

Finnair
www.finnair.com

KLM
www.klm.com

Malaysia Airlines
www.malaysiaairlines.com

Qatar Airways
www.qatarairways.com

Thai Airways
www.thaiairways.com

North America–Japan

American Airlines
www.americanairlines.co.uk

Cathay Pacific
www.cathaypacific.com

Delta
www.delta.com

Japan Airlines (JAL)
www.jal.com

United
www.united.com

East Asia–Japan

AirAsia Japan
www.airasia.com

Jetstar Japan
www.jetstar.com

Peach
www.flypeach.com

Vanilla Air
www.vanilla-air.com

Ferries

This is not an exhaustive list; check online and locally for further options.

From China

Shanghai Ferry Company
www.shanghai-ferry.co.jp
Shanghai–Osaka (approx 48hr, weekly)

Japan-China International Ferry Company
www.shinganjin.com
Shanghai–Kobe (approx 48hr, alternate weeks)
Shanghai–Osaka (approx 48hr, alternate weeks)

From Korea

JR Beetle
www.jrbeetle.co.jp
Busan–Fukuoka (approx 3hr, daily)

Camellia Line
www.camellia-line.co.jp
Busan–Fukuoka (approx 7hr or 11hr overnight service)

From Russia

Eastern Dream/DBS Cruise
www.dbsferry.com
Vladivostok–Sakaiminato via Donghae, Korea (approx 36hr, seasonal)

Internal travel

www.alpen-route.com/en
Official website for the Tateyama Kurobe Alpine Route

Rail

www.hyperdia.com
Essential for checking train times

www.japanrailpass.net/en/index.html
Great value rail pass for foreign visitors

https://global.jr-central.co.jp/en
Official website of JR Central; click 'Service Information' to check for service disruptions. JR East, West and other regions have similar websites

Buses

https://japanbusonline.com/en
Nationwide bus booking website

www.willerexpress.com/en
Long-distance and night buses

www.alpico.co.jp
Local and long-distance buses in Nagano

www.nouhibus.co.jp
Bus services in the Hida Takayama area

Car hire

Hertz
www.hertz.com

Toyota Rent-a-Car
www.rent.toyota.co.jp/en

Air travel

All Nipon Airways (ANA)
www.ana.co.jp/en

Skymark
www.skymark.co.jp/en

Weather

www.jma.go.jp/jma/indexe.html
Japan Meteorological Agency website, for weather forecasts and natural disaster updates

www.mountain-forecast.com
Accurate forecasts for mountains around the world including many in Japan

Hiking resources

www.fujisan-climb.jp/en
Up-to-date information for climbing
Mt Fuji

www.env.go.jp/en/nature/nps/park
Official Ministry of the Environment
website for Japan's National Parks
(includes North Alps, Mt Fuji, and South
Alps information)

https://japanhike.wordpress.com
English-language information on hikes
around Japan

https://climbjapan.blogspot.com
English-language information on alpine
rock climbing around Japan

www.yamareco.com
Hiking information and recent photo
reports (all Japanese)

www.yamakei-online.com
Popular mountain resource (Japanese link)

www.kamikochi.org
Official website with news and regular
posts (in English) about the Kamikōchi area

www.go-nagano.net
Official tourism website for Nagano
Prefecture, includes hiking section

www.azumino-e-tabi.net/en
Official website of Azumino City and the
Hotaka area

www.ridgelineimages.com
Interesting and varied Japan-focused
articles

www.outdoorjapan.com
Quarterly outdoor magazine, can read
online

Luggage forwarding services

Yamato
www.kuronekoyamato.co.jp/en

Sagawa
www.sagawa-exp.co.jp/english

Language

https://translate.google.com/m/translate
For translating text from web pages

www.google.co.uk/intl/en/chrome/
browser/desktop
Browser with automatic translator for
reading Japanese websites

https://rikaichan.en.softonic.com
Free popup Japanese dictionary add-on

www.jisho.org
Good online dictionary

APPENDIX F
Further reading

One Hundred Mountains of Japan by Kyūya Fukuda, translated by Martin Hood (University of Hawaii Press, 2015) – First published in 1964, Fukuda's list of 100 favourite summits has gone on to become the definitive list of Japanese mountains, known as the *hyakumeizan*. Short, poetic essays on each mountain (including many in the Japan Alps), often with a focus on name origins or historical/cultural notes, now superbly translated into English.

Mountaineering and Exploration in the Japanese Alps by Walter Weston (John Murray, London, 1896) – Fascinating and historical account of the English missionaries' attempts to summit many of Japan's biggest, and at that time, relatively unclimbed mountains. Another book by the same author, *The Playground of the Far East*, recalls further climbs.

Hiking in Japan (Lonely Planet, 2009) – Out-of-print and now fairly difficult to find, describes various hikes around Japan. Some complain about a lack of photos, too many multi-day hikes and occasional understating of the severity of the routes, but nevertheless contains some good information.

Hiking in Japan by Paul Hunt (Kodansha International, 1988) – The first guidebook dedicated to hiking Japanese trails, this book is long out of print and very outdated, but interesting notes on geological and cultural points are still relevant.

The Roads to Sata by Alan Booth (Kodansha USA, 1985) – Seminal and influential Japan travelogue. Booth crosses Japan on foot, with interesting muses on the places and people he encounters.

Four Pairs of Boots by Craig McLachlan (Paradise Promotions, 2013) – An entertaining account of the author's walk from one end of Japan to the other in the early 90s, with a short section in the Japan Alps. McLachlan is an accomplished walker and has hiked extensively in Japan.

10 Classic Alpine Climbs of Japan by Tony Grant (Climb Japan, 2016) – Ebook and paperback guide to some of Japan's best alpine rock routes, written by an experienced British rock climber based in Japan. Routes include the Kita-dake Buttress, the Kitakama ridge on Mt Yari-ga-take, and other more serious climbing routes (usually requiring a rope).

NOTES

NOTES

DOWNLOAD THE ROUTES
IN GPX FORMAT

All the routes in this guide are available for download from:

www.cicerone.co.uk/947/GPX

as GPX files. You should be able to load them into most formats of mobile device, whether GPS or smartphone.

When you go to this link, you will be asked for your email address and where you purchased the guide, and have the option to subscribe to the Cicerone e-newsletter.

www.cicerone.co.uk

LISTING OF CICERONE GUIDES

SCOTLAND

Backpacker's Britain:
   Northern Scotland
Ben Nevis and Glen Coe
Cycle Touring in Northern Scotland
Cycling in the Hebrides
Great Mountain Days in Scotland
Mountain Biking in Southern and
   Central Scotland
Mountain Biking in West and North
   West Scotland
Not the West Highland Way
Scotland
Scotland's Best Small Mountains
Scotland's Mountain Ridges
The Ayrshire and Arran Coastal Paths
The Border Country
The Borders Abbeys Way
The Cape Wrath Trail
The Great Glen Way
The Great Glen Way Map Booklet
The Hebridean Way
The Hebrides
The Isle of Mull
The Isle of Skye
The Skye Trail
The Southern Upland Way
The Speyside Way
The Speyside Way Map Booklet
The West Highland Way
Walking Highland Perthshire
Walking in Scotland's Far North
Walking in the Angus Glens
Walking in the Cairngorms
Walking in the Ochils, Campsie Fells
   and Lomond Hills
Walking in the Pentland Hills
Walking in the Southern Uplands
Walking in Torridon
Walking Loch Lomond and
   the Trossachs
Walking on Arran
Walking on Harris and Lewis
Walking on Jura, Islay and Colonsay
Walking on Rum and the Small Isles
Walking on the Orkney and
   Shetland Isles
Walking on Uist and Barra
Walking the Corbetts
   Vol 1 South of the Great Glen
Walking the Corbetts
   Vol 2 North of the Great Glen
Walking the Galloway Hills
Walking the Munros Vol 1 – Southern,
   Central and Western Highlands
Walking the Munros Vol 2 – Northern
   Highlands and the Cairngorms
West Highland Way Map Booklet
Winter Climbs Ben Nevis and
   Glen Coe
Winter Climbs in the Cairngorms

NORTHERN ENGLAND TRAILS

Hadrian's Wall Path
Hadrian's Wall Path Map Booklet
Pennine Way Map Booklet
The Coast to Coast Map Booklet
The Coast to Coast Walk
The Dales Way
The Dales Way Map Booklet
The Pennine Way

LAKE DISTRICT

Cycling in the Lake District
Great Mountain Days in the
   Lake District
Lake District Winter Climbs
Lake District:
   High Level and Fell Walks
Lake District:
   Low Level and Lake Walks
Mountain Biking in the Lake District
Outdoor Adventures with Children –
   Lake District
Scrambles in the Lake District – North
Scrambles in the Lake District – South
Short Walks in Lakeland Book 2:
   North Lakeland
The Cumbria Way
The Southern Fells
Tour of the Lake District
Trail and Fell Running in the Lake
   District
Walking the Lake District Fells –
   Langdale
Walking the Lake District Fells –
   Wasdale

NORTH WEST ENGLAND AND
THE ISLE OF MAN

Cycling the Pennine Bridleway
Cycling the Way of the Roses
Isle of Man Coastal Path
The Lancashire Cycleway
The Lune Valley and Howgills
The Ribble Way
Walking in Cumbria's Eden Valley
Walking in Lancashire
Walking in the Forest of Bowland
   and Pendle
Walking on the Isle of Man
Walking on the West Pennine Moors
Walks in Ribble Country
Walks in Silverdale and Arnside

NORTH EAST ENGLAND,
YORKSHIRE DALES AND
PENNINES

Cycling in the Yorkshire Dales
Great Mountain Days in the Pennines
Mountain Biking in the
   Yorkshire Dales
South Pennine Walks

St Oswald's Way and St Cuthbert's
   Way
The Cleveland Way and the Yorkshire
   Wolds Way
The Cleveland Way Map Booklet
The North York Moors
The Reivers Way
The Teesdale Way
Trail and Fell Running in the
   Yorkshire Dales
Walking in County Durham
Walking in Northumberland
Walking in the North Pennines
Walking in the Yorkshire Dales:
   North and East
Walking in the Yorkshire Dales:
   South and West
Walks in the Yorkshire Dales

WALES AND WELSH BORDERS

Cycle Touring in Wales
Cycling Lon Las Cymru
Glyndwr's Way
Great Mountain Days in Snowdonia
Hillwalking in Shropshire
Hillwalking in Wales – Vol 1
Hillwalking in Wales – Vol 2
Mountain Walking in Snowdonia
Offa's Dyke Map Booklet
Offa's Dyke Path
Pembrokeshire Coast Path
   Map Booklet
Ridges of Snowdonia
Scrambles in Snowdonia
Snowdonia: Low-level and easy
   walks – North
The Cambrian Way
The Ceredigion and Snowdonia
   Coast Paths
The Pembrokeshire Coast Path
The Severn Way
The Snowdonia Way
The Wales Coast Path
The Wye Valley Walk
Walking in Carmarthenshire
Walking in Pembrokeshire
Walking in the Forest of Dean
Walking in the Wye Valley
Walking on the Brecon Beacons
Walking on the Gower
Walking the Shropshire Way

DERBYSHIRE, PEAK DISTRICT
AND MIDLANDS

Cycling in the Peak District
Dark Peak Walks
Scrambles in the Dark Peak
Walking in Derbyshire
White Peak Walks:
   The Northern Dales
White Peak Walks:
   The Southern Dales

For full information on all our guides,
books and eBooks, visit our website:
www.cicerone.co.uk

Explore the world with Cicerone

walking • trekking • mountaineering • climbing • mountain biking •
cycling • via ferratas • scrambling • trail running • skills and techniques

For over 50 years, Cicerone have built up an outstanding collection o
nearly 400 guides, inspiring all sorts of amazing experiences.

www.cicerone.co.uk – where adventures begin

- Our **website** is a treasure-trove for every outdoor adventurer. You
  can buy books or read inspiring articles and trip reports, get technica
  advice, check for updates, and view videos, photographs and mapping
  for routes and treks.

- **Register this book** or any other Cicerone guide in your member's
  library on our website and you can choose to automatically access
  updates and GPX files for your books, if available.

- Our **fortnightly newsletters** will update you on new publications and
  articles and keep you informed of other news and events. You can also
  follow us on Facebook, Twitter and Instagram.

We hope you have enjoyed using this guidebook. If you have any
comments you would like to share, please contact us using the form or
our website or via email, so that we can provide the best experience for
future customers.

CICERONE

Juniper House, Murley Moss Business Village, Oxenholme Road, Kendal LA9 7RL

✉ info@cicerone.co.uk   cicerone.co.uk

IPSWICH
HISTORY TOUR

Dedicated to my nephew and godson, Jonty Howgego.

First published 2016

Amberley Publishing
The Hill, Stroud,
Gloucestershire, GL5 4EP
www.amberley-books.com

Copyright © Caleb Howgego, 2016
Map contains Ordnance Survey data
© Crown copyright and database right
[2016]

The right of Caleb Howgego to be
identified as the Author of this work
has been asserted in accordance with
the Copyrights, Designs and Patents
Act 1988.

ISBN 978 1 4456 5583 3 (print)
ISBN 978 1 4456 5584 0 (ebook)

British Library Cataloguing in
Publication Data.
A catalogue record for this book is
available from the British Library.

Origination by Amberley Publishing.
Printed in Great Britain.

ACKNOWLEDGEMENTS

As always, I would like to thank God, my family and friends for their continued support and encouragement. Thanks go to my uncle, Richard Davies, who provided help and advice with some of the contemporary photographs featured here.

My thanks also go to the Ipswich Transport Museum and Suffolk Record Office for the use of images from their collections, as well as to Colchester and Ipswich Museums Service, who provided images from the collections of Ipswich Borough Council. The image of the Willis Building is reproduced with the kind permission of Willis Towers Watson.

Efforts have been made to identify and seek permission from the copyright holder for all of the images featured in *Ipswich History Tour*.

INTRODUCTION

Ipswich is an ancient town – certainly one of the oldest continually established settlements in England. Indeed, so old is the street layout of much of the town centre that a modern resident can recognise it and many of the town's landmarks from a quick look at John Speed's map of 1610. Speed's map, which is the earliest known surviving of the town showing its street layout, has been reproduced here for purposes of comparison with the modern Ordinance Survey map; it's worth noting that the street pattern was established long before this, with the town's history stretching back over 1,000 years prior to its charting. For all this venerability, a visitor, or even a local resident, would be forgiven for not perceiving Ipswich's rich heritage. This book, in a small way, aims to redress this imbalance.

The tendency to lose sight of Ipswich's antiquity is largely due to the cycles of decline and prosperity the town has seen in its long history. Put simply, whenever the town was in prosperity, those who could afford to make their mark on it did so, often at the expense of older constructions. Ipswich has time and again embraced change and adapted in order to prosper so that what is left today often appears something of a hotchpotch of old and new. Therefore, perhaps more than for most places, a guide to its history may be useful.

This book offers a short introduction to the history of Ipswich and some of its notable inhabitants by taking you on a tour of the town centre and docklands. Each location is marked on the Ordnance

Survey map at the front of the book, and a mixture of historic images and modern-day photographs of the places are featured so that you can read the tour at home or venture out to follow the tour route.

Due to limitations of space, this book only touches the surface of the rich and varied history of the town but I hope it goes some way to encourage you to explore further for yourself.

Caleb Howgego
June 2016

IPSWICHE

Orwell flu.

The Salt water

A	Chrifts church	G.	S.Laurence	N	S.Mary Key
B	S.Georgs chap.	H	S.Stephens	O	Stoke church
C.	S.Margarets	I.	S.Helens	Q	Stoke Bridge
D	S.Mathews	K	S.Clements	R	Stoke mill
E	S.Mary Towre	L	S.Nicolas	S	The Key
F.	S.Mary Elms	M	S.Peters.	T	Graye Friers

A SCALE OF PASES

V	Black Friers	4	Barre Gate
W	Chriſt Hoſpital	5	Old Bar gate
X	Gramer Schole	6	Fiſhe market
Y	Poores houſes	7	Kings Stret
Z	Hanford mill	8	Corne hill
3	Bull Gate	9	Broke Stret

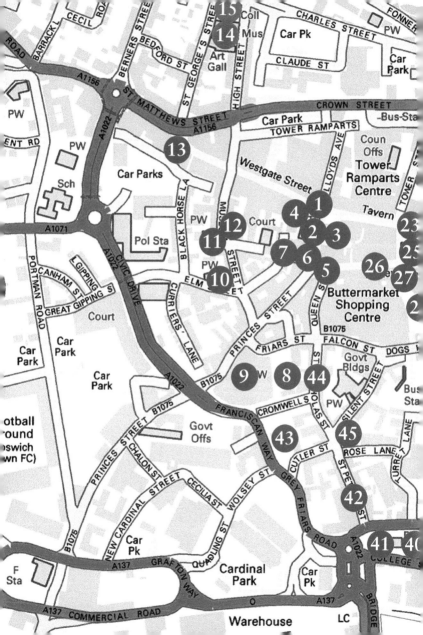

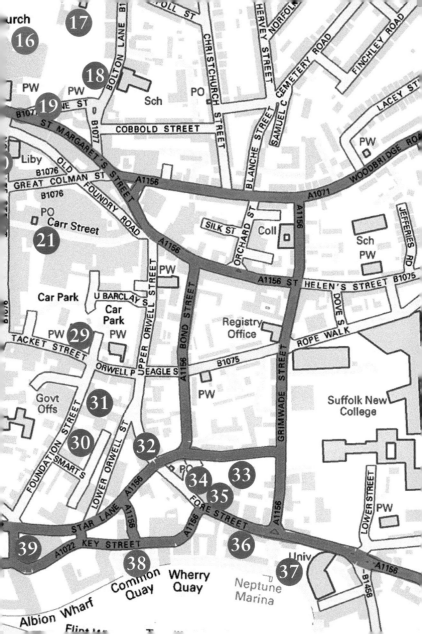

1. CORNHILL

This historic central space in Ipswich goes back a long way and can be seen on John Speed's 1610 map of Ipswich. Successive generations have continued to rebuild Cornhill, so that it is now hard to recognise how ancient it is. The oldest recorded building on this site was a church named St Mildred's, which stood around the site of the present town hall from around AD 700.

2. TOWN HALL

This is a photograph of the former town hall. The current town hall was built in 1866–67. It housed much of Ipswich's civic life for a century, but in the 1960s, due to lack of space, various borough council departments began to move out. Today, most civic administration takes place in other offices such as Grafton House. The town hall still plays a municipal role in Ipswich, housing the mayor's office.

3. OLD POST OFFICE

In 1881, as part of a wide-ranging attempt to revitalise a growing
Victorian Ipswich, this new enlarged post office was opened. The
building is no longer used for its original purpose, but if you look up
at the upper frontage of the building you should still be able to see
four female figures that each represent important pillars of a Victorian
economic vision: industry, electricity, steam and commerce.

4. THE GOLDEN LION

The two oldest buildings that remain today on Cornhill are the public houses – the Golden Lion and Mannings – which date back to at least the eighteenth century. This photograph shows a group of servants outside the Golden Lion Hotel in the 1850s. However, after centuries of pint-pulling, the Golden Lion closed in 2016 and is at the time of writing currently unoccupied.

5. THE GILES STATUE

This statue was unveiled in 1993 to commemorate the work of Carl Giles, the newspaper cartoonist who enjoyed a distinguished career working in Ipswich. The statue is placed so that his famous character 'Grandma' is looking up at the office window where he used to work. Throughout the important events he covered, Giles became well known for his brand of wit and humour. In 2000, Giles was voted 'Britain's favourite cartoonist of the twentieth century'.

6. CORN EXCHANGE

The public houses the Sickle Inn and the King's Head, which feature in this photograph, once stood here. This part of the town centre was considerably altered in the 1870s when these buildings were torn down to make room for the creation of the new corn exchange. Part of the former corn exchange building now houses the independent cinema, Ipswich Film Theatre.

KING'S HEAD COMMERCIAL INN

LOT 5   LOT 6   LOT 7

7. KING STREET AND ARCADE STREET

Arcade Street was built in the 1840s, cutting through what was then the offices of the Ipswich and Suffolk Banking Company. This is also where the author Jean Ingelow once lived during her childhood, her father being the manager of the aforementioned bank. Beyond the archway is Birketts Solicitors, used by Wallis Simpson during her divorce hearing at Ipswich Assizes in 1936. Edward VIII went on to abdicate in order to marry her.

8. UNITARIAN MEETING HOUSE

The Unitarian meeting house is the oldest surviving timber-framed chapel in East Anglia. This Grade I-listed building owes its existence to the religious turmoil of the seventeenth century when many new Christian groups emerged. The Act of Tolerance of 1689 encouraged these groups to create their own places of worship, sometimes in converted houses or in new purpose-built buildings, as in this case.

9. WILLIS BUILDING

In 1975, the most influential building Ipswich has produced in recent times was completed: the black glass edifice of the Willis Building. It was Norman Foster's first major commission and is considered a pioneering piece of social architecture, complete with a roof garden, gymnasium and originally an Olympic-sized swimming pool. Since 1991 it has been one of the country's youngest Grade I-listed buildings.

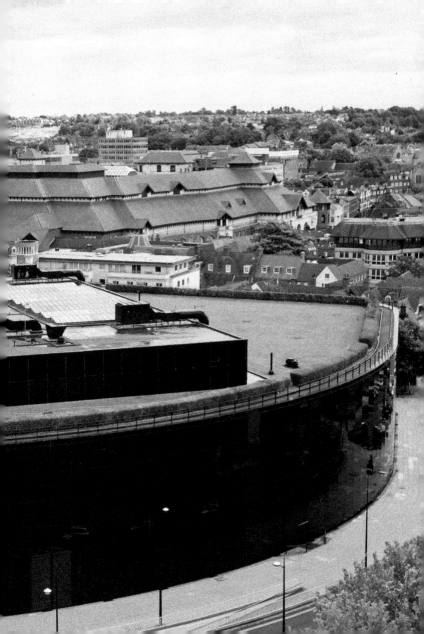

10. ST MARY AT THE ELMS

This church was constructed in the 1440s and acquired its name from the trees in its churchyard. It was built on the site of an older church dedicated to St Saviour and the stone doorway in the south porch is likely to date back to Norman times. Henry VIII visited St Mary's and the shrine of Our Lady of Grace. A replica of this shrine is now housed in this church and is visited annually by the people of Nettuno, Italy.

11. MUSEUM STREET METHODIST CHURCH

The foundation stone of this church was laid in 1860 by William Pretty, a successful businessman in the town. Methodism was a comparatively late arrival in Ipswich, however the congregation continue to meet here and the church is still active in community life today, including playing host to guest speakers on topics such as local history.

12. ARLINGTONS

This was the original premises of Ipswich Museum. From early on, the museum proved itself to be a prestigious institution, being visited by Prince Albert who, according to Queen Victoria, talked of scarcely anything else for several days afterwards. In 1881 when the collections were moved to a new museum on High Street, this building was used, amongst other things, as a dance hall. Today, it houses Arlingtons Brasserie, a restaurant and café bar.

13. LADY LANE

Perhaps no place in Ipswich has fallen further from favour in Ipswich than Lady Lane. A representation of Mary once stood upon this site in the Chapel of Our Lady of Grace for around 300 years from the mid-twelfth century, attracting pilgrims from across Europe. Henry VIII himself visited the shrine as a pilgrim. After the king's break with Rome, the shrine was sent to London as an example of idolatry to be burned. However, many believe that the shrine was saved from the flames and smuggled out of England, and is now located in Nettuno, Italy.

14. IPSWICH MUSEUM, HIGH STREET

Opened in 1881, the museum on High Street was greatly expanded from its previous premises on Museum Street to include a library and schools of science and art. The collections have continued to grow and the museum now has galleries featuring natural history, artefacts from Anglo-Saxon East Anglia, Ancient Egypt and world collections, as well as displays telling the historic story of Ipswich.

15. IPSWICH ART SCHOOL GALLERY

Ipswich Art School was originally based in Northgate Street from 1859, but in 1874 a decision was made to link the town's schools of science and art in one location on High Street. This building was constructed in the 1930s but was closed in 1997 when all the teaching moved to the main Suffolk College campus. Maggi Hambling, Leonard Squirrell and Brian Eno all either worked or studied at the school. Today, it is open to the public as an art gallery.

16. CHRISTCHURCH PARK

Christchurch Park was part of the grounds of the Priory of the Holy Trinity that was established in the twelfth century until it was suppressed in 1537. The park was formally opened to the public in 1895, but long before this the higher arboretum was freely open to the public. It was a popular retreat in the town, where people came to enjoy the immaculately landscaped space and even gathered to watch games of tennis.

17. CHRISTCHURCH MANSION

The history of Christchurch Mansion goes back as far as the 1540s when the Withypoll family began its construction on the site of the former Priory of the Holy Trinity. The mansion and grounds in turn passed into the hands of the Devereux and Fonnereau families. Felix Cobbold took possession of the building and generously presented it to the town in the 1890s. Christchurch Mansion opened as a museum soon after and public admittance is free to this day.

18. ST MARGARET'S CHURCH

Considered by many to have the finest exterior of any church in Ipswich, St Margaret's was built around 1300 by an Augustinian priory for the use of the expanding town. St Margaret's remained the most populous parish well into the nineteenth century. Changes made to the tower as the result of a Victorian expansion can clearly be seen by comparing this photograph, taken in 1865, with the church as it stands today.

19. OLD PACK HORSE INN

This building is thought to date from the mid-sixteenth century but alterations were made during the 1930s to accommodate the widening of the road. It would have been used by visitors to the Priory of the Holy Trinity (now the site of Christchurch Mansion) before its dissolution. It was also used by peddlers who brought their wares to the town on horse, hence the name.

20. PYKENHAM'S GATEHOUSE

This Grade I-listed building was originally constructed in 1471 to serve as the gatehouse for the Ipswich residence of the newly appointed Archdeacon of Suffolk, William Pykenham. The room above the gatehouse was once used as lodgings for the gatekeeper. Today, the gatehouse is owned by the Ipswich and Suffolk Club and is leased to the Ipswich Building Preservation Trust, who carried out restoration work on the building in 1983.

21. CARR STREET

In many ways, Carr Street typifies both the readiness of Ipswichians to continually rebuild their town and their historic lack of sentimentality to retain the town's ancient heritage. As early as the seventh century, 'Ipswich Ware' pottery was being made on this site and exported as far as Kent and Yorkshire. Walking down the street today, it is hard to spot many long-standing buildings at all.

22. THE GREAT WHITE HORSE HOTEL

This former hotel is perhaps best known for featuring in the Charles Dickens novel *The Pickwick Papers* (1837). Dickens visited the hotel himself, as did Lord Nelson in 1800 and George II in 1736, indicating the status of the Great White Horse as Ipswich's premium hotel in times past. The Great White Horse has recently been converted into shops, but the building retains its well-known façade and lettering.

23. TAVERN STREET

From the eighteenth to mid-twentieth century, Tavern Street was filled with alehouses and inns, thus gaining its name; for centuries, the street has been a site of revelry and repose for the people of Ipswich. Geoffrey Chaucer's family were selling wines on this street over 700 years ago. In modern times, Tavern Street has become pedestrianised and its alehouses have mostly given way to shops and cafés.

24. ST MARY-LE-TOWER

St Mary-le-Tower is the site at which the people of Ipswich gathered in 1200 to receive their town charter – one of the earliest royal town charters in English history. The tower itself wouldn't have been there at that time, as it is a Victorian addition to a church that has been remodelled and rebuilt throughout its long history. It remains the town's civic church.

25. ST LAWRENCE CHURCH

The tower of St Lawrence was the tallest in Ipswich, and the only one with bells, from at least the 1440s to around 1500. The bells that ring today are original, making them the oldest ring of five bells in use in the world. In 2008, the building reopened after thirty years of closure as the St Lawrence Centre and is now in use as a community centre, restaurant and gallery.

26. BUTTER MARKET

This is another ancient part of the town. A market existed in this area in one form or another from Anglo-Saxon times up until 1810. Fish, meat and dairy products, including butter, were sold on stalls outside buildings such as the Ancient House, which still stands on this street. The Buttermarket Shopping Centre now sits on the site of what was once a Carmelite friary dating from 1278–79.

27. ANCIENT HOUSE

This building's history goes back to at least the second half of the fifteenth century. The seventeenth-century pargeted front is one of the finest examples of the technique on a building in England. It depicts the world's four then-known continents: Africa, America, Asia and Europe (Australia was not yet known to England). It has been used as a place of business by fishmongers, booksellers and printers.

28. ST STEPHEN'S CHURCH

A church of St Stephen in Ipswich is mentioned in the Domesday Book of 1086. The current structure is less ancient than that, but was likely rebuilt on the same site as its predecessor between the fourteenth and sixteenth centuries. This medieval church, after being declared redundant in the 1970s, has found a successful new use as the town's tourist information centre.

outh Prospect of

ens Church

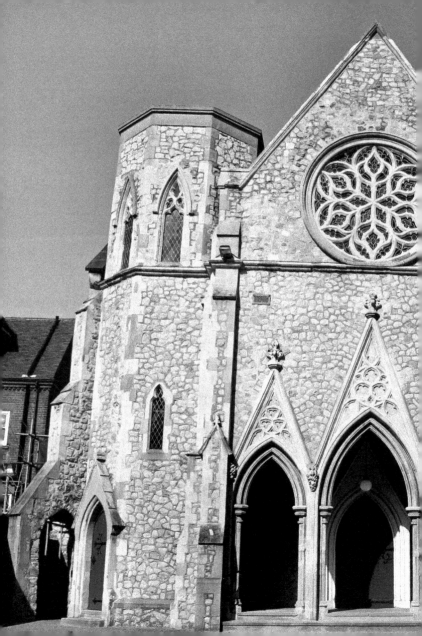

29. TACKET STREET CHAPEL

The Tacket Street chapel was built in 1858. However, the history of this congregation can be traced back to the 1680s, much before this Gothic Revival style building. The church's two spires were removed in the 1960s when they were considered to be unsafe. Now named Christ Church, it remains a place of worship and community today.

30. ALMSHOUSES, FOUNDATION STREET

This ancient Ipswich Street is named for the almshouses that have stood here since the 1550s that were known as the 'Foundation'. Some were built with money from a wealthy sixteenth-century portman of Ipswich named Henry Tooley. These buildings were originally used to house townsmen who had fought in the king's wars and were now either too injured or too old to continue in service. The current houses were rebuilt on the same site in the 1840s.

31. BLACKFRIARS RUINS

Little remains of the once-considerable Dominican friary that stood on this site. It was founded in 1263 and continued to grow steadily until the mid-fourteenth century. Dominicans were known as Black Friars for the black cloaks they wore over their white habits. Blackfriars maintained a presence in Ipswich until the dissolution of the site under Henry VIII.

he Worshipful the BAILIFFS the
nd COMMON-COUNCEL MEN, of the
Ipswich
pect is humbly Inscrib'd by
their most Obedient Servant

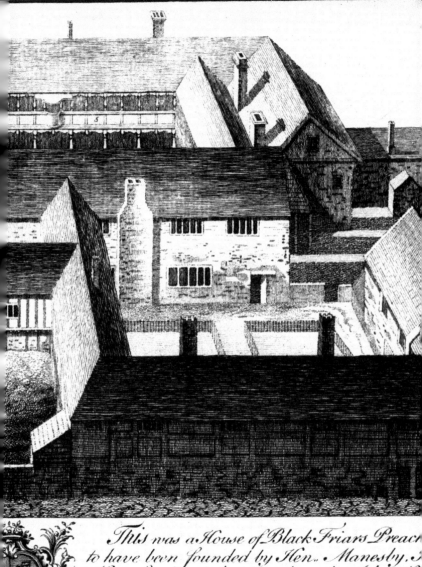

This was a House of Black Friars Preach
to have been founded by Hen. Manesby. I
Hen. Loudham, but by others, by John Ha
was granted at the Suppression to Mr. Joh.
it was purchased by the Corporation for C.

1 House 2 Chapel 3 Bridewell 4 Grammar School 5 Cloister & C

32. FORE STREET

Pictured here is one of many merchant houses that were abundant in Fore Street centuries ago. Some of these buildings date back to at least the seventeenth century and often incorporated living quarters, a shop and warehouses. One of the first female British pilots, Edith Maud Cook, also lived on this street, as did Thomas Eldred, who set sail as navigator for the second English circumnavigation of the globe in 1586–88.

33. ST CLEMENT CHURCH

Secreted away behind its surrounding foliage, this church is something of a hidden gem. In times past known as the 'Sailors' Church', it had many prestigious congregation members including Sir Thomas Slade, designer of HMS *Victory*, who is buried in the churchyard. The building was declared redundant in 1979. There is hope for the church coming back into use as plans are progressing to transform it into an arts centre.

34. SWIMMING BATHS, FORE STREET

The Victorian Fore Street swimming bath, containing a 25-by-7-yard pool, was built in 1894 with money provided by Felix Cobbold – the same member of the Cobbold family to present Christchurch Mansion to the town. Although Crown Pools is now Ipswich's main central swimming pool and leisure centre, Fore Street Pool, as it is now known, is still open to the public and is run by Ipswich Borough Council.

35. LORD NELSON INN

This pub was once called Noah's Ark before changing its name to The Lord Nelson Inn in 1805 after the maritime hero of the same name was appointed High Sheriff of Ipswich. In fact, Nelson only visited the town on one occasion and, upon doing so, stayed at the Great White Horse Hotel.

36. THE OLD NEPTUNE INN

The current building was constructed in 1490 and extended in 1639, although the oldest parts of this house date back perhaps as far as the early 1400s. The building was originally a merchant's house with a shop and warehouses but, in the eighteenth century, the building became an inn. Since 1937, the building has been used as both a workplace and a private house.

37. WET DOCK AND WATERFRONT

The newly revitalised wet dock of the Victorian era was at the epicentre of Ipswich's trade economy. In recent times, it has been reimagined as a marina to relax in and enjoy. It is also now a place to study; University Campus Suffolk was founded in 2007, with its main buildings on the waterfront, as a collaboration between the University of East Anglia and the University of Essex. In 2016 it gained its independence and became the University of Suffolk.

38. OLD CUSTOMS HOUSE

This solid building was constructed in the 1840s as part of the renewal of Ipswich's docks after a period of decline during the eighteenth century. During its history, it has housed the Ipswich Dock Commission and the Ipswich Port Authority as well as being partly used as a police station. Today, the customs house is part of Associated British Ports and still handles around 3 million tonnes of cargo each year.

39. ST MARY-AT-THE-QUAY CHURCH

This is one of Ipswich's medieval churches that served the maritime town. Construction of St Mary-at-the-Quay began in the fifteenth century. The building has recently undergone renovation by the Churches Conservation Trust, which has worked with Suffolk Mind to transform this long-neglected building into a wellbeing and heritage centre, hopefully securing a long-term future for St Mary-at-the-Quay.

40. WOLSEY'S GATE

This is the last remaining fragment of a grand Tudor college planned by Cardinal Wolsey at the height of his power in the 1520s. He founded Cardinal College, Oxford (now Christ Church College) and made plans for feeder colleges around the country, with the main one to be in Ipswich. However, construction was abandoned before the building of the college was completed due to Wolsey's fall from power.

The
S

41. ST PETER'S CHURCH

This was to be the chapel for Wolsey's college before the cardinal's fall from power. The current building was constructed in the fifteenth century on the site of an even older church. It is thought that St Peter's probably occupies the site of the earliest church building in Ipswich; a church with such a name dates back to at least Norman times, referred to in the Little Domesday Book of 1086.

42. ST PETER'S STREET

Originally, St Peter's Street ran all the way from St Nicholas Street and past St Peter's Church. The road is a good deal shorter now due to the Star Lane traffic scheme, which cut off its southern end. The names of the shops and cafés along this pleasant street may have changed over the years, but many of the buildings themselves remain quite venerable.

43. ST NICHOLAS CHURCH

St Nicholas is another of Ipswich's medieval churches, built in the early fourteenth century upon the site of an older Saxon church. The young Thomas Wolsey would have attended this church with his parents, who are buried in the graveyard. For some twenty years, St Nicholas' stood empty, but in 2001 it was reacquired by the Church of England and converted into a resource and conference centre for the diocese of St Edmundsbury and Ipswich.

44. ST NICHOLAS STREET

Taking its name from the nearby medieval church, this street is thought to be the location of Thomas Wolsey's birthplace and childhood home. Although some of the houses are Tudor, some were constructed in the 1920s and 1930s, sometimes using timbers from much older houses. A recent addition is the statue dedicated to the memory of Russian-born Prince, Alexander Obolensky, who played rugby for England and was buried in Ipswich.

45. SILENT STREET

The distinctive name of the street may have been bestowed for its heavy loss of life during the plague outbreak of 1665–66. Another suggestion is that the road was lined with straw to reduce the noise of carts travelling to a hospital based on the street in the mid-seventeenth century. It remains home to some of the most attractive timber-framed buildings in the town.

Also Available from Amberley Publishing

This fascinating selection of photographs traces some of the many ways in which Ipswich has changed and developed over the last century.

Paperback
180 illustrations
96 pages
978-1-4456-3631-3

Available from all good bookshops or to order direct
please call **01453-847-800**
www.amberley-books.com